TEN HILLS FARM

C. S. MANEGOLD

TEN HILLS FARM

THE FORGOTTEN HISTORY OF
SLAVERY IN THE NORTH

PRINCETON UNIVERSITY PRESS   PRINCETON AND OXFORD

Published by Princeton University Press, 41 William Street,
Princeton, New Jersey 08540
In the United Kingdom: Princeton University Press, 6 Oxford Street,
Woodstock, Oxfordshire OX20 1TW

Library of Congress Cataloging-in-Publication Data

Manegold, C. S., 1955–
Ten Hills Farm : the forgotten history of slavery in the North / C.S. Manegold.
p. cm.
Includes bibliographical references and index.
ISBN 978-0-691-13152-8 (hardcover : alk. paper) 1. Ten Hills Farm (Mass.)—History.
2. Slavery—Massachusetts—History. 3. Slave trade—Massachusetts—History.
4. Slaves—Massachusetts—Social conditions. I. Title.
E445.M4M36 2010
974.4'03—dc22
2009030875

British Library Cataloging-in-Publication Data is available

This book has been composed in Sabon Family text with Centaur MT Display
Printed on acid-free paper. ∞
press.princeton.edu
Printed in the United States of America
3 5 7 9 10 8 6 4 2

For
ROSE

The bird is above, and below
Its shadow is running bird-like.

A fool becomes the hunter of the shadow
Running so much that he runs out of breath.

Ignorant that this is the picture of the air-born bird
Ignorant of where the origin of the shadow is.

Rumi, *Masnavi* I, verse 425

Contents

Letter from
Antigua

◆

History in this hot and weathered place lies scattered in plain sight. I touch something with the toe of my shoe. It is a piece of china, a cup shard, a glint of ancient porcelain, blue and white against the brown. And here, a fragment of a bowl decorated in delicate patterns of leaves. Trash amid the stones. I pluck several pieces from the dirt that makes a sidewalk just outside Antigua's National Archives in St. John's, startled to discover such bounty underfoot in this most public of spaces. No less than the papers inside, these shards tell a story. It is the story of whites who lived in style and luxury and built great fortunes on the backs of other men.

I've been drawn to the path by the seductive thump of drums. It pulls me from my work inside, reviewing fuzzy microfilm and brittle texts. As I head out, Dr. Marion Blair—the director of the archives, her hair cropped almost to her scalp, her gaze that of a woman who has seen it all, and more than once—says she believes it is a march by students in a protest against crime. Dr. Blair ("Marion" to a young black woman exploring her family's past) addresses me rather formally with a rich Antiguan roll. The words sound strange to my more northern ear, and I must pause to let them translate in my head.

Outside in the keen noon light the drumming is boisterous and hundreds of students fill the road, blocking all traffic. They are marching in their various school uniforms—not a white face among them—making a sea of red and blue and gold and black.

Some carry placards. A few are singing. Hand-lettered signs call out for better times: *Let there be peace on earth and let it begin with ME*. These are shards that tell a different story. It is the story of blacks whose ancestors were slaves who labored without freedom on a soil far from home.

An editorial in the *Antigua Sun* coinciding with the march reflects upon a recent study showing Caribbean youths between the ages of 15 and 17 as more likely to die by homicide than any other group their age around the world. "We need to add nothing more," the newspaper's editors conclude. Yet people do: It is the bitter legacy of slavery, say some. The crap left behind by a corrupt government, say others. "Cultural," one older white man says without elaboration. I write it all down as it comes.

Rich and poor. Black and white. Protected, vulnerable. Divisions on this small Caribbean island are not as clear as they once were. In the affluent seaside community where long ago a New Englander named Isaac Royall made his home and built his fortune, it is impossible to tell whether a black family or white sits down to dinner back behind new walls and heavy gates. The community is racially mixed, and fairly affluent. The houses are built well. The grounds are trim and neat. Gardens receive care and plenty of water and give reward in crazy explosions of color and perfume. Yet there is a constant sense of vulnerability as well. In the absence of effective policing most residences are protected by huge dogs—rottweilers, ridgebacks, bulldogs, mutts—who, though gentle with their masters, could rip an intruder to pieces in a single, unforgiving flash of teeth. They thunder toward the fences, jaws open, haunches tucked, whenever strangers wander by. Though the fences hold them back, the strangers always flinch, and I do, too, and begin to drive even short distances, against a lifelong habit to the contrary.

In the houses the dogs are much discussed: the breed, the loyalty, the temperament, the potential to inflict a lethal wound. Where I stay there are three acres and six dogs. One is old and blind and nearly lame. Three others are massive coils of muscle and vitality. A pup has joined the crew. He will be big when fully grown. There is another puppy, too, brought home this week, a silly blur of black and white that will never grow much bigger than a cat. She cuddles like a child and stays mostly upstairs.

In poorer enclaves the dogs run free and fight for scraps. There, the population is a monochrome, every face caught somewhere on a broad continuum of dark. In those places life is hard and the most pressing task is just the struggle to make do. Cars are luxury. Buses run infrequently. Water, always an issue on an island with a chronic scarcity, is hauled about in buckets. Sewage slides in open gutters. Houses are spare in the way that houses of the very poor are spare in warmer climates everywhere: shacks made simply with a room or two and not much in them but the breathing, laughing, quarreling of many. Down one severely rutted deep back road that proves harder to navigate by car than on foot, a man in copious dreadlocks marshaled by a knitted hat in Africa's red, yellow, green, emerges from a shack at dusk to brush his teeth with water from a large tin bucket. Yards away a group of children plays soccer in the dust and a woman in her forties, who looks older, is almost home, her shoes worn nearly through.

A few miles south lies another extreme, the Mill Reef Club, a storied playground of social ascendancy open only by invitation to those of finest pedigree and flawless manners tuned at dinner tables and boarding schools around the world. There, pale families tucked beside clean, azure waters are cosseted by black hands (and the occasional white yoga instructor) from dawn to well past dusk. It is generally a simple matter to spot the people heading for that walled-off life. In the waiting room at the international airport in Puerto Rico, a woman with shoulder-length carrot hair wearing perfectly pressed khakis and a navy blue jacket adorned with big gold buttons disdainfully flicks a soiled Kleenex to the floor, then rests her brilliant orange new suede shoes atop the seat across from her. When her daughter leans in close to reprimand, the woman—who appears not long out of boarding school herself—puts one foot up to her daughter's face, perhaps to show how *her* feet, amazingly, are never dirty, or at least to tell the child to back off. The feet remain at altitude while the woman busies herself on her Blackberry and the girl chats sullenly with a brother.

The father, a towering dark-haired American dressed exactly like his wife (but for the shoes and bright gold buttons) is distracted, calling someone in New York to inquire without preamble: "How is the market?" Hours later, disembarking in the noontime heat at the Antigua airport, the family stops beside a stately black woman holding a small sign printed with the club's name. Though several of my favorite people vacation at the Mill Reef every year, and have for decades, this pair fits every ugly stereotype I harbor. Then again, I know too much to ever see the club as just a simple place of sun and sand.

As John Fuller, an attorney in St. John's, so aptly puts it, "Then it was sugar. Now it is sun. All we changed is what we sell."

I am staying with John and his wife at Hodges Bay near land Isaac Royall once controlled. It is Isaac Royall, long dead, and his legacy, still very much alive, that call me here to this place near Beggars Point. I have learned that man's history and followed his trajectory and engaged myself with his ambition and his flaws and now I sift the sand of his beach between my toes and speak with people whose forebears in another time he might have owned. Today there is no Royall listed in the phone book. But the name and legacy are still attached to a tiny bay, a shop, a housing cluster, a dot on fraying maps.

John and Sarah Fuller, émigrés from England and America, have made a full life here and hold a complex view of the island and its history. Mostly, though, like anyone, they simply live their lives, hosting a constant flow of children, friends, gardeners, assistants, birds, puppies, lizards, mosquitoes, mongooses, and, of course, the dogs. Laughter often spills out of their house. Visitors come and go throughout the day. They are black and white, related, not related, British, American, and Antiguan.

Here on this hot and gritty land a short sail from the equator I am finishing a book about America. For three years I have known my work would draw me to this place. It takes a book to explain why. This is that book. It is not a history in the classic academic sense. It is, instead, a story, and a true one, about a six-hundred-acre farm just north of Boston. In writing this story I have done my best to find the truth and ensure the accuracy of every detail of the telling. That, as any historian knows so well, is a daunting task. Surely I have made mistakes. I apologize for them here. They are not for lack of trying but are born instead of a scarcity of documents and the maddening task of trying to recreate a time almost four hundred years ago. Still, I have done my utmost to confirm each fact and double-check my perceptions. I leave the more pointillist detailing to scholars with more training in the field than I, and perhaps more patience for the minutiae upon which the finest scholarship is built and on which I have gratefully depended during much of my own process of discovery. Leaving history to the historians, I offer this instead. It is the story of a piece of ground near Boston, today a busy metropolis with part of its memory wiped almost clear.

May this book restore that memory.

csm
Hodges Bay, Antigua

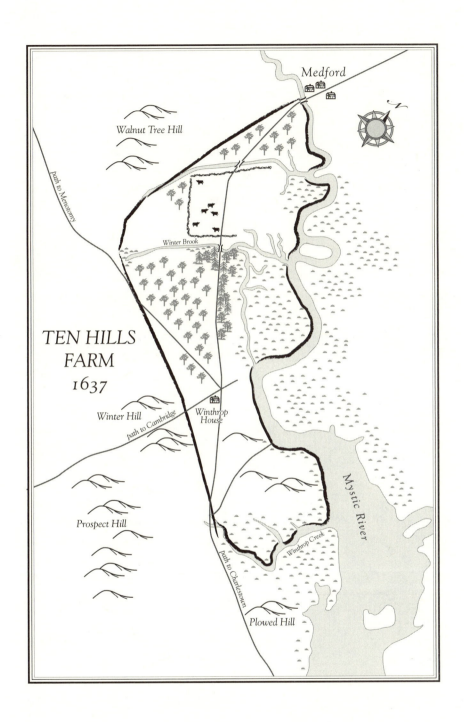

Medford

Walnut Tree Hill

path to Menotomy

Winter Brook

TEN HILLS
FARM
1637

Winter Hill

path to Cambridge

Winthrop
House

Prospect Hill

Mystic River

Winthrop Creek

path to Charlestown

Plowed Hill

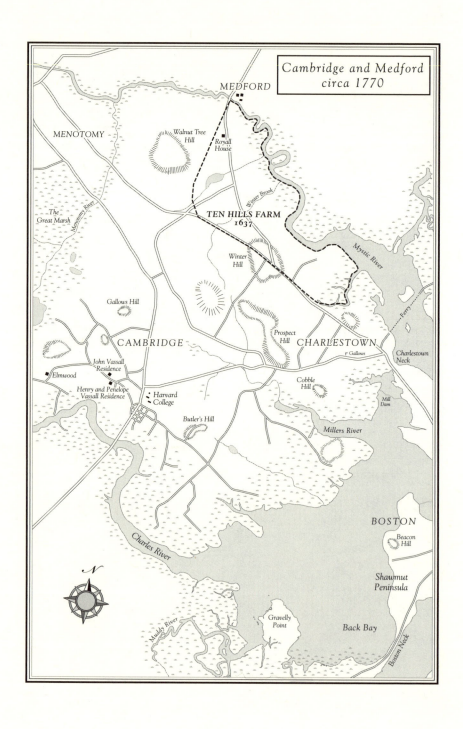

Cambridge and Medford
circa 1770

MEDFORD

MENOTOMY

Walnut Tree
Hill

Royall
House

The
Great Marsh

Winter Brook

TEN HILLS FARM
1637

Mystic River

Winter
Hill

Gallows Hill

Ferry

CAMBRIDGE

Prospect
Hill

CHARLESTOWN

Gallows

Charlestown
Neck

John Vassall
Residence

Elmwood

Cobble
Hill

Henry and Penelope
Vassall Residence

Mill
Dam

Harvard
College

Butler's Hill

Millers River

BOSTON

Beacon
Hill

Charles River

Shawmut
Peninsula

N

Muddy River

Gravelly
Point

Back Bay

Boston Neck

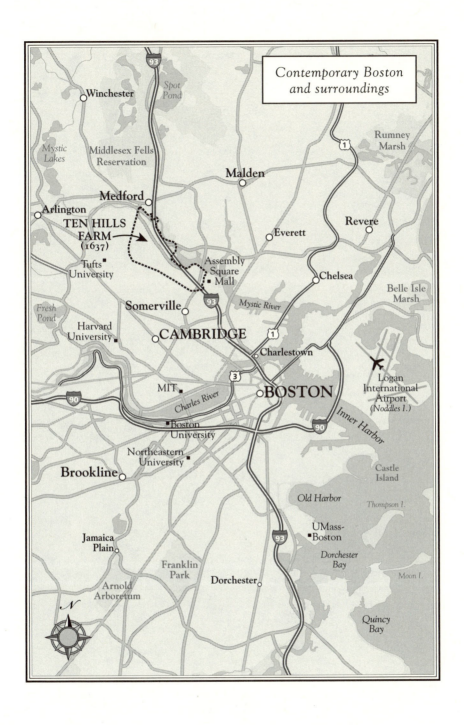

Contemporary Boston and surroundings

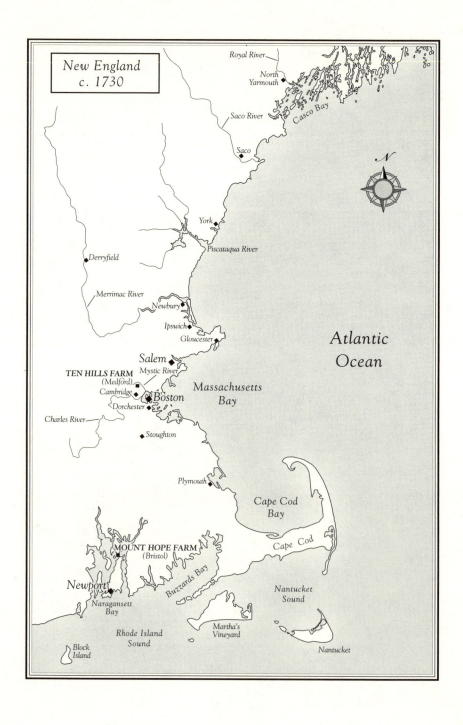

New England
c. 1730

Royal River
North
Yarmouth
Saco River
Casco Bay
Saco
N
York
Piscataqua River
Derryfield
Merrimac River
Newbury
Ipswich
Gloucester
Atlantic
Ocean
Salem
TEN HILLS FARM
(Medford)
Mystic River
Cambridge
Boston
Massachusetts
Dorchester
Bay
Charles River
Stoughton
Plymouth
Cape Cod
Bay
MOUNT HOPE FARM
(Bristol)
Cape Cod
Newport
Nantucket
Sound
Naragansett
Bay
Buzzards Bay
Rhode Island
Sound
Martha's
Vineyard
Nantucket
Block
Island
Nantucket

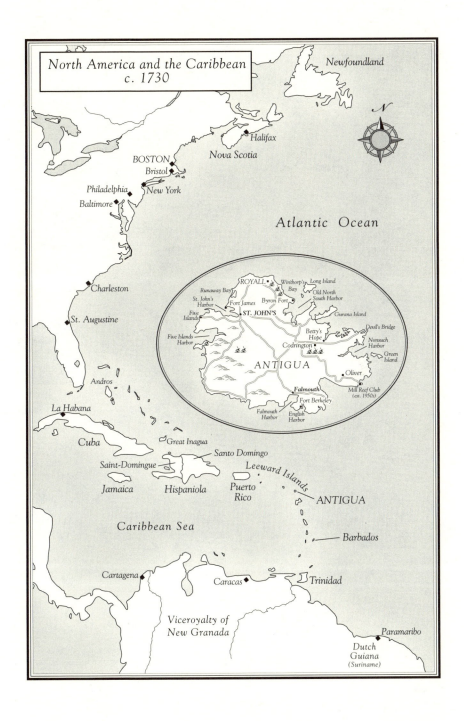

North America and the Caribbean
c. 1730

N

Newfoundland

Halifax
BOSTON
Bristol
Nova Scotia
Philadelphia
New York
Baltimore

Atlantic Ocean

Charleston

St. Augustine

Andros

La Habana

Cuba

Great Inagua

Santo Domingo

Saint-Domingue

Jamaica
Hispaniola
Puerto Rico

Leeward Islands

ANTIGUA

Barbados

Caribbean Sea

Cartagena
Caracas
Trinidad

Viceroyalty of New Granada

Paramaribo

Dutch Guiana
(Suriname)

ROYALL
Winthrop's Bay
Long Island
Runaway Bay
Byron Fort
Old North
South Harbor
St. John's Harbor
Fort James
ST. JOHN'S
Five Islands
Guiana Island
Betty's Hope
Devil's Bridge
Five Islands Harbor
Codrington
Nonsuch Harbor
Green Island
ANTIGUA
Oliver
Mill Reef Club
(est. 1950s)
Falmouth
Fort Berkeley
Falmouth Harbor
English Harbor

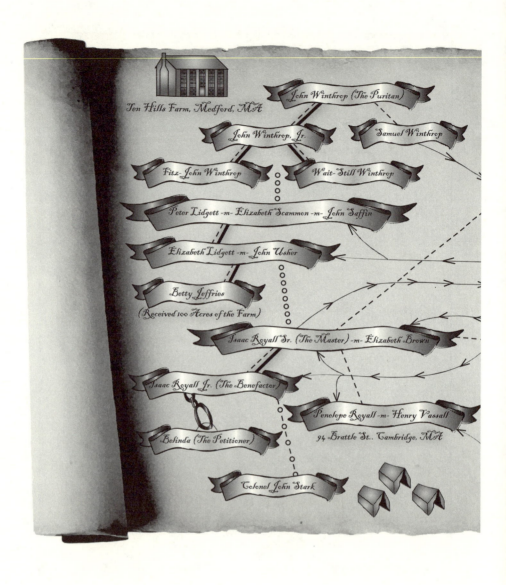

Ten Hills Farm, Medford, MA

John Winthrop (The Puritan)

John Winthrop, Jr.

Samuel Winthrop

Fitz-John Winthrop

Wait-Still Winthrop

Peter Lidgett -m- Elizabeth Scammon -m- John Saffin

Elizabeth Lidgett -m- John Usher

Betty Jeffries
(Received 100 Acres of the Farm)

Isaac Royall Sr. (The Master) -m- Elizabeth Brown

Isaac Royall Jr. (The Benefactor)

Penelope Royall -m- Henry Vassall
94 Brattle St., Cambridge, MA

Belinda (The Petitioner)

Colonel John Stark

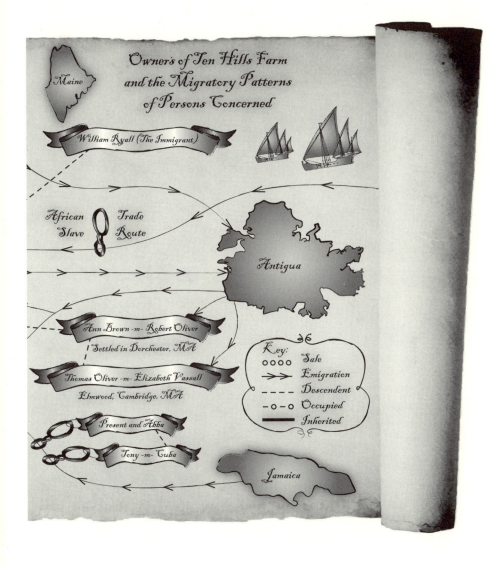

Owners of Ten Hills Farm
and the Migratory Patterns
of Persons Concerned

Maine

William Ryall (The Immigrant)

African Slave Trade Route

Antigua

Ann Brown -m- Robert Oliver
Settled in Dorchester, MA

Thomas Oliver -m- Elizabeth Vassall
Elmwood, Cambridge, MA

Present and Abba

Tony -m- Cuba

Jamaica

Key:
ooooo Sale
→→ Emigration
- - - - Descendent
-o-o Occupied
▬▬▬ Inherited

PART I

THE
PURITAN

The Land

On this ground a thousand years ago, the woods embraced a people called the Massachusett. They made no books, no maps, no monuments to their achievements, no lasting record of defeats. No history of these people was described in stone or set on silk or sheepskin for posterity. No library preserved their lore. Instead, season by season, year by year, long nights around great bonfires glowed with the legends of the place, the battles won, the heroes honored. But these were only stories, as ephemeral as the flowing waters of the nearby Mystic River. With the coming of white explorers, that record started burning in the fevers of disease. Then came the crack of musket shot and the stifling language of a distant court. In a blink of geologic time, a population withered. What had been saved and shared so long was lost, the people of those legends broken. By the time the Puritans and their stern, committed few arrived to stake their claim, an eerie silence was already spread across the ground. A veil of illness lingered. More tragedy would come.

Until the 1400s, literate, seafaring civilizations understood the space beyond their knowing as but a cipher and a dream, a nightmare, really, made of falling over the earth's edge. Ancient mariners who ventured into the New World spoke of brown-skinned men and gray-blue waters full of fish. But were they to be believed? Elegant maps with whale spouts and huge monsters at their edges showed just a frightening void beyond the boundary of what they had explored. By the 1500s it was filled. Yet even then Europeans knew more about the Caribbean and Mexico than vast territories stretching north of Florida. The famous cartographer Sebastian Cabot in 1544 showed New England and everything to the north of it as a literal *terra incognita,* filled only with grasses, bears, a mountain lion, and several Indians with sticks. While royal records in their spindly hubris and self-interest described man's greedy sweeps across the arc of Asia, Africa, and Europe, neither scholars nor explorers bothered yet to mark North America's lush acres in dark ink or fine gold leaf.

Then came fishermen, laborers, ministers, and warriors. And finally the region's history, already well advanced upon the land itself and written in the hearts and memories of a people who had made their lives upon that ground for a millennium, began to twist into another form, a form best suited to the egos and the interests of white tellers, newcomers all, armed with the great power of the pen. Almost imperceptibly, a complex history was casually erased, as though the god of memory had simply closed his eyes.

These newcomers would spin a tale of bold adventurers, men of honor and deep principle who came to settle a "new" land. Among them was a forty-two-year-old chronicler whose journals would frame and define our knowledge of this land for centuries to come. "For 350 years Governor John Winthrop's journal has been recognized as the central source for the history of Massachusetts" in its first decades, wrote Richard S. Dunn in an introduction to the Harvard University Press edition of those journals printed in 1996. Sweeping as the statement is, Dunn might have minimized the impact. For it was not just Massachusetts that the leader of the Puritans helped to define, but America's very understanding of itself. Almost inevitably, much of that understanding came from Winthrop, whom Dunn rightfully acknowledges as "both the chief actor and the chief recorder" of the Puritans' bold experiment. He left behind a body of observations and a manifesto of intention that is quoted even now, across the span of centuries. In that sense, Winthrop's writings were both a gift and the seed of a conundrum posed to later generations struggling for a broader view.

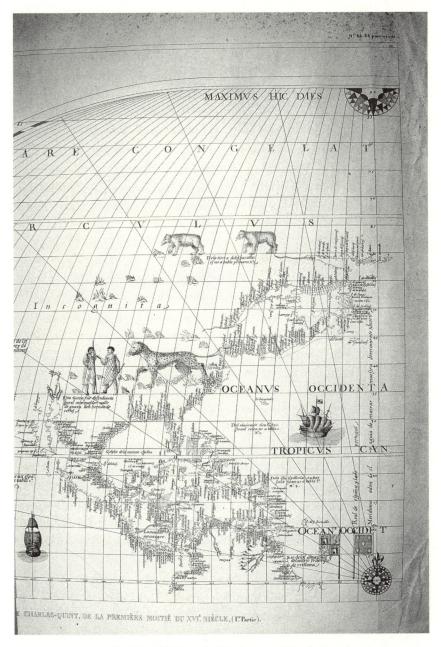

1.1 Detail of World Map, 1544, showing North America as "Terra Incognita." Courtesy American Antiquarian Society.

Winthrop's journal, or those parts of it that have survived the years and the vicissitudes of weather and poor treatment, opens on March 29, "*Anno domini 1630,*" an Easter Monday. The new governor of the Massachusetts Bay Company was aboard the 350-ton *Arbella* in Southampton along England's southern coast in preparation for his sailing then. He had been on the ship more than a week when he sat to write his opening words and he felt a keen impatience. As he settled at a table to make that first entry, the vessel rode heavy at anchor off the Isle of Wight not far from England's shore, her hold jammed with provisions for the journey ahead and the hard, lean months to follow. Within earshot on that day, three other ships, the *Ambrose, Jewel,* and *Talbot,* their sails furled tight and stately masts spiking in the harbor air, also bobbed uneasily at their waterlines, ready and at rest.

All four vessels would leave that sheltered sanctuary within days, wrenching their anchors out of harbor mud before rolling out of sight in a roar of musket shot and flapping canvas. Again and again throughout that year, one heaving schooner after another would head west, splashing across the Atlantic until a thousand souls were dumped as strangers on a strange and distant shore. Within two decades twenty thousand immigrants would uproot to make that journey. Even as Winthrop dipped his pen and tapped a drop of excess ink that day, the *Charles,* the *Mayflower* (not of Pilgrim fame), the *William and Francis,* the *Hopewell,* the *Whale,* the *Success,* and the *Tryall* were being readied under the bark and whistle of ship's captains elsewhere. The governor noted each with a delicate hand. In brown ink on the first page of a small notebook lashed with leather, he started his great story. What he did not say, perhaps what he did not yet clearly see, was that history was shifting, and he would shape it in his image.

The first order of business was to establish a clear line of mastery and control. As governor of the new colony, he would need it. "Upon conference it was agreed that these 4 shippes should consorte togither," Winthrop wrote. Now and for the duration of the voyage, a strict hierarchy would hold. Governor Winthrop's ship, the *Arbella,* was selected for the lead. It would sail as "admiral." The larger *Talbot* would be "vice admiral." The *Ambrose,* "rear admiral," and the *Jewel*, "captain," would round out the fleet. Together, they would push history before them like a wave.

With that decided, Winthrop organized himself and paced the decks. In the last days before the fleet embarked, the new governor observed the *Arbella's* captain, Peter Milborne, with all his many preparations for the sailing. A crew of fifty-two was hard at work, heaving barrels, mending sails, and stowing last-minute provisions. Twice that number of passengers shuffled aboard and found their way to cramped and musty spaces down below. By slow degrees as these last hours clicked by, Winthrop gently turned away from the rolling hills of England and all that he had ever known to point his will and energy toward his new life in a new land.

A country gentleman and an accomplished lawyer who served as justice of the peace in Suffolk County, John Winthrop was new to thoughts of a vast social experiment in a distant hemisphere. Having been raised in a prominent family amid a flow of titled visitors and important guests, he was "lord of the manor" in a literal sense, hardly the sort whom fate might pluck for great adventure. On the contrary, his path seemed set, and comfortable. His boyhood home at Groton Manor with its great fireplaces and yawning mastiffs was a picture of English stability. His choice to serve as a magistrate showed nothing of a taste for thrill. Even John Winthrop's life as a father and a family man was accompanied more by the drumbeat of responsibility than the cymbal clash of risk.

When the Pilgrims sailed, Winthrop hardly made a note of it. Instead, he left the chaos of new colonies to others, including his second son, Henry, who in December 1626 (well before these thoughts of Massachusetts crossed his father's mind) sailed away with Captain Henry Powell to help establish a colony in Barbados. The ship arrived at its sandy and unkempt destination February 17, 1627. Henry was not yet in his twenties then, a young man full of promise, blessed with means. He loved the place, and for two years he had a great adventure. Yet Barbados was a young colony and dogged with problems, and he could not make a go of it. By the time his father packed his bags and walked on board the *Arbella*, Henry was back home again (though hardly chastened), preparing for another gamble, this time with the great John Winthrop, off to try a new experiment.

As the chisel-faced Puritan gazed out across England's gray shoreline in that spring of 1630, perhaps he understood Henry's urgent impulses as never before. Surely, he knew the risk. Henry had already fumbled. But just like his son, John Winthrop also knew the promise: life on his own terms in a world that he could fashion.

The tales of the two men's voyages echo eerily.

It was two years after the English established a foothold in Barbados that eighteen-year-old Henry crossed the Atlantic to start a tobacco plantation and assist with the island's administration. It was two years after the Massachusetts Bay Colony was conceived and John Endecott planted England's flag in Salem that John Winthrop would arrive, settle a farm, and manage the colony's administration.

Inflated family accounts of Henry's achievements identify him as "chief proprietor and commander-in-chief of Barbadoes." Court records and histories identify his father as chief magistrate and governor of Massachusetts. Though they stood at different stations in the hierarchies they helped create, each well understood the lure of leadership in a colony just taking shape.

In Barbados, Henry found sandy ground inhabited by a handful of Englishmen and slaves. He immediately pronounced the place "the pleasantest island in all the West Indies." Yet he would not prosper. John Winthrop discovered a colder, richer landscape inhabited by a greater number of Englishmen living beside Indian tribes already decimated by disease. Like Henry he spoke movingly of the region's beauty and extolled its boundless possibility. But there the echoes end. John Winthrop thrived where Henry failed. But of course it did not start that way.

In the first few months of Henry's adventure in the Caribbean, the young man was mentioned fondly and often in family letters. "We are very glad to hear so good news of our son Henry," Margaret Winthrop wrote optimistically after receiving news of her stepson in the summer of 1627. Doting family members applauded his gumption and wondered how to send him shoes and other goods. But shoes were hardly what young Henry needed. Henry urgently needed men. And in a raw and unsettled island culture that would soon become notorious for the sadistic abuse of workers, "men" meant either indentured servants or, more often, African and Indian slaves.

"I have found two sturdy youths that would go to him," John Winthrop wrote in a letter from that period. Henry wanted more, and shipped some rough tobacco as a preliminary payment in exchange. His father rejected it, complaining in uncharacteristically florid language that the leaf was so "ill-conditioned, foul, and full of stalks, and evil colored" that no English grocer would deign touch it. Even Henry's uncles would not buy. Nor was John Winthrop in any position to provide additional help. "I have no money," the Puritan said sharply in a letter to his son that has survived the years, "and I am so far in debt already, to both your uncles, as I am ashamed to borrow any more." The reason for his penury was perfectly clear. Even so, John Winthrop spelled it out, sparing Henry nothing in the telling: "I have disbursed a great deal of money for you," he chided, "more than my estate will bear." The ten men Henry asked for would not come. Henry's life as master of a new plantation would be short. "I can supply you no further," announced the father. Though he had generously backed the Barbados venture for some time, young Henry's demands had strained John Winthrop's personal finances to the limit. Nothing more would flow.

Back in England, enthusiasm for the experiment cooled. Tobacco use was out of favor among the Puritans. In any case, the crop Henry produced was bad stuff hardly worthy of the name. John Winthrop, his third wife, Margaret, and eldest son John Jr. (later the governor of Connecticut) now pinned their hopes instead on the North American mainland. Two months after the Puritan cut his son Henry off from further subsidies, the Massachusetts Bay Company was formed with a wealthy London merchant and family associate, Mathew Cradock, named as governor. John Endecott and scores of settlers embarked at once. Though they were part of a broad land grab in a time of growing empire, their settlement would be an experiment unlike any other. According to the Massachusetts Bay Company's charter, the wheels and cogs of governance would be given to the colony itself, not controlled at a distance from counting houses and stuffy courtrooms back in London. These men "were not . . . adventurers or traffickers," explained the Puritan's descendant Robert C. Winthrop, a long-time president of the Massachusetts Historical Society (and great-great-grandfather of Massachusetts senator John Kerry), in his "Life and Letters of John Winthrop." Nor were they going "for the profits of a voyage . . . [or] the pleasure of a visit; but to 'inhabit and continue' there" and build a world. Self-governance on a distant shore represented a structural shift many historians would read in hindsight as of profound, and finally revolutionary, consequence. These men would rule themselves.

John Winthrop was originally called into the project merely to mediate differences between several bickering New England officers and John Endecott, the Salem-based official who had set up camp in Massachusetts while Henry struggled in Barbados. Yet Winthrop's role quickly expanded. Over a series of meetings held in London, it was Winthrop who emerged as a clear leader. For him the venture came at a good time. His finances were a mess. He had just left (or was pushed from) a position as attorney at the Court of Wards, the body charged with overseeing the estates of wealthy orphans who might otherwise fall prey to guardians inclined to put their own self-interest first. He feared for his religious freedoms. A beloved brother-in-law, Thomas Fones, and his mother (who had always lived beside her son at Groton Manor) died within days of each other. The family estate seemed suddenly bleak and lifeless. Winthrop fell into a severe depression.

"We see how frail and vain all earthly good things are," he wrote his wife while shaking off the deaths of those he loved. "Only the fruition of Jesus Christ and the hope of heaven can give us true comfort and rest."

Why, then, not leave England for a new life in His service? When the Massachusetts Bay Company called on the forty-two-year-old magistrate to join in that adventure he was prepared in more ways than his associates could have guessed. His needs were great. His standing commitments were frayed or severed. The thought of relocation must have seemed less daunting after Henry's recent travels. And surely where the wayward son had failed, the father might succeed. In any case, freedom, opportunity, and a fresh start clearly lay offshore.

By mid-October of 1629 John Winthrop, then staying in London with his sister Lucy and her family, was so engrossed in the Massachusetts Bay Company's business—and so entranced by its potential—he could find "not one quarter of an hour's time to write," he told his wife. Settling a new territory with a charter from the king was an enormous task. Recruiting investors and "adventurers" willing to take the gamble, calculating stores of goods and livestock, arranging for a cross-Atlantic passage, and luring families to join the exodus consumed all of his time. And yet the work bore fruit. "We are now agreed with the merchants," the Puritan told Margaret in a scribbled note, "and stay only to settle our affairs." By the time the matter of leadership came to a vote, he had consolidated his position and settled his intention. On October 20, 1629, John Winthrop—with a show of hands—came out first among four candidates for governor. He started his duties the same day.

That night the newly appointed governor retreated to his sister's elegant house at Peterborough Court, just off Fleet Street. There, in a cramped and musty space that had once served as the residence of a prince of the church John Winthrop had come to hate, Lucy and Emmanuel Downing embraced the plan and offered whatever help they could provide. Theirs was no empty promise. For three decades the couple would house and feed the Winthrops as they stopped in London in their wanderings. They would advise the men on business matters, tweak distant levers of power, and cheer the Massachusetts Bay Colony's success. The Puritan's brother-in-law Emmanuel, a committed Puritan himself and a colleague at the Court of Wards, proved shrewd and indefatigable. He would guide the governor's business enterprises in England and help John Winthrop's sons as they ventured near and far. But that was all for later. For now, the family merely reveled in the news and looked with awe upon its meaning.

John himself was clearly humbled, and at least a bit afraid. Settling by candlelight after others went to bed, he dipped his pen and bent his head to inform Margaret of the unexpected news. "So it is," he wrote, "that it hath pleased the Lorde to call me to a further trust in this business of the Plantation than either I expected or find myselfe fitt for." Over the span of only thirty days his life—and that of his entire family—had turned abruptly on its head.

Henry was just back from Barbados then and looking for some new adventures. Among them was romance. He married his cousin (a liaison, some wags joked, that precipitated her father's death). He immersed himself in the London party scene. He made it clear he was available. With his parents and older brother now dismissing the tobacco operation in Barbados as a hasty rush to riches in a place of sin, Henry was counseled instead to stay in England as his father prepared for a rather holier experiment. "I have conferred with him," the governor said in a letter written in October 1629. "What he will do, I know not yet."

If Henry wrestled with that decision, events in the Caribbean must have helped to sway his mind. News out of those waters at the time was news of war. The island of St. Christopher (now St. Kitts) "is taken by the Spaniard," John Winthrop wrote his wife. Barbados seemed headed for a similar fate. European powers were tearing at each others' fragile, distant borders. Perhaps Massachusetts might prove as vulnerable. The new governor gambled everything that it would not. "Some would discourage us with this news," John Winthrop wrote, "but there is no cause. . . ." Henry, meanwhile, made himself busy in his father's service, acting as a middleman in the provisioning of the company's ships and doing his father's bidding when he was not distracted by the many seductions London offered. Soon his days in Barbados would fade as a new set of thrills and challenges emerged. His wife, Elizabeth Fones, was pregnant. A novel set of expectations and responsibilities held his attention and sharpened his focus. He poured himself into his new task. And so while his father sat aboard the *Arbella* writing in his journal, Henry was ashore, racing to finish final tasks, rounding up an ox and ten sheep to fill out the store of livestock. Yet while the governor's second son was gone, a vicious storm blew up. It kept Henry from returning to his ship.

On board the *Arbella* at that time, John Winthrop wrote and paced. For him setting off meant steering a new colony in a wilderness barely scratched by what he knew as human culture. But it also meant—and here was the sweet song of it—preserving and spreading the work of God as he understood it. Throughout that winter and spring John Winthrop encouraged friends and fellow Puritans to make the trip. Here was a chance to build a refuge for the religiously oppressed, escape England's corrupt and teeming population, and take and settle a new land. Here was God's experiment, a worthy challenge with a clear reward.

As the Puritan prepared himself to face this new frontier, words to shape a nation were then churning. The image that he held was one of liberty, justice, and godliness, an image that would abide across the centuries. "We shall be as a city upon a hill," the governor said in a sermon likely delivered just days before the fleet embarked. "The eyes of all people are upon us." Thrive or starve, win or lose, the group's extraordinary undertaking, he said prophetically, would be "a story and a by-word throughout the world."

Those words would echo over history. He was, the scholar Richard Dunn would write in 1962, "the first keeper of the New England conscience." And in that sermon he made clear the stakes.

In the last few days of waiting, John Winthrop said his final goodbyes. Mathew Cradock, the company's first governor and owner of two of the four ships sailing, came on board. A wealthy merchant and member of the East India and Virginia companies, Cradock had a keen interest in every aspect of the voyage. Though he would never cross the Atlantic himself, he stayed close until the ships embarked. Visit by the "late governor," Winthrop noted dryly in his journal's opening entry. A volley of gunshots marked Cradock's farewell, but a week later the old man was back, full of news and worries. As he left, John Winthrop wrote, the captain gave him "three shots out of the steerage for a farewell." With the dying sound of musket fire, the fate and fortune of the voyage shifted. Now the Puritan more securely took the reins. He would be the spiritual and administrative leader of the enterprise. Two days later they sailed off.

In the dim light before dawn on April 8, a fine chop shivered at the *Arbella's* hull. Henry had not made it back on board. Though he tried to cross the choppy water with his servants, the governor noted, "the winde was so strong against them as they were forced on shore." Now, as the *Arbella's* crewmen hoisted anchor, Henry Winthrop and his servants were left to scramble for another passage. "We have left them behind and suppose they will come after," the governor wrote. "We were very sorry they had put themselves upon such inconvenience," he mused, "when they were so well accommodated in our ship."

Henry, though, was just the sort to take that sudden change of plans in stride. Indeed, he had been so anxious for another voyage that John Jr. had to talk him out of making a "quick" round-trip to Barbados before the *Arbella* set her sails. Henry agreed and stayed in London for those months of preparation, drinking in his last days in high society by outfitting himself as a bit of a fop in a bold scarlet suit and cloak. As the moment of departure neared, however, he must have felt a spike of pure adrenaline. He would not be left behind. Instead, he scrambled hard to catch another ship. Meanwhile, someone else took up his berth on board the admiral of the fleet. "We have many young gentlemen," John Winthrop advised proudly, "who behave themselves well, and are comfortable to all good orders." The young man's bed would not go empty. As the last checks were made, Henry found his way aboard another ship, the *Talbot,* sailing as "vice admiral" of the fleet.

In that last morning well before the sun was up, with all hands at last accounted for, there was a rise of energy within the fleet and a bustle in the captains' quarters. The wind was running fine and steady. A line was yanked. A great expanse of canvas filled. It flapped open in a flash of white, then paused, then billowed in the tug of a light breeze. Up on the *Arbella's* decks there was a heave and push, an almost imperceptible advance, and then the crew and passengers were freed from life ashore. The ordered chaos of departure was repeated through the fleet.

Winthrop kept good records of the voyage, and an almost childish thrill emerges in the opening pages of his famous journal. Yet there were frustrations, too, and they began before the first day's sail was done. As the governor described it, the wind would be a tease in that first day. It moved from an inviting breeze to dead calm to violent storm and back to calm again. When the sun came up the wind died down. By 10 a.m. all four ships slowed to a trot, then wobbled on their keels, lurching like great stallions confined behind a stable door, restless, going nowhere. The gurgle of water gave way to the sickening creak of ships becalmed. Nothing to be done for it. Frustrated passengers watched as the *Arbella's* sails deflated and her lines hung limp, dragging useless in the water. The great wood rudder wagged listlessly beneath. The day passed. They waited. At last, some time after dusk, John Winthrop wrote, the wind rose briskly from the north, and flying in a "merry gale" they left the gentle hills of England in their wake.

Back on shore it was a busy time for Cradock and other men with interests in the colony. Seventeen ships would cross the Atlantic bound for the Massachusetts Bay in that first year. Seventeen holds would release their pale, disoriented cargo—pouring one thousand settlers into a strange and largely unexplored "New World." As those ships came, a time of discovery would fast become a time of conquest and control.

Winthrop would eventually christen and bury more children on that soil, lose his wife, marry for a fourth time, die at the age of sixty-one, and lie forever in that ground. For now, though, the challenge was immediate and simple to the point of crudeness: Get to that far shore. Survive the gales. Use the sun and stars as guides. Keep your eye on the other vessels in the fleet. Conserve rations. Tend to the sick and women in childbirth. Keep steady on the rolling deck and make it safely to the other side.

On the *Arbella*, the deck was crowded, and the hold beneath it full. Among the passengers were men like William Vassall, a son of wealth and power, who had signed up with his wife and their four children for the voyage. Men of polish and sophistication and servants without means moved side by side, pacing with the shared concerns of those at sea. Each felt the lurch and lull of that long journey, ate and slept, and felt their fates entwined. As they studied the weather and the waves, each waited for fresh shoreline far from land they knew.

The new governor, bearded, stern, and leathered by life's losses, was father to seven sons and a daughter by then, yet he left most of his family behind. His third wife, Margaret Tyndal, and his nineteen-year-old daughter, Mary, would travel later, on another ship, with John Winthrop Jr. as their chaperone. With Henry bunking elsewhere, the Puritan had only two of his seven boys, eleven-year-old Adam and twelve-year-old Stephen, for company. Still, the governor was hardly alone. And if he missed Henry's companionship he did not say so in his journal. Nor did he show that he suffered from the loss of Henry's help. And why would he? Eight servants traveled with him, tending to his needs. Charles Edward Banks, in his book *The Winthrop Fleet of 1630*, showed them on the passenger list with his best approximation of a void, the stark notation of a dash for everyone who went ———,——— and then the briefest note: "Eight servants of Gov. Winthrop, names unknown."

As the *Arbella* pushed ahead, the larger *Talbot* struggled to keep up. The lead ship's fleetness and the *Talbot's* lumbering splash were not a match. From the first day out, the fleet's admiral had to struggle just to keep the *Talbot* within view. "Towards night," John Winthrop wrote on the Wednesday after sailing, "we were forced to take in some sail . . . for the vice admiral . . . was near a league to the stern of us." One day later, the admiral of the fleet would lose its clumsier companion in a storm.

On the morning of April 15, Winthrop's ship bobbed in nearly windless air while the *Talbot* idled far downwind. Passengers and crew aboard the two vessels eyed each other at a distance. So far to go and getting nowhere! The tedium of morning gave way to the tedium of afternoon. Then a wind caught the sails in a clap and the *Talbot* and *Arbella* maneuvered almost close enough to touch—a hazardous operation that had already led to one hair-raising collision in the open water. "We bore up towards her and having fetched her up and spoken with her . . . we tacked about and steered our course west, northwest, lying as near the wind as we could," Winthrop wrote of the encounter. Did Captain Milborne warn them of a storm ahead or say the slower ship should fall behind? Did he speak of whales or flying fish or what they'd had for dinner? Did they trade gossip or establish orders? Winthrop made no note of it beyond the simple fact of meeting.

With the wind freshening, her sails tight and the captain steering close into the growing breeze, the *Arbella* made good time. But as night drew on, the wind strengthened and the makings of a storm were clear. Rain began to pelt the ship. Some time before midnight Captain Milborne barked an order to his crew. The topsail fell. The mainsail and foresail came down next. The ship steadied under less canvas, but a furious sea slammed at her sides. While she struggled through the water, a giant wave rose overhead and then crashed across the deck, tossing passengers about and costing the *Arbella* one of her dinghies, which went overboard, wrote Winthrop, along with some fresh fish. "The storm still grew," he said, "and it was dark with clouds."

Captain Milborne ordered a light hung from the shrouds lest the *Arbella* lose the other ships or ram them in the dark confusion of the storm. Even so, reported the Puritan, "before midnight we lost sight of our vice admiral."

The wind stayed high all night, screaming through every crack it found. At first light it finally slackened, but the waves did not lose strength. High and dark, they "tossed us more than before," wrote Winthrop. Captain Milborne assessed the churning water and ordered only the mainsail kept aloft. Progress was slow and the passengers were quiet. "Yet our ship steered well with it," the governor observed with pride, "which few such ships could have done."

Once the air cleared, passengers and crew stumbled to the deck to review the storm's damage. Aside from the lost dinghy everything was secure aboard the *Arbella*. She had made it through the weather beautifully. Nearby, the *Ambrose* and the *Jewel* held close. They appeared undamaged, too. Henry's ship, however, was nowhere to be seen. Water stretched to the horizon at all sides without her reassuring spike of white. As the little fleet moved forward through a second gale-whipped night, the *Arbella*, the *Ambrose*, and the *Jewel* held close in a watery triangle. They would hold that loose formation for the duration of the trip. There was no further sign of the vice admiral.

❖ ❖ ❖ ❖ ❖

The last days of the crossing were spent in a thick fog. Sensing land, the crew called to their captain for a sounding. Nothing but water. Even so, everyone could feel a shift. Suddenly it seemed that rock, sand, and vegetation—the far side of the ocean—lay somewhere near. "The fog continued very thick and some rain withall," wrote Winthrop. "We sounded in the morning and again at noon and had no ground." At last they hit "a fine gray sand" and shifted course. That night another gale came up, but even so, the fog remained. On Friday, June 4, 1630, the governor reported air so dense "we could not see a stone's cast from us, yet the sunne shone verye bright." Now the crew was sounding every two hours. Only water met the weights. Again and again they tried until the drill became a new form of monotony. Then suddenly a shout went up: *sand at 80 fathoms*! The mist dissipated and the passengers and crew saw a line of green off in the distance. Land. Over the next few days the fleet bumped unsteadily on a southerly course, making its way down the coast of Maine, sounding all the way.

Monday, June 7, almost two months to the day from setting out, Winthrop reported the landing of a great fish, a cod that he described—incredibly—as stretching four and a half feet from tail to snout, a signal of great bounty. That evening the weather turned raw and a woman aboard gave birth to a dead child. Then on Tuesday, the air changed again. In "fair sunshine" they approached their destination and the governor made note of a new quality in the air he breathed: "a sweet ether . . . like the smell of a garden" met those weary travelers. A wild pigeon and another bird the governor did not identify landed on the ship and stared about with curiosity. Salem lay before them.

On Saturday, June 12, John Endecott, who had settled in Salem several years before and served as governor on site, boarded the *Arbella* with a small welcoming party. While Endecott and Winthrop met, some passengers climbed into bobbing skiffs and rowed ashore to stand on solid ground and eat fresh food for the first time in several months. John Winthrop did not join them. After meeting with John Endecott he stayed aboard to spend the holy day in prayer. Great hardship lay ahead, he knew. Endecott had shared disturbing news. Of the three hundred settlers who had ventured to the Massachusetts Bay so far, more than a quarter—eighty men, women, and children—were already rotting in the ground. Many others were sick or running out of patience, or they lacked the will to make it through another winter. The planting season had begun, but harvests were still far away. More people arriving now meant more mouths to feed. This was no time to celebrate. Monday morning the *Arbella* emptied with a salute. And so the journey ended and the work began.

Nothing was heard of the *Talbot* for several weeks. Then at last on July 1 a sail broke the horizon line. Theirs had been a difficult passage. Water and wind had battered the ship. Sickness had dogged their days. Fourteen of the *Talbot's* passengers were dead. The vessel's rigging, sails, and fittings showed the price of a hard journey. Yet Henry was in high spirits and he was anxious to explore. On the morning after landing the Puritan's second son went for a walk with several officers. The day was hot. Fresh water sparkled invitingly after so long spent at sea. The group spotted an Indian canoe on the other side of a swift river. Henry offered to swim for it. It was a long way to the nearest point where they could cross on foot, he argued, and Henry was the only man among them who could swim. Impulsively, he stripped off his shoes and dove into the river. But as he made his way across, a riptide caught him. Then a leg cramp yanked him down.

Two weeks later, John Winthrop wrote a letter to Margaret, Henry's stepmother. "We had a long and troublesome passage," he began. "The Lord's hand hath been heavy upon myself in some very near to me. My son Henry! My son Henry! Ah, poor child!"

In his journal the Puritan scratched only the stark message: "My sone H. was drowned at Salem."

Historians and Winthrop buffs have tended to paint John Winthrop's second son as an irresponsible playboy, a rough cut of the more sober and religious father. There is some truth in that. Yet

Henry's adventure in Barbados and John Winthrop's in New England were two cuts of the same cloth. As members of the gentry, they embodied the great hubris—as well as all the tangible and intangible benefits—of their time and birth. Each felt entitled to a life of intellectual independence and material success. Each had the means and the confidence to try to build a colony. Over many generations, others would extend the family's reach. John Winthrop Jr., the eldest, would be governor of Connecticut, as would his son (the Puritan's grandson), Fitz-John. Samuel Winthrop, who was only three when the *Arbella* sailed, would explore the Caribbean, settle in Antigua, rise to the post of deputy governor, and buy a fine plantation he named Groton Hall in homage to his boyhood home in England. Samuel would marry well by the standards of the time, joining the ranks of slave owners who enjoyed a world of wealth and leisure on that island. In Antigua he would leave behind a bay and town bearing the family name, each of them spelled Winthorpe.

In New England, meanwhile, a prosperous new world was born. John Winthrop helped to make it thrive. Had Henry lived, his story and his fate might well have been the same. As it was, what the father helped create, surviving sons would turn to their advantage.

TEN HILLS FARM

◆

A season of bounty met John Winthrop and his shipmates. Months of green stretched lazily ahead. "Here is as good land as I have seen . . . sweet air, fair rivers, and plenty of springs, and the water better than in England," the governor told his eldest son in a letter sealed that summer. "Here can be no want of anything."

He lost no time before exploring. Salem was chaotic, busy, and already overrun. The arrival of the *Arbella* and her companions made matters worse, dumping an additional four hundred men, women, and children in a wave. Six hundred other new arrivals would step off more ships in that season. Yet after a hard winter and a year of desperate want, many in the town were already fed up with the experiment. And so when the *Arbella* and her crew turned once again toward to the sea, scores of defeated, sad-eyed settlers were on board. Spitting on the dream, they gathered their belongings, turned their backs on Massachusetts, and went forlornly home.

John Winthrop wanted nothing to do with that despair. Instead, he sought new land and a genuine new start. Three days after he stepped ashore, the Puritan and a small party of his most trusted mates scouted about the edges of the Massachusetts Bay, then turned inland to explore the course of a wide river, searching for a place to stay. Rounding a marshy bend several miles from the open sea, they came across an enchanting landscape. Painted with hills and meadows, softened by low-lying marsh, green and so fresh in those first days of June that it fairly glimmered in the sun, it epitomized John Winthrop's notion of a welcoming ground, a place where God and man could join to do good work.

"Here," he must have thought as he stood beside the Mystic River. *Here*!

To him it seemed a special place. No rocks disturbed the Mystic's course. The water ran both clear and deep. The current made a highway to the sea. Eight feet to the bottom at its lowest mark, the Mystic River rose enough to float the keel of a great ship when tides ran high. Beneath the heave and gurgle of the party's oars flashed a multitude of fish. Alewives, shad, and bass, bright sparks of perch, pickerel, and smelt lay hidden in the weed. As the tide rose, saltwater rippled over the broad wetlands, working on them like a lung, the men reported, drawing clean saltwater in, then flushing summer toxins out. In his journal, Winthrop scribbled his first note since landing in New England: "We went to mattachusettes to find out a place for our sitting down," he said, indicating the area around the bay named after a federation of local tribes. "We went up Misticke River about six miles."

At the end of a day's exploring, the governor and his party stopped for the night at Noddles Island (now the site of Logan Airport), where a settler named Samuel Maverick had made his home six years before. Maverick, noted historian Edmund S. Morgan in an account of the Puritans published in the 1950s, lived there "like a king, offering hospitality to all who came." Unlike the settlers at Salem, this man was no Puritan. He was there for profit only and "seemed to have passed his six years in the wilderness as comfortably and civilly as if he had been in London. If one man could do so well in his own cause," observed Morgan, "how much more could a thousand do in the cause of God?" So Winthrop must have thought. The group rushed back to Salem where news of petty disputes, wolf predations, and the need to organize the leadership took up the governor's time and pages. Cryptic as the mention of the Mystic River exploration was, centuries later Richard Dunn, James Savage, and Leititia Yaendle, the editors of John Winthrop's famous history, would find it "among the most tantalizing in the whole journal," since it seemed to show the governor's intention to settle his whole group in a single Godly enclave.

Surely Medford seemed well suited to their needs. The river offered easy passage to the sea and other colonies, shelter from the worst of storms, and ample fish and fowl. On ground nearby, four gushing streams provided plenty of fresh water. The forest floor was restless with the patter of rabbits, beaver, fox, and deer. Overhead, birds wheeled in bursts against the sky, among them "flocks of wild pigeons this day so thick that they obscure the light," one early settler observed. Surely God abided there. John Winthrop must have heard Him in the drone of bees, the whistling clamor of migrations, and the call of distant whippoorwills at night. There, "sweet air" came rich with the heady scent of loamy soil, of leaf mold warming in the sun, a trace of bayberry, the tang of sea, a tease of wild rose. Hardships would come. And they would multiply. But here, the governor reported to his fellow immigrants, was a place to make a start.

"Possibly they were planning to build a single community for all the incoming colonists," Winthrop's editors observed. Or perhaps the governor just wanted a base for his core group. Neither outcome was to be. Instead, the Puritans spread out to settle in Charlestown, Watertown, Cambridge, Boston, Dorchester, Roxbury, and, yes, Medford, too.

Thomas Dudley, Winthrop's deputy governor, described the process in a letter to a patron back in England: "We began to consult of the place of our sitting down, for Salem, where we landed, pleased us not." The governor and his scouting party favored "a good place upon Mistick [River]," Dudley said. But Dudley and others argued that the immigrants should join the nascent settlement of Charlestown, four miles to the east, at the mouth of the Mystic River, nearer to the bay. Dudley won whatever argument they had. By mid-July Winthrop's goods and stock were being floated there, not further up the river. Other settlers scattered according to their needs and predilections. In the end, Dudley favored Newtowne, later renamed Cambridge. "This dispersion troubled some of us," Dudley conceded, "but help it we could not."

In any case, there was precious little time for argument. Summer was short and there was far too much hammering and sawing to do to think on it much longer. No consolidated Puritan community would rise beside the Mystic River or anywhere else. Instead, as the governor established himself in those first days, it became clear that Charlestown and later Boston would be the intellectual and spiritual hubs of this new colony, just as Dudley (who chose Cambridge) wanted it.

Preparations now moved to the increasingly urgent concerns of food and housing. Two hundred settlers would die in that first winter and eighty more would pack and leave once warmer weather came. And yet that summer, cautious optimism and a frenzied rush were all they knew. By August, the sound of hammering was everywhere. Families raced to build their shelters and to put up stores of game and vegetables. But then winter came and the wind blew and a deadly toll began. In journal pages full of a steady drum of funerals, disease, freezing temperatures, deep snows, starvation, and internal strife, Winthrop left few hints that he ever again thought about the verdant ground he spied in those first days ashore.

Yet he never did forget it. Nor would he let it go.

That November before the dying started, the governor of Massachusetts, furiously busy but confident in his magnificent risk, wrote to Margaret, still in England: "My dear wife, we are here in paradise!"

He wanted a piece of it. And he set about obtaining it, cheering, as he did so, the providential fact that thousands of Native Americans throughout the region "are swept awaye by the small poxe, . . . So as God hathe hereby cleered our title to this place." Before another year was up the governor of the Massachusetts Bay Colony would take the ground that he liked best, granted, as he was, a gracious swath of land beside the Mystic, not for the noisy center of a grand experiment, but rather as a place for peace and contemplation. For him that ground was a release from worldly cares, a country retreat sweetened by four miles of river frontage, spanning hills and meadow claimed and transformed today by the busy cities of Medford, Somerville, and Charlestown. He called the place his "Ten Hills Farm."

Yet how could any man—even a governor—claim property in a region where the very concept did not hold? To many students of the period, the answer is easy enough: Look to the provisions of the charter. Like many other bits of English enterprise, the Massachusetts Bay Company was structured according to a set of norms familiar to and respected in the old country but wholly unanticipated in the new. Every major family moving to New England in the colony's first years expected to be landowners. And they had cause to think it. That business was attended to well before the settlers left. Indeed, Winthrop used the promise to lure emigrants on that great journey. Because of this, wrote Charles Brooks, the author of a nineteenth-century history of the region, "we may . . . fix upon June 17, 1630, as the time when our Anglo-Saxon ancestors first came to Medford, and determined upon the settlement of the town, *and thus took possession.*" That interpretation is something of an oversimplification, but it does not miss the finer details by much, and in his 1855 *History of the Town of Medford* Brooks describes the scheme with relative clarity.

Officials of the Massachusetts Bay Company were empowered by the king to divvy up the land as they saw fit. This was the plan the Puritans devised: two-hundred-acre grants should go "to each adventurer" who purchased £50 of common stock so long as they improved the land with fields, houses, and other buildings. In addition, "adventurers" who traveled to the colony and brought workers along with them were allowed fifty acres more for each person so transported.

John Winthrop, taking a liking to the land beside the Mystic that first summer, would have been well acquainted with these laws; indeed, they fell under his purview as governor. To attend to his desires all he really had to do was exercise his option and divvy up the land—in this case, to himself. And that he quickly did. First, though, he had to sell Groton Manor. "My good son," the elder Winthrop wrote John Jr. from his house in Charlestown on August 14, 1630, "I can now only write a word or two for direction about our affairs. . . . First, for the land (if it be not already sold,) you must sell it speedily, for much debt will lie upon us." The rest of the letter was taken up with the matter of supplies and provisions. The winter would prove hard on everyone.

By the spring of 1631 the family estate at Groton Manor was sold for £4,200, an amount rather less than the family expected, and proof, according to Winthrop descendant Robert C. Winthrop, of the significant sacrifice the leader of the Puritans made on behalf of the new colony. Much of that money went to settle existing debts. But enough was left over for Governor Winthrop to develop a peaceful country estate well outside the buzz and squalor of the growing villages of Charlestown, Boston, and Newtowne. Under the terms of the charter, Winthrop would have been allowed two hundred acres of land plus fifty more for each of the eight servants (———, ———) he transported, making a total of six hundred acres. Many thousands more would flow to the family in time. But the land beside the Mystic he took first. Records of the Court of Assistants of the Colony of the Massachusetts Bay show the following deed—the very first for land along the Mystic—granted to the governor on September 6, 1631: "Six hundred acres of land, to be set forth by metes and bounds, near his house in Mistick, to enjoy him and his heirs forever." That grant, with its view of ten hills and known throughout colonial days as Ten Hills Farm, was conferred to the governor by the governor, giving him a roughly four-mile stretch of waterfront and rolling fertile soil: prime land in a prime location for his sole enjoyment.

Once he secured that property, Winthrop "recommended Gov. Cradock's men to plant themselves directly opposite him on the north side of the river. They did so," explained Medford historian Charles Brooks. Having Cradock as a neighbor (even as the absentee he was) would have suited Winthrop well. Good neighbors made good sense. Isolation in a land filled with bears, wolves, quick-running rivers, and a native population not always charmed by the encroachment of this latest band of Europeans was often risky, sometimes fatal; while having a community of woodsmen, hunters, carpenters, shipwrights, brick makers, and other skilled tradesmen at one's beck and call was nothing but a boon. That

2.1 John Winthrop. Portrait attributed to the school of Sir
Anthony Van Dyck. Courtesy American Antiquarian Society.

was true even if the neighbors never bothered to show up. "This
arrangement," Brooks said dryly, "brought the Governor and these
workmen very near together . . . [to] the interest and convenience
of both."

And so the land was dealt like cards on tables owned by men of
influence. Cradock, with a bigger financial stake in the Massachusetts Bay Company (and perhaps more real estate savvy from his
experience in the East India Company and other colonial enterprises), was served well even in absentia. His land along the Mystic
River's northern shore was gradually developed. There, according
to Brooks, Cradock's servants were tasked to create an elegant deer
park to match the great estates in England. Soon the rolling hills
beside the Mystic were noisy with the sound of great trees falling.

The erstwhile lord of Groton Manor, when not distracted by
colonial affairs and the effort to establish his own sprawling new
estate, kept his eye on trade and the Massachusetts Bay Company's
economic viability. A new colony must have ships to move its

people and its merchandise, he reasoned. And so he commissioned the *Blessing of the Bay,* one of the first oceangoing vessels constructed in North America. Made of locust, the thirty-ton barque was launched into the Mystic River at high tide at Ten Hills Farm on what would become that most quintessentially American day, July 4. The year was 1631.

Winthrop's work was dazzling and swift. He had stepped onto New England soil for the first time just thirteen months before. No record of his grant had yet been signed. That particular detail would take another sixty days to have in place. Yet already that summer there was a house at Ten Hills Farm, and the energy of a rudimentary shipyard, too. Why wait? By the colonial leaders' estimate, the land was theirs for the taking. And so they took it. For much of the colony's first half century, deeds were signed years— and sometimes many decades—after homesteads were secured and fields already farmed and settled.

The governor's possession of Ten Hills Farm reflected this pattern. He had obviously begun developing the property well before it was formally written that he should have six hundred acres *"near his house. . . ."* Shelter came first. Legal niceties could follow.

They *would* have land. That much was established early on, before the settlers ever left the shores of England. "There is more than enough for them and us," John Winthrop argued in a remarkable text titled "General Considerations for the Plantation in New England" written in London in 1629. In language that was alternately soaring and legalistic, the Puritan laid out the group's objectives and responded to some early critics. Among his more compelling arguments was this: God had already "consumed the natives with a miraculous plague," he wrote, "whereby the greater part of the country is left void of inhabitants." Why then, he asked, "should we stand starving here," when across the sea a good Puritan might have "many hundres of acres, as good or better" than England had to offer? At Ten Hills Farm he took his own.

Buoyed by their profound—and in many cases newfound— sense of authority, settlers quickly organized the landscape to their liking. Houses, fields, vineyards and orchards sprouted across an ancient landscape. As the white population secured the food and shelter they required they gained a measure of stability. And with stability came growth. The great experiment was headed for success. It was also, inexorably, heading for a brand of capitalism that cut out the native population, a people unfamiliar with the rules of English law and the ways of coinage and of profit. For them it must have been a dizzying new world filled with weird and inexplicable behavior. At the Mystic River crossing, Mathew Cradock's agents constructed a small bridge with one foot at Ten Hills Farm. Anyone who passed there had to pay a toll. What once was free increasingly came only at a price.

By the colony's second decade, tens of thousands of immigrants had come ashore beside the Massachusetts Bay. They now fanned out across the region. The population boomed. To marshal their behavior, a set of legal norms and economic practices took hold. Rules and expectations shaped the place. Those rules and expectations favored a single group: white settlers, white leaders, the men who wrote the rules. In Brooks's view these settlers were a laudable bunch, fastidious, profoundly moral, and committed to the common good. Yet their sense of honor, while detailed and profound, was also inescapably something else. It was self-serving, based on laws and attitudes that worked aggressively, if not exclusively, to their own advantage. Two centuries after Winthrop's turn as governor, Brooks's reading of that history perfectly reflected the ethnocentrism that lay within that basic structure.

"Here let it be remarked," he boasted, "that there is not connected with the first steps of our Medford plantation the slightest trace of injustice, violence, or crime. In the minute accounts of the best historians, there is no mention of treachery, idleness, or dissipation. If any violation of good neighborhood, or civil law, or gospel morality, had existed, we should certainly have heard of it; for every man was emphatically his brother's keeper, and was Argos-eyed to detect the offender, and Briarian-handed to clutch him. We therefore confidently infer, that they who had concluded to make this place their home, were noble adventurers, conscientious patriots, and uncompromising Puritans; men whose courage dared to meet the panther and the tomahawk, whose benevolence would share with the red man its last loaf. . . ."

Like generations of historians after him, Brooks took pride in men like Winthrop, "the first keeper of the New England conscience" in Dunn's more contemporary iteration, and claimed that they did right by others even as they did well for themselves.

It was the tomahawk that was the sticking point. Settlers moved fast to fix the framework of their occupation. They did so underneath a heavy cloak of morals, speaking in a language and applying alien precepts few Indians could understand. By the time New England's tribes realized they'd been swindled, the first great land deals were already closed and sealed; and there was a system in place to see the law was heeded.

This system was clearly reflected in the complex deeds native peoples "signed" with crude marks and simple drawings. Such agreements, giving land away to whites for free, or selling it off for a pittance, occurred *after* the ink had already dried on legal papers whites shared among themselves. The rationale for this seemingly problematic timing was simple enough—if you were English. The Puritans "refused to recognize the legitimacy of Indian claims to hunting grounds or to uncultivated land adjacent to beaches, lakes and streams," explained historian Alfred A. Cave in his 1996 book, *The Pequot War*. Instead, taking note of how the inhabitants seemed to move fluidly from place to place, the settlers declared these acres "waste" and invoked the principle of *vacuum domicilium*. Under that principle, Puritans could declare any lands not heavily populated, consistently farmed, or already turned to pasture unimproved-therefore-unclaimed. The twist was roughly this: You (*who are already here*) are not using the land (*as we would*) therefore you have no legitimate right to it.

Remember, God Himself had cleared the title, John Winthrop argued. Great sweeps of plague had stilled the tongues of men who might object. So many "are swept awaye. . . ."

Of course there was a softer version of this claim. It hinged on the notion of a benevolent and protective people coming to do good. That image was captured perfectly in an upbeat account of the Massachusetts Bay Colony printed in London well before John Winthrop sailed. That pamphlet, *New England's Plantation*, was written by Francis Higginson, a minister from Leicester who had sailed to America one year before the governor and sent back stories of a wondrous, fertile world inhabited by a native people who "like well of our coming and planting here; partly because there is abundance of ground that they cannot possess nor make use of." *Vacuum Domicilium. Anno Domini 1630.*

Those soothing words at once reflected English law and set up an echo chamber to repeat and reinforce it. But Higginson added another thought, too, one bound to appeal to the better natures of the immigrants. The Puritans' arrival, he advised, "will be a means both of relief to them when they want and also a defense from their enemies." As a minister and an ardent defender of the Puritan cause, Higginson envisioned a benign patrimony led by wise men who would protect and feed the innocents even as they seized their land. Yet though that optimistic minister cheered the abundance of idle ground, he made it oddly plain that the ground was not "waste" at all, but already "cleared by the Indians." In fact, so much land near Salem lay bare that three miles outside the village a fellow could stand upon a hill, the minister explained, and look out over vast fields of cultivation that made "divers thousands of acres of ground as good as need be, and not a tree in the same." That land was farmed, not fallow. Yet the notion of a woodsy wilderness waiting to be tamed was more in keeping with the legal strategy of *vacuum domicilium* than the presence of enormous fields of corn. And so the idea of an untamed virgin land won out in the legal theorizing and popular imaginations of the 1600s as well as in the capturing lens of history; and much as historians have worked in recent decades to correct this misimpression, the notion of a native land unspoiled still often holds the popular imagination.

Settlers who traveled with John Winthrop's fleet had doubtless read Francis Higginson's account of *New England's Plantation* and were predisposed to play their part in claiming their own piece of that abundant ground. They did not stop too long to ponder open spaces. Nor were they weighed down by moral conflict. On the contrary, they were glowing with self-righteousness. Why,

God Himself had blessed their venture! He had sent the miracle of plagues. And the king had blessed them, too, with the colony's new charter. In any case, they were taking only vacant ground, property Higginson himself had stressed the Indians "cannot possess nor make use of."

Winthrop used not one but two arguments to justify the taking. He invoked the Old Testament by speaking of Abraham among the Sodomites (moral right), then added "a secular, legalistic argument," noted Cave, declaring that "the 'natural right' of hunter-gatherers" was trumped by the governor's "civil right" to enhance the land "for the raising of crops and the domestication of livestock." Since Winthrop intended to use Ten Hills Farm to plant crops, build a home, and raise cattle, he deemed himself completely justified, both legally and morally, a view nineteenth-century historians like Brooks were all too happy to repeat.

In the confusion that inevitably attended matters like land deeds signed without a common rule of law, language, or set of cultural expectations, local Indian tribes consistently lost out. Examples of that dynamic litter colonial history, but Medford land deeds tell the tale as vividly as any historian might wish. Several documents signed years *after* Winthrop's land was "set forth by metes and bounds" show Indian sachems, or leaders, signing away Medford acres for next to nothing—and in at least one case literally no tangible exchange at all but "to acknowledge their many kindnesses by this small gift."

One Winthrop deed discussed in a history of Middlesex County explicitly acknowledged the hand of the local magistrates even as it legitimized the transfer after the fact. Signed by the rough mark of a female sachem, or queen, that deed was written not in language she might have naturally produced or even understood, but in the arch and tortured verbiage of English jurisprudence. To "the inhabitants of the towne of Charlestowne," the female sachem allowed, should go "all the land within the line *granted them by the Court,*" except for those specifically reserved for Indians "to plant and hunt upon . . . and to fish at while the squaw liveth." Once the sachem died, her lands, too, were Winthrop's to use or otherwise "to dispose of, and *all Indians to depart.*"

And what did the sachem gain in return? Twenty-one coats. A large quantity of beads. Three bushels of corn.

Viewed across the span of many centuries, this seems a neat trick. But perhaps somewhere in John Winthrop's mind such dealings did not sit well. In any case, within a year of the Puritans' arrival there were hints of tension. Winthrop noted them in his journal and unquestionably felt them in his life upon that ground.

One of the few stories of Ten Hills Farm to survive the centuries is of the governor losing his way in the dark. It is an odd tale of a man becoming disoriented in the woods near his house, finding shelter, and then withholding that shelter from someone who, arguably, had much more reason to claim it than he. Brooks and other early historians tell the story as an example of the Puritan's fortitude and ingenuity. But it is possible to read the tale—recounted briefly in John Winthrop's journal—another way, as the story of a man sorely afraid of a people whom he does not really know and yet has grievously wronged. For what, in a time of peace, was a man with a gun to fear from a woman without one?

❖ ❖ ❖ ❖ ❖

On the evening of October 11, 1631, after taking his supper at Ten Hills Farm, John Winthrop left his house carrying just a match, a compass, and a gun. He was after a pack of wolves that had been killing swine and calves on his estate, but he failed in his hunt and soon became lost in the gathering darkness. Feeling his way along unfamiliar trails, he searched in vain for familiar landmarks until he found himself at the house of an Indian leader, Wonohaquaham, whom the English settlers called "Sagamore John." By then it was too late to make his way back home.

A powerful figure and a handsome young leader, Wonohaquaham was known to and respected by Winthrop. The governor, finding no one at home, decided he would pass the night there. The house was raised off the ground on stilts and hard to enter, so Winthrop gathered some mats, "made a good fire . . . and so spent the night sometimes walking by the fire, sometimes singing psalms and sometimes getting wood." Yet he could not rest, and by morning a light rain began to fall. Cold and sleepless and "having no cloak," at last he grabbed a long pole and used it to hoist himself up to the platform and into the dwelling.

At daybreak his peace was disrupted. "There came thither an Indian squaw," Winthrop wrote. Whether she needed shelter or something else was never clear. Certainly, John Winthrop never knew. He barred the door to her, though "she stayed there a great while essaying to get in." At last, she vanished back into the woods. By midday the governor was home again and welcomed there by servants who had cried and hollered and searched through the night, "but he heard them not."

Once home, Winthrop doubtless played down whatever fear he had experienced. But the event stayed with him powerfully enough that he recorded it at some length in his journal. Reading that entry against the backdrop of other entries from that period, it begins to come clear why he may have acted as he did. One month earlier, on the very same day his six-hundred-acre land grant was made, Winthrop and his fellow magistrates had ordered the severe whipping of a man "for enticing an Indian woman to sleep with him." For a Puritan, especially the governor, to be alone with an Indian woman in a deserted house in the night would have raised questions at least. And the law was about to turn harder. One week after Winthrop's night out on the land, the colony's main court ordered that any man caught committing adultery would be put to death. Perhaps it was lust the governor feared.

Or it may have been violence. For violence was a growing problem, a darker one, that emerged with equal clarity around that time. Journal entries and other records from 1631 show a pattern of trade swindles by unscrupulous Europeans answered by an escalating cycle of kidnappings, murder, and mayhem on the part of local tribes. If the Puritans arrived in a blush of peaceful coexistence, that time was fading fast. In the spring of 1631 Winthrop reported Mohawk Indians were preparing to massacre settlers and any Indians who made allegiance with them. It was a false alarm. The Mohawks lived hundreds of miles to the south, and the rumored attacks by that tribe, or tribes in alliance with them, never came. But other trouble would.

Writing in his journal just a week after his forest mishap, Winthrop noted that a trader and his companion staying on an island north of Boston were slaughtered by a group of Indians who "burnt the house . . . and carried away their guns and what else they liked." Angry traders asked Winthrop to provide twenty men to take revenge. Winthrop refused, citing bad weather but also allowing that the slain trader was "a wicked fellow and had much wronged the Indians." In that atmosphere, perhaps no one would have risked an open door. A time of relative peace was at an end. Undoubtedly, as he took shelter near Ten Hills Farm on that wet October night, John Winthrop felt the shift just as plainly as the rain.

POSSESSION

◆

War did come, and with it slavery. A clash was unavoidable. By 1634, Winthrop and the Puritans were so well established that Sir Simonds D'Ewes, an influential Puritan who remained behind in England, would observe the governor and his company had "raised such forts, built so many towns . . . and so dispersed and enriched themselves . . . [it seemed] the very finger of God" had guided them. Now the colony was bursting at the seams. New houses sprang up along the Charles and Mystic rivers. Existing settlements grew. Meetinghouses were built, fields cleared and planted, forests cut. The Puritans' headquarters moved to Boston, a great city being born. There, in the quiet of John Winthrop's house on the first Tuesday of each month ("att 8 of the clocke," old records say), the Court of Assistants gathered to shape the great experiment that was America.

A metal plaque installed in 1930 on the stone façade of a Charlestown building describes that court's beginnings. On it, a frieze depicts nine men attired in matching jackets, hats, and breeches clustered in the shade of several leafy trees. Beneath the frieze a text explains: "On this site the Assistants of the Governor and Company of the Massachusetts Bay met on August 23, 1630 and organized the Court of Assistants. This was succeeded in 1692 by the Superior Court of Judicature and in 1781 by the Supreme Judicial Court," a body that still functions as the commonwealth's final arbiter. In its infancy, the court's nine judges established the colony's legal system, approved laws, settled disputes, hosted criminal trials, and weighed the major issues of the day. Then they turned their attention to expansion. Territories to the south along the fertile Connecticut River valley seemed ripe for the taking. The court granted settlers permission to start building in that valley. Other populations were there first, however, and resented the intrusion. The ground was bloodied as Connecticut was born.

In 1635, John Winthrop's eldest son, twenty-nine-year-old John Jr., was dispatched to the region and put in charge of this new venture. It was no easy sinecure. For young John Winthrop to consolidate control he had to run a gauntlet of conflicting interests. Dutch settlers in New Amsterdam were anxious to stop the spread of English interests creeping south. Pequot Indians vowed they would hold the Connecticut River valley as their own. Settlers from Plymouth had their own agendas, too.

Sensing the Puritans' vulnerability, John Jr. dreamed of a massive fort to hold the coast and guard the river's mouth. From there, he thought, he could extend the Puritans' reach inland and effectively protect their interests. Upriver, meanwhile, three new settlements were established in quick succession, making a line of power down the broad, flat Connecticut River valley from Windsor, south to Hartford, then to Wethersfield. To the southeast, beside the sea, rough homesteads sprang up in rings around what was then only a raw clearing at the river's mouth. The towns of Lyme, Westbrook, Chester, Essex, and Deep River were soon born. To protect the growing colony, the Puritan's eldest son, now the dashing governor, petitioned his backers in England for an engineer to help devise a system of protection for those isolated villages.

That sudden burst of energy shattered a thin calm. As settlers swept across old Pequot lands, felling the tribe's forests and encroaching upon their villages, localized squabbles over trade, stolen livestock, damaged fields, hunting rights, property, and alcohol erupted up and down the valley. More and more, those arguments were settled with either a bullet or a blade. Pequot warriors gathered and prepared to fight. Puritan leaders spoke of war. Violence would turn the key to the Puritans' continued growth.

Back in England, the new colony's backers asked a skilled designer named Lion Gardiner to join their fledgling enterprise as something of an urban planner, colonial-style. He was granted a four-year commission and a £100 annual salary and told to serve John Winthrop Jr. by "drawing, ordering and making of a city, towns or forts of defence." Gardiner agreed and, after a stop in Holland to be married, arrived on the New England coast in November of that year. An early winter slowed him down, but by March 1636, Lion Gardiner and his pregnant wife had arrived at a rough clearing in what is now the town of Old Saybrook, a stylish if sleepy seaside enclave two hours by Amtrak from Manhattan. The barren scrape of land Gardiner found was hardly the hive of activity he had hoped for. In an account of his adventures penned twenty-four years after that unpacking, he complained he had been promised "300 able men, whereof 200 should attend to fortification, 50 to till the ground and 50 to build houses." Instead his family was met by only two laborers and several traders. His heart sank.

John Winthrop Jr., who had traveled with Gardiner and his wife, did not linger long to hear the man's complaints. Instead, he made a hasty exit back to Boston, where he rejoined his family in a place of power. After bidding the thirty-six-year-old engineer good luck and godspeed, the young governor promised to send supplies, then vanished, as far as Gardiner knew, off the very surface of the earth.

For weeks, Gardiner waited for provisions and of course those promised workers. Nothing came by sea or land. At last he sent a letter to his absent governor, the Puritan's eldest son, pleading for men to help him build and—even more pathetically—for food. And yet his hopes were low.

"To the Worshipfull Mr. John Winthrope Junior Esquire at Bostone in the bay," he groveled, "Worshipfull sir, I have received your letter, wherein I do understand that you are not like to return. . . . I wonder that you did not write to me, but it is no wonder, seeing that since your . . . departure there hath been no provision sent, but on the contrary, people to eat up that small, and now no, store that we had." By the time he wrote this letter, two dozen men, women, and children clustered in the rudimentary encampment.

They had come expecting to make a new home. Yet they arrived on the cusp of war in a time of famine. Now the engineer had more mouths to feed but nothing at hand to feed them with, a point he rushed to make. "Here hath come many vessels with provision to go up to the plantations," he complained. "But none for us. It seems that we have neither masters nor owners, but are left like so many servants whose masters are willing to be quit of them."

Hungry, abandoned, and facing the ever-growing threat of war, Gardiner came to believe John Winthrop Jr. never intended to come back at all or send supplies and would look out only for himself if a war came. In fact, John Winthrop Jr. did exactly that, splitting his time among family visits at Ten Hills Farm, a salt works he was starting up near Salem, and various other schemes that had little to do with either the settlement in Connecticut or the threat of war Gardiner and others were reporting. The engineer, abandoned at Old Saybrook on the eve of the colonists' first major conflict with the native population, told a ship's captain he believed the young governor was a selfish man who would tend to his needs first and "leave [us] at the stake to be roasted, or for hunger to be starved."

Soon, the fort builder and his wife would feel more vulnerable still. Perched at the edge of an unfamiliar sea, on April 29, 1636, the couple welcomed the family's newest member. After a hard labor, Mary Gardiner gave birth to the first white child born in Connecticut. So began a season of planting and desperate scrabbling for survival. In his account of that period, Gardiner wrote that his concern over food grew so intense that he backed off any thought that he might make progress on the fort. "War is like a three-footed stool," he explained. "Want one foot, and down comes all." Of the three ("men, victuals, and munition"), victuals were the leg he most immediately required. That first summer Gardiner determined to tend to stomachs first and worry about men and bullets later. "It will be best," he informed the colony's leaders, "only to fight against Captain Hunger, and let fortification alone awhile." Instead of building a great fort, he labored in the fields.

That July, the murder of a trader brought war closer. Gardiner's mood and sense of betrayal deepened. Of the tribes of the northern coast, the Pequots were among the most powerful and populous. It was widely known they could be brutal. Gardiner's fears were well founded, and his reading of the situation was acute. War would come. Yet soon it became clear anything the Pequots dared to do the Puritans would match, and then exceed in raw brutality. The conflict that followed was quick, deadly, and decisive. But it was the Pequot families, not Gardiner and his lonely charges, who would be roasted in the fires that came with it. The Puritans, convinced of God's protection and certain of His approval, moved toward a strategy of eradication.

Soldiers from the Massachusetts Bay Company streamed south from Boston in the spring of 1637. When they arrived near the sandy shore where Lion Gardiner struggled to establish himself, they joined forces with other settlers from Plymouth and elsewhere to drive their might against a strongly fortified Pequot settlement near a Connecticut estuary called the Mystic River. In a fury, those English soldiers and the Narragansett warriors who had allied with them burned the Pequot village and slaughtered or captured every inhabitant inside. Contemporary historians estimate as many as four hundred to six hundred Pequot men, women, and children perished in the raid. Those who did not die at once but tried to flee were met with musket shot and a ring of swords that pushed them back into the inferno. Gardiner later wrote of the day with gratitude. "The Lord God blessed their design," he said of the Puritans, "so that they returned with victory to the glory of God and honour of our nation, having slain three hundred, burnt their fort, and taken many prisoners."

Soldiers wrote of the stench of charred skin and disembowelment.

In his classic history, *New England Frontier: Puritans and Indians 1620–1675*, published in 1965 and reprinted thirty years later, historian Alden T. Vaughan captured the impact of that massacre: "The destruction of the Pequots cleared away the only major obstacle to Puritan expansion," he observed. "And the thoroughness of that destruction made a deep impression on the other tribes." Broken and humbled, the Pequot fled. Soldiers followed. John Winthrop made a note of it: "The rest are dispersed," he wrote of the Pequots in the immediate aftermath of that vicious swamp fight, "and the Indians in all quarters so terrified as all their friends are afraid to receive them."

To all involved, the violence of this first major conflict revealed something important, something that would reverberate and then, in time, repeat. These newcomers clearly had not come to bring those Indians "relief to them when they want," as the upbeat Puritan minister Francis Higginson so naively predicted in his early pamphlet, nor to provide "defense from their enemies," as he once prophesied (though the Narragansetts and several other tribes were perfectly content to have the Pequots broken). Instead, they proved a ruthless enemy.

Among whites, meanwhile, the bloody rout in Connecticut was perceived largely as Gardiner saw it, as a signal to the colonists of their God-given right to possess and settle a new land. Gradually, a time of deeper conflict would begin. But even as allegiances shifted and the complex tapestry of Indian tribes adjusted to this new awareness, the pattern of war, imprisonment, sale, and conquest would continue, albeit unevenly, for a century and more.

In Boston when news of that great slaughter came, a cheer went up at news of victory. John Winthrop Senior, writing to Governor William Bradford in Plymouth, described the scene with the lusty language of a man who sends young soldiers off to battle but has never seen a war himself. "Our men cut off a place of swamp with their swords" and pressed the Indians into "a narrow compass . . . [the] easier [to] kill them through the thickets," said the master of Ten Hills Farm. In the raging terror of that fight, Winthrop's men escaped unhurt except for those few who sloshed into the swamp and were engulfed by friendly fire or cut to ribbons by the swinging tomahawks of dying men. Winthrop saw God's hand in that success and spread his own interpretation of events. This was "a just war," he assured his people, a war in which God's chosen vanquished all who stood to block their way.

The next order of business was to deal with all the prisoners. Most were sold or given to the Narraganssets, or handed out as favors to serve the colony's soldier class as slaves. Among those prisoners dispatched to Boston in 1637, the Puritan explained, "we send the male children to Bermuda by Mr. William Pierce, and the women and maid children are disposed about in the towns." In his journal, the governor of Massachusetts made a note: seven hundred Pequot men, women, and children slain or captured.

In the aftermath of war, it was often left to the head of Ten Hills Farm to supervise the distribution of these prisoners. As governor, it was he who could determine and divide the spoils. And so he doled out warriors and women as slaves to men who came to him for favors, and saw to it, too, that some among these hapless folk were treated kindly. In a letter to his friend William Bradford written that July, he explained: "Among the prisoners we have the wife and children of [the Indian sachem] Mononotto, a woman of a very modest countenance and behavior. As a prisoner of war, Mononotto had two wishes, that her captors "would not abuse her body," and that her children be left with her. "It was by her mediation," explained John Winthrop, that "two English maids were spared from death . . . and kindly used by her." In deference to that show of mercy, wrote John Winthrop, "I have taken charge of her."

Other prisoners were not so fortunate.

"Much Honoured Sir," wrote Roger Williams, the founder of Rhode Island and a man known for his embrace of Native American rights, "It having again pleased the most High to put into your hands another miserable drove of Adam's degenerate seed, and our brethren by nature: I am bold (if I may not offend in it) to request the keeping and bringing up of one of the children. I have fixed mine eye on this little one with the red about his neck, but I will not be preemptory in my choice."

Given Williams's genuine compassion for native people (and his widely despised call for Puritans to "repent" over the unrighteous taking of Indian lands through royal grants), it seems more than possible that Williams wanted that young boy not for work, but to raise as his own, within a world view and religion he embraced. Even so, the fact of ownership was clear in any case, a matter of intellectual enslavement that did not bear the name. Still, for other supplicants the call for ownership was likely less benign.

"We have heard of a dividence of women and children," wrote another settler, "and would be glad of a share, a young woman or girl and a boy if you think good."

"Honored Sir," began Israel Stoughton, a distinguished officer in the Pequot War, "By this Pinnace . . . you shall receive 48 or 50 women and children." Among them, he explained, "there is one I formerly mentioned that is the fairest and largest that I saw amongst them to whome I have given a coate to cloath her: It is my desire to have her for a servant. . . ."

Stoughton also wrote on several friends' behalf: "There is a little Squa that Steward Calacot desireth. . . . Lieutenant Damport also desireth one, to witt, a tall one with three strokes upon her stomach."

In Boston in the end of that first clang of war, fifteen male and two female war prisoners were bound and manacled and marched aboard the Salem-built *Desire* to be sold as slaves in the West Indies. Once there, the ship's captain, William Pierce, traded them for stores of cotton, tobacco, and a group of Africans. When the *Desire* returned, Winthrop made a note of her cargo. That brief mention is generally taken as the first historical reference to the sale of blacks upon New England soil. The year was 1638. The Massachusetts Bay Company was not yet ten years old. In the uproar of the busy harbor, merchants met and made their deals. Goods and people were unloaded. Bales of cotton and fragrant bunches of tobacco were heaved and checked and traded. Sugar was weighed by the barrel and sold by the bag. Somewhere in the clamor, the huddled Africans were gathered up and hawked to willing strangers. And so it was that slavery set its second foot upon that ground.

Several months after those black slaves arrived, a visitor from England, John Josselyn, stopped at Noddles Island—just as Winthrop once had done—to stay the night with Samuel Maverick, the isolated émigré who had somehow made a life of elegance on a rough island out in Boston Harbor. By then, Maverick had at least two slaves to do his bidding. In Josselyn's 1674 travelogue, *An Account of Two Voyages to New England*, the visitor described a troubling scene. A black woman appeared at his window wailing and distraught. She told the traveler a story of her host. "Mr. Maverick,"

the author explained, "was desirous to have a breed of Negroes." To execute that plan, "will'd she, nill'd she," that woman would provide the womb. By ordering one of his slaves to rape another, Maverick planned to build his fortune.

This is Josselyn's account in its entirety:

> The Second of October, about 9 of the clock in the morning, Mr. Mavericks Negro woman came to my chamber window, and in her own Countrey language and tune sang very loud and shril, going out to her, she used a great deal of respect toward me, and willingly would have expressed her grief in English; but I apprehended it by her countenance and deportment, whereupon I repaired to my host, to learn of him the cause, and resolve to intreat him in her behalf, for that I understood before, that she had been a Queen in her own Countrey, and observed a very humble and dutiful garb used toward her by another Negro who was her maid. Mr. Maverick was desirous to have a breed of Negroes, and therefore seeing she would not yield by perswasions to company with a Negro young man he had in his house; he commanded him will'd she nill'd she to go to bed to her, which was no sooner done but she kickt him out again, this she took in high disdain beyond her slavery, and this was the cause of her grief.

Josselyn did not linger there, but moved his narrative ahead to tell of how that afternoon he bit into a wasp's nest, mistaking it for some odd, sweet fruit of this new world, a pineapple perhaps, "big as a woman's hat." A wasp settled on his lip and set its stinger in the soft flesh there. The woman was forgotten.

When Josselyn returned some years later, he made no effort to learn the woman's fate or whether she had given birth. Her name, her age, the place of her upbringing, the story of her transfer to New England, any tale of life before her time on Noddles Island, any children that she might have had, and also the story of the other slave who was forced "to go to bed to her" and how he might have felt about that rape, and later, if a child was born, how he might have felt about that child—all of this was lost. Of those earliest slaves, only that one paragraph remains and only that because Josselyn was approached and took the time to make a record of the conversation.

Gradually what was novel became commonplace. The people of the Massachusetts Bay Colony condoned slavery in their midst. Merchants spun a web with slave economies elsewhere. By the time New England's earliest newspapers appeared they showed an easy, constant flow: what students everywhere know as the "triangle trade," but what really was more often like a hexagon, a pentagon, a square, a triangle or line, depending on the market, the weather, the captain's orders, and raw luck. Here to there, there and back, ships rode heavy to their waterlines, cargos bulging with huge stores of indigo, sugar, molasses, rum, and humans with dark skin. Still today, disintegrating pages tell a centuries-long story of deals done, men moving, profits made.

Winthrop captured the first tendrils of that intertwining trade in his journal with the offhandedness of a man who knew it well and carried no objection: "Here came a small bark from the West Indies," the governor wrote in his journal in the summer of 1639. "He brought much wealth in money, plate, indico and sugar." The captain sold his goods in Boston, then refilled his hold and left again for the West Indies. Trade built wealth. Wealth blurred borders. In the Atlantic economy of the 1600s, the sails of commerce were stitched with the skins of slavery and blown by the wind of greed. "One of our ships which went to the Canaries with pipe staves in the beginning of November last returned now and brought wine and sugar and salt, and some tobacco," Winthrop wrote one spring. Those products "she had at Barbados in exchange for Africoes, which she carried from the isle of Maio," part of Cape Verde, off the coast of Africa.

Seven months to make a square. Boston. The Canary Islands. Africa. Barbados. Boston again. Pipe staves in exchange for people in exchange for wine, sugar, salt, and some tobacco. The only thing that mattered was how the winds blew, what the market would bear, and how much those ships could carry. The lure of unpaid labor made for an enticement too strong even for the righteous to resist.

On October 3, 1639, the Massachusetts Court of Assistants ruled "the Governor had leave to keep a Narragansett Indian and his wife." Slavery by that time was black and brown, routine, accepted, fixed. The practice would hold in Massachusetts for a century and a half—longer by a decade than in Georgia, which was settled later, though it held on longer.

Two years after the governor was "given leave to keep" and three years after Captain Pierce returned from his West Indies mission, Massachusetts became the first colony in North America to formally endorse the ownership and sale of human property. The law made legal what was already true. Black and Indian slavery, though not the norm, was well established. Now it would be sanctioned, too. The Massachusetts Body of Liberties of 1641 defined slavery in a way that satisfied Puritan pieties; yet the language made it clear that slavery would be welcome at more than a ship's distance.

There should never be any bond slavery, item 91 declared, *"unless . . ."*

> *It be lawful captives taken in just wars.*
> *And such strangers as willingly sell themselves.*
> *Or are sold to us. . . .*
> *This exempts none. . . .*

Legal. Accepted. Rewarded. Desired.

More than twelve hundred Native Americans were enslaved in New England before the 1600s closed. The number of blacks was not recorded, and historians struggle for an accurate count. In his 1866 study of slavery in Massachusetts, George H. Moore wrote that he believed there were at least two hundred African slaves in the colony in the 1600s, more still in the century after. Contemporary scholars tend to double those figures, yet they acknowledge that the work is painstaking and the end result almost certainly inaccurate. It is difficult, after a span of centuries, to make a count of a phenomenon that was prevalent but never adequately tabulated. The word "servant" was often substituted for "slave," as though the two conditions were the same. Records are scattered, damaged, and lost. Considering the ravages of mildew, flooding, fire, sun, negligence, ignorance, shame, acidity, insects, dry rot, simple carelessness, and the basic sense among most whites that *this* history did not merit preservation, the magnitude of the task of reconstruction becomes clear, and Josselyn's briefest clue more valuable.

Those few records that did survive show black and Indian slaves in settlers' homes, fields, and businesses. Some drove carriages or served as footmen. Some made bricks and some built houses. Some wore formal livery. Others were clad only in rags. Some cooked. Some farmed. Some cleaned. Some worked as carpenters, blacksmiths, woodsmen, weavers. Others, deemed too unruly or too angry to be tamed, were shipped south to serve harsh masters as their punishment or sold back to the West Indies, where plantation life was ruder, days were longer. At Ten Hills Farm and his more formal residence in Boston the governor "had leave to keep . . ." and that he did. Along with land, John Winthrop in an early will made it clear that to Adam, his fourth son, "I give my Indians. . . ."

It is hard to reconstruct the total number of slaves John Winthrop may have had, or what happened to those slaves upon his death, or how he treated them in life. As a result, contemporary readers are left to analyze only the barest clues while knowing they show just a fragment of reality.

The notion of such property came easily to men already well acquainted with the slave system. The service of one man to another was expected and banal. Yet not all service was the same. White men like Lion Gardiner (who complained so bitterly that he was abandoned in the wild like a servant with no master) tended to work with contracts. Those contracts sometimes led to independence, property, and wealth. After his time of service was complete, in exchange for a black dog, a gun, powder and shot, several blankets, and a bit of rum, Gardiner bought a 3,300-acre island off the eastern tip of Long Island from the Montaukett tribe and won a King's grant for tens of thousands of acres in East Hampton. Four centuries later, impressive echoes of that wealth remained. When ninety-three-year-old Robert David Lion Gardiner, the self-described "16th lord of the manor," died in East Hampton in August of 2004, Gardiner Island was still in family hands. So was a legacy of wealth and privilege. In a half dozen obituaries, the old man was reported as having routinely dismissed the Fords, the Rockefellers, and the Du Ponts as nouveaux riches. One article put it more colorfully still, saying that to *Gardiner's* clan, George Washington came off as something of a parvenu.

Of course not all families were as successful. But in early America, where economic systems were so loose the General Court could get away with minting money in direct defiance of royal orders for almost thirty years, land and liberty were the most reliable coins of this new realm. Even a small bit of money went quite far, and as the Gardiner example shows, the legacy of land could last through generations.

To the freemen went the spoils. And to the freemen went the servants. Writing from Barbados in 1627, young Henry Winthrop had asked his father to please send him men "and they be bound to serve me in the West Indies some three year or five." In another letter he informed his uncle that he was quite content with island life. It was his intention, he explained, "always to have a plantation of servants." Of course the rub came in paying those men's wages. Get them, Henry wrote his father, not for £100 a year, as Lion Gardiner was paid, or even £50, but "as reasonable as you can, promising them not above 10 pounds a year."

But why pay ten pounds when slaves worked for free? Basic economics argued against it. And in a colony still struggling for a start, how were such slaves to be obtained? In 1645, John Winthrop's brother-in-law and business wizard Emmanuel Downing presented a bold notion, championing the idea of a new war with the Indians, this time against the Narragansett tribe, those same warriors who had sided with the English against the Pequots a decade earlier. In war, he argued, the colony could obtain a fresh supply of prisoners to sell in exchange for blacks or, as he called them, "Moores," purchased in the Caribbean.

"Sir," Winthrop's brother-in-law began, "A war with the Narraganset is very considerable to this plantation, for I doubt whether it be not sin in us having power in our hands to suffer them to maintain the worship of the devil, which their powwows often do." And war, he hastened to add, contained powerful business advantages the colony should not neglect. "If upon a just war," he argued, "the Lord should deliver them into our hands, we might easily have men, women and children enough to exchange for Moores." That trade, he said, was "gainful pillage." Besides, how else should the colony prosper? "For I do not see how we can thrive until we get into a stock of slaves sufficient to do all our business." Downing was a practical man in this, and he argued skillfully. "I suppose you know very well," he told the master of Ten Hills Farm, "how we shall maintain 20 Moores cheaper than one English servant."

Winthrop did not go to war. But slavery grew in any case.

And so a deep imbalance was then set. Like a poisonous snake gliding off a river rock, it laid its curse without much trace. In that first decade, the language of freedom was deformed. While Winthrop and his brethren spoke in stirring terms of liberty and godliness, what was possible for some was never within reach for others. That proved as true on John Winthrop's six hundred acres as it was anywhere across the South. Though slavery never took hold in New England on the same epic scale as in rural Virginia, South Carolina, Georgia, Tennessee, and elsewhere, the practice was just as firmly planted in the minds of northern settlers accustomed to white rule, and just as ravaging for those who suffered the consequences. As it was in the North, so it was in the South. Those who came in chains or were sold as bounty in a war were branded with a deficit that would last through generations. And for generations the system firmly held its grip.

Part II

The
Immigrant

THE KING'S FORESTER

◆

William Ryall came to Massachusetts with a contract to cut wood. He stepped ashore in 1629 with no important stature, no promise of a sizable estate, no grand inheritance or intricate web of social influence. A workingman, he never knew the taste of privilege. But neither did he wince under a master's order that he breed, or bend before the whip, or wordlessly obey. He was just a fellow with a skill, a handful of possessions, a letter of introduction, and a job. From that humble seed, descendants fought their way to wealth and power. His grandson Isaac would embody the American Dream before the notion even formed. One might even say that he invented it.

Early accounts of the family's rise often refer to Ryall only as "the Immigrant," as if America itself had given birth. And in a way, it did. What came before was lost. What was built, what was won, all that was achieved on that new ground was proudly kept. At a time when literacy was rare and spellings fluid, even the family name would change from the humble Ryall to the more baronial Royall, all within two generations.

One year before John Winthrop sailed, the master of the *Lion's Whelp*, "a neat and nimble ship" of 120 tons carrying forty planters, six fishermen, a full hold of provisions, and four braying goats, prepared to sail from Gravesend, England, to America. The great fever of migration was hardly then a blush on England's cheek. John Winthrop had not yet signed up. He was busy at a wedding and several funerals. His mother died. His son Henry married. His brother-in-law was laid into the ground. In London on the day the *Lion's Whelp* unfurled her sails, the lord of Groton Manor was watching as his son and niece exchange their vows. Hardly yet a man, Henry at the time believed he would return to the young slave colony at Barbados where he had made a stumbling start, this time with Elizabeth Fones, his cousin-bride, in tow. The Puritan had his doubts about the marriage. He had his doubts about Barbados, too, but the Caribbean venture had not yet been written off as failed. As Vincent Harlow explained it in his 1926 history of Barbados, Winthrop, that "great nation-builder . . . had been quick to see the possible advantages of trade therewith." Henry, though boasting only poor results so far, was ready for a second try. His father grudgingly supported him. The pregnant Elizabeth Fones was game as well. A restless generation was unmoored.

At a distance on the day Henry Winthrop and his cousin bowed their heads and exchanged rings, a shout went up in Gravesend harbor as scores of men of lesser means set off for Massachusetts. Their prospects were not as bright as Henry's. Most among them had no wealthy fathers to send men. Surely they never imagined they would "always have a plantation of servants," as Henry once so casually remarked. For the most part, these men were servants, and they nursed few expectations. Still, they were young and adventurous and, like Henry, eager for a risk.

William Ryall was among them on the *Lion's Whelp*. He was a strapping figure, capable, curious, strong-willed, healthy, and ambitious. To pave his way in that new land was a letter from one governor, Mathew Cradock in England, to another, John Endecott in Salem, relatives who served the Massachusetts Bay Company's interests on two shores. The letter was full of practical instructions. Among them was the request that Endecott clear the way for this young Englishman to do his work. Please welcome him, the letter urged, extend whatever favors he might need. As the *Lion's Whelp* tacked west in steel-gray seas, Ryall looked ahead at what his life might be. Once he satisfied his contract's terms he could move and find some land and make his start. His time of servitude

4.1 Original seal of the Massachusetts Bay Company. Courtesy of the Public Records Division, Commonwealth of Massachusetts.

would end. Then, in the wilderness that beckoned, he could shape his fate on his own terms.

Sailing nearby on the *Talbot* that same summer was the Reverend Francis Higginson, that cheerful purveyor of the image of a fertile land inhabited by friendly Indians who, struggling desperately with the ravages of smallpox, were now waiting for salvation from the very interlopers who imported the disease. Higginson possessed a sparkling optimism that found its way onto the colony's new seal. Produced in London, the seal depicted a bare-chested Indian standing in an empty field, bow in one hand, arrow pointing downward in the other in a sign of peace. The image promised safety and good times ahead. And if that message did not shine out clear enough, a clever designer added a sweet touch: a streamer snaking from the Indian's mouth, over his head, and protectively encircling his naked shoulders with the plea: "Come over and help us."

It was a neat bit of marketing. For godly Puritans looking for a holy ground, the promise of religious freedom and boundless opportunity twined ever so smoothly with the declaration of a moral purpose. They would save the heathens' souls, these Puritans declared, even as they stripped the woods, secured the land, and shaped a distant world to white men's liking.

To prepare for that untidy flood, several hundred men went on ahead in early voyages to clear the land and set first seeds. Ryall was among them. At the end of June 1629, when the *Lion's Whelp* anchored at Salem, the Immigrant found a primitive encampment busy with new life on ancient ground. The village was bustling with the bang of carpentry. Fields were full of men. A company store was then in business, too. John Endecott's ship had carried enough goods to clothe one hundred men. One year later the *Talbot, Lion's Whelp,* and *George* brought more. As a result, rough-hewn shelves in Ryall's day, according to a fascinating study of daily life in those first years written by George Francis Dow, were crammed with simple necessities: hundreds of dark suits, eight hundred sturdy shoes, great stacks of matching shirts, five hundred red knit caps, a hundred black hats trimmed with leather, piles of green waistcoats, eight hundred socks, and a very few indulgences. Garters, handkerchiefs, small throw rugs were the several luxuries available. For a generation, settlers dressed with numbing uniformity.

For men like Ryall, even such basic purchases were an indulgence that would have to wait. Old shoes, old coats, old pants, hats, socks, and belts would all wear down to ribbons in hard work, and soon enough. But for now, more important matters pressed. The Immigrant's first challenge was simply to stay dry. He had his clothes. What he needed was a roof. Men like him "burrow[ed] . . . in the Earth for their first shelter," one early resident remarked, as though they wished to cleave the loamy soil in relief upon their landing. If Ryall did that, there is no record. More likely he set about building a simple "English wigwam," a primitive dwelling constructed of tall saplings bent into a frame, then covered up with sod or bark to shape a curved and windowless hut finished with a door standing sentry at one end and a chimney smoking at the other.

But where to build it? Salem was unkempt and cluttered. Ryall instinctively moved away from it, heading north, across the river. At a place called Ryall Side, today the town of Beverly, he built himself a home. Then he sought an audience with the governor.

Imagine him arriving at the Endecotts' door early in this great experiment, a supplicant, hat in hand, the sound of chickens clucking in the background. All around him settlers like himself rushed to make the most of summer's benediction, to build a home, till a field, chop wood for winter warmth. Every path was busy. Conversation turned to matters of survival. True enough, the outpost was crowded. But life outside it could be dangerous. Everywhere the story was the same: The wolves were at the chickens. The deer were in the corn. The wilderness was near. The crops were dry. They needed rain. Everything felt tenuous. At night when work was done and fires lit, the haunting cries of wild animals sounded close in the deep silence of that land. Beyond them lay the glacial heaves, the wide unknown, the unexplored, the native tribes, a natural world they did not know. Few men had time to spend exploring. Survival in that season was an all-consuming enterprise.

Ryall's meeting with John Endecott would have been a quick exchange. With several ships having just disgorged hundreds of disoriented passengers, it was a hectic time, and full of urgent business. Ryall's orders hardly needed explanation. The contract binding him to company service carried all the stiff formality of court. William Ryall and another servant, "coopers and cleavers of timber," the letter announced, "are entertained by us in halves. . . . Pray join others that can assist them . . . and let them provide us some staves and other timber of all sorts, to be sent by the Talbot, Whelp or the other two ships that come after." Get these men into the woods! Let them plunder those towering riches! Let them grab the new land's wealth, then send the bounty back to us.

With those instructions and an axe, Ryall started his new life. In time he met a girl named Phoebe Green. They married. For several years he spent his days in great cathedrals of old hardwood. In the brilliant, speckled light that flickered down from canopies of forest green, he felled huge towers of the straightest locust, maple, walnut, elm, alder, ash, and oak. In the salty air of passing seasons, the smell of cedar was his ether. The deepest woods became his home.

While Ryall worked, the ever-buoyant Puritan minister Francis Higginson remained behind in town, tending to his flock and making extensive notes. By mid-July he was voted teacher of the congregation. His future in the colony seemed sure. His place within it brought him joy. In lengthy breathless prose, he recorded details of the land and of beauty he could scarcely grasp. Here one might find "plenty of strawberries in their time," he wrote in that seductive account of New England life published in England on the eve of John Winthrop's sailing, "and pennyroyal, winter savory, sorrel, brooklime, liverwort, carvel and watercress . . . leeks and onions. . . ." On and on he scribbled, precisely marking each detail, his spirit fairly humming with the lushness of that summer. "Here are also abundance of other sweet herbs delightful to the smell . . . and plenty of single damask roses very sweet. . . . Also, mulberries, plums, raspberries, currants, chestnuts, filberts, walnuts, smalnuts, hurtleberries and haws of whitethorn. . . . For wood there is no better in the world I think."

Higginson had found what Winthrop soon would find. Such riches! His pamphlet whetted the appetites of many, and the new governor used it extensively to whip up interest in the project. Yet the land could be as harsh as it was beautiful, and in the minister's second winter, after great new waves of immigrants washed in, cold and disease would take him. The optimistic teacher was among some two hundred settlers who perished in that awful season.

William Ryall thrived. The woods were to his liking. His term of service had an end. In time he looked ahead and wondered at the boundaries of a new frontier. Salem grew with every passing summer. It was too densely settled for his taste. The social ladder mattered. He was barely on it. There were petty annoyances, too. Sewage fouled the air. Wolves came. Livestock shifted and bleated in the night. Fierce enmities were everywhere. A ring of new laws tightened. Still more settlers poured ashore. In that first decade, more than sixteen thousand immigrants arrived and struggled for a way to make a life. For a man who came to love the quiet majesty of an untrammeled world, it seemed high time to leave.

"The King's Forester," as William Ryall was dubbed by a Salem native writing to John Adams more than a century later, quickly vanished from town lore. Though early Salem records (and even MapQuest) recognize a Ryall Side in the seaside town of Beverly, no history details the life and fortune of the immigrant who gave the spot his name. Instead, by 1638 another newcomer of roughly the same age but graced with a far superior pedigree claimed the land where Ryall made his start. That second man, thirty-three-year-old John Winthrop Jr., was granted "liberty from his father Gov. Winthrop to set up salt works at Ryal Side." The Massachusetts court granted the governor's son sixteen acres for his project.

As to Ryall, he had already moved on. Only his name remained, while the Puritan's eldest son took the land. Parentage, patronage, and royal patents ruled the day. William Ryall understood that well enough and had already traveled north, moving deeper into a region not yet claimed or tilled by whites. Eventually, he found his place. By the time John Winthrop Jr. took over at Ryall Side, William Ryall and his wife Phoebe were sitting down to dinner on the rough, unsettled coast of Maine.

Less than a decade after leaving England, the Immigrant (Ryall, Ryal, Rial, Royall, or Royal, as the name was variously spelled in documents that survived the centuries) carved 250 acres out of the frontier and claimed it as his own. He and his new wife, the stepdaughter of Boston's first tavern owner, Samuel Cole, planted themselves boldly in the wilds. It was a leap of faith in a new marriage. On the broken shores of Casco Bay, Phoebe's neighbors would not be Puritans, families of the elite, or even rough and like-minded pioneers, but sandpipers, snipes, seagulls and egrets, seals and sea hawks, wolves, and bears, and everywhere, the Abenaki people (better known now as the Penobscot), "men of the East" as other tribes knew them.

William and Phoebe set up a rudimentary camp at a point of land between the Indian-named (and also variously spelled) Westgusttugo and Chusquissacke rivers. They would use that land to farm. A stone's throw to the north, at a place called Fogg Point, they built a home that looked across a landscape patterned like spilled milk, a solid landmass broken into fingers stretching into tidal waters, past glistening sand flats, and then gone. In the distance only the occasional dot of rock and a scattering of bumpy islands topped with pine gave way to open sea. This was a colder place than Ryall Side, but just as bountiful. Fish and lobster were abundant. Sweet mussels, clams, and oysters littered the shoreline and sliced the thickest leather underfoot. The woods were lively with an ancient walk.

The Ryalls were the first whites to settle in Wescustogo, an area that now encompasses the towns of Yarmouth, North Yarmouth, and Freeport, Maine, the last of which today is most famous as the home of L.L. Bean's 160,000-square-foot homage to the American frontier (2.7 times the acreage of a football field), with its bright profusion of canoes, moccasins, fishing poles, tents, tarps, traps, headlights, flashlights, lanterns, knives, axes, saws, camping tools, coffee mugs, cookbooks, compasses, global positioning devices, bows and arrows, and a thousand other outdoor pleasures, open for business "24-7, 365, and yes, including Christmas," said a fleece-shod salesclerk in the spring of another century.

Ryall and his family epitomized the rough-and-ready spirit L.L. Bean so deftly markets. The family subsisted in that frigid, spartan outpost using mostly brawn and ingenuity. For forty years they called it home. During most of that time, white settlers and the Abenaki managed a fretful coexistence. Cycles of farming and trade began. Routines emerged. It was a hard life in a beautiful yet barren place. Just to grow a carrot and a cabbage in those early years, the Ryalls had to heave rock, turn soil, smooth the ground beneath rough plows, and weed by hand. They rushed to build a cabin, put up stores of food, gather and cut wood enough to make it to first thaws. In time, they created a large homestead for themselves. Then, as the family grew, the couple left Fogg Point to settle on their farm beside the lapping waters of a river that now bears their name—the Royall River—a narrow crystal flow along Interstate 95 that passes under eighteen-wheelers in a blink.

Not long after the family claimed the land, William Ryall moved to subdivide it. What mattered to him most a decade after arriving in North America was not relief from the silly posturing of town, or even freedom from England's unforgiving social structure, but safety in numbers. Isolated on a wild frontier, the couple came to crave community. In 1639, like Lion Gardiner before him, the Immigrant was about to be a father. A second generation would be born. Yet word of the Pequot War had set its seed of terror. Phoebe craved protection for her baby. He would be a boy, the first of seven children, an infant they called William.

To keep that baby safe, the Immigrant devised a plan. He would invite new settlers north and make a ring of whites to keep the Indians at bay. And so the Immigrant wrote a letter to the Puritan and asked him to send men.

Favors to the Few

"One Mr. Ryall," wrote John Winthrop in his signature spidery scrawl in 1639, "having gotten a patent at Sagadahoc out of the grand patent . . . tendered it to our government, so as we would send people to possess it."

The governor informed the court.

The court did nothing to pursue it.

"We were not ready for such a business," explained Winthrop, "having enough to do at home."

In Cambridge then Harvard College was established. Land disputes were negotiated, colonial boundaries argued and redrawn. Cycles of farming and trade became routine. At last the new community was prospering. But as it stabilized, new threats emerged. Some came from tribes anguished over white incursions. Some came from supposed friends. Success bred not just more success, but challenges to the Puritans' design. In London, the powerful Lord Saye and Sele, a viscount and expansionist planter with his eye on building riches in the Caribbean and Connecticut, used both his wiles and his considerable influence in an attempt (much like young Ryall's) to divert new immigrants from Massachusetts. Winthrop was outraged.

Partly, the hurt was personal. Lord Saye condemned Massachusetts for its rocky soil and cold winters. What was Winthrop thinking when he landed there? Why not let new immigrants come settle in a warmer place, the influential Puritan viscount wheedled, a temperate land more suited to the leisurely accumulation of new wealth?

"It came over by divers letters and reports," Winthrop sputtered, "that the Lord Say did labor, by disparaging this country, to divert men from coming to us, and so to draw them to the West Indies." Though Winthrop himself had once supported such endeavors (and several of his sons were then exploring business possibilities in Barbados and Antigua), the usually stoic governor responded with a bitter tongue-lashing. He was in no mood to let his people go. Not for a pompous viscount, and certainly not for an untitled immigrant who held some minor toehold on the coast of Maine. The Ryalls would have to wait for neighbors. John Winthrop and his New England cohorts would spread their message—and their manpower—in the way best suiting them.

Eventually that would mean enduring links to the rapidly growing slave economies of Antigua, St. Christopher, and Barbados. But those ties emerged in a way that fit the Puritan's aims far better than the raw siphoning of new settlers to fill out someone else's dreams. The Puritan's youngest son, Samuel, a member of Harvard's class of 1646 (though he did not stay to graduate), would settle in Antigua at the age of twenty and stay for the remainder of his life. There he would make his home in grand style at his Caribbean Groton Hall, rise to the position of deputy governor, and manage scores of slaves. In all his years in Antigua, though, he kept close ties to family, to New England, to Ten Hills Farm, and Cambridge. Leaving might promise adventure, and riches perhaps. But it came at some personal cost. Perhaps to acknowledge that, before he left in 1646, Samuel Winthrop gave his college (then housed in a single, shingled building) a small gift. Before he sailed away, Samuel and three friends (among them his cousin George Downing) gave Harvard a cow pasture they had planted out with fruit trees. They would call this field their *Pomarium Sociorum*, Latin for the Fellow's Orchard. Today it is the site of Harvard's Widener Library. The university acknowledges the bequest on its website, calling that small plot of land "the first gift of real estate by alumni."

For many years, Samuel thought he would return to live back home at Ten Hills Farm, where he had ambled from the age of four until he left the colony as a college student of eighteen. Letters in his later years speak to that desire. Yet following a pattern common at the time, he would remain instead at his warm island post, trading and investing with his brothers on the mainland, completing a circle of trade that long persisted between those farmlands and the North.

But it was not yet time for such adventures. In 1640, Samuel was just a lad of thirteen, and the colonies of the Caribbean had not yet found their feet. Meanwhile, New England's patriarch was distracted by events at home. For Samuel Winthrop's father then it was a time of crisis, not expansion. In that year tremendous debts incurred by a reckless manager at Ten Hills Farm left the Puritan reeling. Instead of looking outward, at opportunity, he withdrew, and considered only his survival.

While up in Maine the Ryalls built a crib and looked optimistically ahead, John Winthrop struggled with the news that James Luxford, his manager at Ten Hills Farm since 1633, had so bungled the business of running the estate—forging the governor's name to questionable documents, accepting loans at usurious interest rates, and selling produce and cattle well below fair market value—that the governor hovered near financial ruin. Instead of carrying a debt of about £300, as he supposed, Winthrop faced obligations nine times as great in debts that stretched across the sea. The hapless Luxford (who was also condemned as a bigamist in court proceedings of the time) was exposed, jailed, and punished. Having crossed the colony's top official, he was unlikely to find leniency. And he did not. Records show he was found guilty of "forgery, lying & other foule offences" and sentenced to be bound and whipped in public. To seal that punishment, his ears were lopped off and he was driven from the colony.

After Luxford was dispatched, Winthrop surveyed the devastation. Creditors in New England and Britain were clamoring for payment. Yet just as he most needed a steady stream of income from his farms, prices plunged. A decade after the governor's arrival, the colony was producing well. As a result, goods were "plentiful now in the Bay," Winthrop reported, "and very cheape." That was welcome news to struggling newcomers. But it hit some families hard. In 1640 the price of cattle plummeted by 82 percent (from a high of £28 a head to a low of just £5). The price of corn and other crops fell, too, settling at little more than half their previous value. With creditors dogging his every move, the governor could only look to selling property to meet his debts. Worse still, he was sideswiped in his public life, losing his post as governor to an old rival, his former deputy, Thomas Dudley, who claimed Winthrop held too much power for the general good. Winthrop would later regain the post and serve as governor until his death. But one decade after he stepped foot in North America, it suddenly took all the Puritan's considerable energies just to stay afloat.

Supporters, stunned by this reversal, scraped together £500, paying Winthrop the equivalent of five years' salary though he'd just been booted out of office. The outgoing governor accepted the perk, but none too gracefully, finding the sum too small to meet his obligations. Political cronies next threw in three thousand acres near the mouth of the Concord River in a place known as Billerica. To safeguard that gift the land was placed in Margaret Winthrop's name, thus ensuring creditors could not demand the property as payment for her husband's mess.

John Winthrop seems to have expected just such help. Indeed, he seems to have expected more; for in a culture carefully designed to benefit the already well endowed, the distribution of perquisites was common. Lords who fell upon uncertain times were explicitly allowed such benefits, explained a book of English jurisprudence published in 1579, when they required "advantages and profittes" beyond the norm. As a one-time clerk of the wards, Winthrop knew about such dealings and likely felt himself entitled to the same leniency. Thus, while a common man succumbing to a significantly smaller debt would have been thrown in jail (and called upon to pay for his own upkeep while incarcerated), the Puritan was spared the trauma, showered with cash, and granted lands three times the size of New York's Central Park. In his journal, the Puritan made note of this shower of good fortune in his usual cheerless style, referring to himself, as always, in the third person: "the court (having no money to bestow, and being yet much indebted) gave his wife three thousand acres of land, and some of the towns sent in liberally, and some others promised, but could perform but little, and the most nothing at all. The whole came not to £500."

It was a fifth of what he owed.

Humbled, land poor, and running out of options, John Winthrop now revoked his latest will and started selling land. Some went for a nominal price to Winthrop children who, through effort, marriage, or inheritance, had money of their own to spend and wanted to keep the family holdings intact. Some went on the block. In Boston, the Winthrop house was sold and family servants started packing up. In a sober flurry, pewter dishes, a brass kettle, simple lamps and iron pans, a mortar and pestle, books and papers, chamber pots and writing desks, stools, a featherbed, blankets, breeches, stiff-brimmed hats, bonnets, hairbrushes, the family Bible, the famous journal, ledgers, a musket, several swords, a box of trinkets, aprons, candlesticks, lead pencils, and other odds and ends—some of the things that would appear in the Puritan's inventory upon his death—were packed and bumped along in wheelbarrows down busy streets. Having spent their first decade in New England living in one of the finest houses then to grace young Boston's narrow lanes, John and Margaret Winthrop now squeezed themselves into a smaller home.

Four miles to the north, however, the land the Puritan first loved was spared. John Winthrop's attachment to Ten Hills Farm (and the low offer presented when he did attempt to put it up for sale) left the property in family hands. Responsibility for its upkeep now would fall to John Jr. And he would change it. From 1640 forward, instead of serving the Winthrops merely as a place of respite from the press and wear of life, the family's simple stone house below the slope of Winter Hill, so often before busy only with the scrabble of mice and pound of rain, would ring loudly with the constant sound of children.

The governor had always intended to give his firstborn the best land. In a will signed not long before he learned of his financial crisis, the Puritan allowed that if his wife survived him she was to have half the farm and be maintained there in a "comfortable and honorable condition" for the remainder of her life. The other half was for John Jr., Margaret's stepson and guardian, for whom the governor cared, he wrote, "more . . . than for myself." With the will suddenly canceled, John Jr. moved much closer to that prize.

Married and in his mid-thirties then, the younger Winthrop at that moment needed a new home. Ryall Side was not for him—the salt works was too far from the thick of things—nor was the town of Ipswich (then called Agawam), which John Jr. had helped found. His residence there was even more remote and its history carried personal grief. Young Winthrop had buried his first wife Martha Fones in that cold ground, and her stillborn child lay beside her. John Jr. held no special love of the place, and his second wife, Elizabeth, demanded something better. With Elizabeth several months pregnant in the summer of 1641 and John himself preparing for a lengthy business trip abroad, he suddenly found himself with an urgent need for housing. Taking a pregnant woman and three children under the age of six on an arduous voyage across the Atlantic was unthinkable; yet Elizabeth made it plain she had no intention of waiting for him in Agawam.

Ten Hills Farm provided a convenient solution. By leaving his growing brood a short sail from Boston, John Jr. knew the elder Winthrops would be close. Cousins, in-laws, and old friends were also near. The children would have room to roam. Perhaps just as important, in a culture that encouraged the preservation of dynastic wealth, the Puritan's most cherished acreage remained in family hands, at least for now.

The oldest map of the property (one that Winthrop scholar Francis Bremer speculates was sketched by John Jr. himself several years before this move) shows the farm as it was in 1637. A simple sketch penned carefully on a long, rectangular silk panel, the map establishes the property's northern terminus at Cradock Bridge in Medford. Viewed from a north-south orientation (which means twisting the panel upright with Medford at the top and the river making a jagged boundary to the right), the property takes the rough shape of an apple slice, its northern tip starting at the bridge with one border bumping downriver over oyster banks, marshland, Two Penny Brook, Winter Brook, and lesser streams until coming to a full stop at a band of water known then as Winthrop Creek. From the same starting point upriver, a second, more rounded boundary branches left to make the curved side of the apple, moving from the foot of Cradock Bridge southwest in a straight line, then south, then turning in again to intersect with Winthrop Creek further up its bending course.

Given the size of the property and its enviable location, it was not only for the Winthrops to pass there. Rather, the land included several thoroughfares that allowed for a quiet flow of goods and livestock through that landscape. Beginning at the foot of Cradock Bridge, a dirt road cut Ten Hills Farm directly down its length. Anyone going from Medford south would have had to take that way.

Imagine a man passing there in summer; an Indian on his way to make a trade in town or perhaps a servant heading to Charlestown to conduct some business for his master. Traveling on foot with a heavy pack, the traveler makes his way across Cradock Bridge, his footfall echoing on the wood planks of a simple structure suspended on pontoons to allow for the surge and fall of eight-foot tides. After paying a small toll and stepping across those rushing tidal waters, he steps onto dry land on the Mystic's southern shore. There, he walks along a wide dirt path that heads southwest at first through an orchard marked on the map with a neat triangle of trees. Then the road jogs left. Soon the traveler comes to a point where the landscape opens into a graceful field where Winthrop's servants, taking advantage of a watery U-shaped boundary (made of two streams and the marsh beside the Mystic) have fenced some pasture to create a rectangular enclosure. Here the traveler must stop to wrestle with a gate. He makes his way through the opening, fastens it tight behind him, and turns toward a gently sloping landscape made of waving grass.

The road bisects the field, and the traveler raises his head and takes in a deep breath, his senses aroused by the mingled scents of hay and wild thyme and the sweet, warm scent of cow dung. The sun blazes across a landscape speckled with brown and black cattle that low and munch and eye this random interloper with bovine disinterest. If the traveler gazes left, toward the river, his eyes follow a green sward dotted with great stones. Beyond lies marsh and then the glinting ribbon of the Mystic. Looking right, he sees another wide expanse, more cows, a neat fence line, and the rise of Walnut Tree Hill (today, the site of Tufts University). The animals around him are mostly Winthrop stock, kept for family use or being fattened up for market. But there are some animals, too, that John Winthrop is putting up for friends who have shipped fine stock ahead while finishing preparations for their own passage. Some in this herd belong to Winthrop's brother-in-law, Emmanuel Downing, who intends to move his family to New England. But Downing has frequently delayed the trip, since his wife Lucy (the Puritan's sister) enjoys her home, does not share her brother's religious fervor, and fears there might not be enough opportunity to adequately "enrich oneself in the Bay." And so the cattle graze. Eventually, the Downing family will emigrate. But theirs is a faint commitment, and like so many others of that era, they give up on the experiment after only several years.

The traveler does not know all this. He only sees a handsome herd, a sloping field, the unmistakable signs of wealth in this new land. Everywhere he looks, the ground and even some of the people tending it are property of someone else, someone richer and more powerful than he; and he cannot help but feel the distance between his station and theirs. Across the meadow, the traveler stops again to make his way through a second gate. Beyond it he crosses a narrow footbridge over Winter Brook, then steps into a dark overhang of forest. If he is moving quickly, the sky soon opens again as he passes into a second orchard, where low fruit trees stand in tidy rows.

This orchard is bigger than the last and leads to a small cluster of buildings. The traveler sees them in the distance: a simple house with a massive chimney at its center; a barn; three outbuildings. Winthrop's house is made of stone, and even in the distance, it appears substantial. It had better be. The Puritan's first dwelling collapsed in heavy rains, since workers fixed the joints with clay. Now the men have built again using sturdier mortar that ensures the structure will withstand the elements. The traveler approaches, admiring a large garden, thick with vegetables and vines, the careful craftsmanship of outbuildings. Here, though, he is distracted by a decision he must make. Beside the house (no hint of which remains these centuries later) this single path branches into three. One lane is a switchback that would take him to Menotomy, now Arlington. Another angles right, moving uphill toward what, in the distance, will become the choked streets and busy alleyways of Cambridge. The traveler takes the third option, staying straight, leaving Medford behind him and keeping to the main road as he marches off toward Charlestown and the far-off glint of Massachusetts Bay.

As he leaves, the traveler hears a dog. There beside the house it stretches, yawns, and shakes itself awake. It is a tremendous beast, shaggy gray, his muzzle heavy, his face a mass of fur. Standing on its hind legs, the animal could rest his paws on the man's chest and tower well above him. Lanky, fast, and deadly, the ancient breed is kept for hunting wolves. The traveler unconsciously picks up his pace. Even at rest, the dog conveys a fearsome power. As the traveler looks back, he sees the beast is one of several.

Five years before, Emmanuel Downing had shipped four Irish Wolfhounds to John Winthrop. The dogs were a special present, at once both practical and powerfully symbolic. Known by Irish warriors as the Cu, the hounds were ancient dogs of war, bred and cherished by royalty some centuries before the birth of Christ. The mythic Irish chieftain Fionn mac Cunhal was said to have deployed at least three hundred of the dogs in combat. Feared and admired, they were impressive in the field. Nothing stopped them in the blur of battle. Indeed, so dangerous were they that Irish law allowed only noblemen the right of ownership, and it was strictly rationed. Lesser nobility could keep only one or two of the great hounds, while kings and chieftains bred and kenneled scores. Set loose upon the enemy, they were a poem of destruction, thundering, brutal, and remorseless. Ancient tales of war spoke of them beheading soldiers on the run.

By the 1600s, these majestic dogs were more regularly used to guard livestock and property than to hunt a human foe. Still, they played a crucial role in country life. Winthrop may have enjoyed the nod to royalty but undoubtedly valued the animals more for the bloody service they provided late at night when wolves came padding near. With sparsely settled lands nearby, so many sheep and cattle standing vulnerable on open ground, and the family itself in residence at Ten Hills Farm in summer and for holidays, the dogs performed a necessary chore. So compelling was their reputation and so efficient their attack that gentlemen in the Irish countryside let the dogs out only late at night, after guests were safely tucked in bed.

With the wolfhounds well behind him, the traveler slows his step and looks about. At his back lies a stretch of hills, before him, open meadow. He has arrived at the mouth of Winthrop Creek. Here, at the foot of an undulating sweep of open ground, the map ends, and the traveler leaves the property behind. Up ahead, he spies his destination, Charlestown, a young village, gabled, thatched, and built of wood and brick, with a tree line chopped with chimneys and the spiking masts of distant ships. Walking steadily, he has crossed the farm in an hour and twenty minutes.

Winthrop Creek is just a memory for mapmakers today. The creek is gone, paved over, and the ground that lay there long ago— a land of oozing tidal flats burping with the smell of rotting vegetation and the bubbling of clams—is now asphalt-covered fill. Where once an open hill stood on the map, today there is a checkerboard of narrow streets rising beside a shaggy park where kids from the local housing projects launch canoes at the Boys & Girls Club to take a break from summer heat. Nearby, a paved trail barely wide enough for two moves north along the riverbank to hug a narrow strip of ground. A jogger padding on that trail today might see the same things Winthrop saw: a seagull drifting over open water, a log adrift, a redwing blackbird resting in a scrubby tree and, at the water's edge, the regal silhouette of a great blue heron fishing. But of course there is something new as well. To the jogger's immediate left today there lies the urgent blur of traffic on Interstate 93. In some spots, those cars seem almost close enough to touch.

Today, on average, more than 1.4 million cars cross Ten Hills Farm each week—and that is just counting the traffic on I-93. Not far beyond the northern end of the tunnels created by Boston's scandal-plagued "Big Dig," a driver on that route might peer down to see the boundaries of the property. At the southern border, where the traveler left the land as he crossed the narrow surge of Winthrop Creek, the modern traveler finds a vast expanse of parking lot stretching seamlessly from a multiplex to a Home Depot. The marsh is filled. The river's course has been subdued. What's left of it lies hidden now behind a low expanse of nondescript buildings and low trees. Though one nearby apartment complex is rather hopefully called "Mystic View," there is no Mystic view to speak of, just the sight of a workmanlike berm with a major highway stretched on top. Nor are there orchards, pastures, or ancient woods along the farm's long eastern boundary, just a weave of residential streets built tight with triple-decker houses, small businesses, and shops. Further to the north, the ground beneath the highway gives way to the treeless boulevard of Medford's all-work Mystic Avenue and quiet neighborhoods that mix architectural styles from three centuries. Tufts University lies at the property's northeastern edge, and at the very top, where the seventeenth-century traveler began his walk, Cradock Bridge remains. Of course that has changed as well. Today the bridge, though old, is a sturdy stone and asphalt crossing no traveler from Winthrop's day would recognize.

And yet look closely and there are clues. In Somerville, beneath Route 93's six-lane expanse, tucked tight into the shoulder of a Kmart, TJ Maxx, a Loew's theater, and that Home Depot (big enough to fit a field of corn), a hill dotted with modest houses displays a chiseled marker that proclaims: Here once lay John Winthrop's residence. Another sign nearby tells visitors America's first ship, the *Blessing of the Bay*, was built along this shore; and street signs mark Ten Hills Road, Governor Winthrop Road, and Puritan Road in silent homage to the past. Yet the signs are something of a mystery. Though the ground was clearly part of Ten Hills Farm, the 1637 map shows the governor's house built further north and slightly to the west on the water side of Winter Hill. The neighborhood that claims him is shown on the Winthrop map as just a patch of hilly ground.

To the nearly quarter million drivers who pass this way each day, the densely populated expanse of Ten Hills Farm is nothing but a quick glance out the window to a tangle of tight housing and concrete. Perhaps today's commuter would see the bright red time-and-temperature display on the Century Bank building. Perhaps he idly notices a sweep of undistinguished landscape common to almost any stretch of the urbanized East Coast. With a tap on the gas, he crosses the Mystic River and is gone. On a day without much traffic, the trip through Ten Hills Farm takes not an hour and a half as it would have done for a traveler in John Winthrop's time, but just about the time it takes to hear a song on the car radio—four minutes.

❖ ❖ ❖ ❖ ❖

On August 3, 1641, John Winthrop Jr. boarded a small ship bound for England. His wife and children were settled then at Ten Hills Farm. He had given last instructions to the servants. His father and stepmother would help look after the small children. The governor's eldest son expected to be gone a year.

The vessel that would carry John Winthrop Jr. across the Atlantic was crowded, and it stank of fish. But John was on a mission and anxious for his start. Tucked away in his luggage was a heavy box filled with stones and minerals. It did not look like much. But John intended to lug it around Europe and display the contents at some of the finest homes he could. Having abandoned his salt works and moved away from the settlement at Agawam, he filled his head now with plans for a new ironworks. Over the next eight months, in one meeting after another, he would produce those stones with charming flourish, laying them down on fancy desks and well-turned tables as he struggled to convince skeptical investors that America's riches lay ready for exploitation. Some of these riches could be theirs, young John Winthrop Jr. persisted with a smile, if they would only help him build the ironworks he planned in Saugus, eight miles east of Medford.

For a man of many talents, tremendous restlessness, and a deep entrepreneurial spirit, it was a grand adventure, the latest of many. Life in the colonies was growing more inviting. For those with ambition and some startup capital, new opportunities were everywhere. As his father's misfortune at Ten Hills Farm so clearly showed, it was not enough to merely amass land and hire someone to watch after it. No. A forward-thinking settler must look ahead and make his own good luck. Young Winthrop saw himself as such a man, and historians have generally shared the view. If his saltworks at Ryall Side failed, if his experiment running the new community at Ipswich led to personal tragedy and the burial of a first wife and child, if his stewardship of Connecticut all came up somehow short, he would simply try again.

"Among second-generation New Englanders," the scholar Richard Dunn would say of him, "there was no more attractive figure than John Winthrop Jr." Surely the governor's son and namesake epitomized the zeal of young America. "Founder of three towns, industrialist, scientist, doctor, governor, diplomat, farmer, land speculator," crowed Dunn in *Puritans and Yankees*, penned in 1962, the younger Winthrop "reflected almost every aspect of his burgeoning society."

Or perhaps he represented something far more limited: the almost boundless advantage that attached itself to the elite.

John Jr., born in England in 1606, grew up at Groton Manor attended by at least nine servants. When he embarked for America with his first wife, mother-in-law, and several siblings in 1631, he did so with several hundred barrels of goods stored safely in the hold. When his ship arrived in Boston Harbor on November 4, it was not the usual bedraggled crush of sea-weary travelers that disembarked, half lost and wondering what awaited them, but the governor's family, well turned out and welcomed by a cheering throng. An honor guard stepped sharp. A noisy salute was fired by the militia. A crowd of lesser folk pressed close with offerings of food. "Well-wishers," wrote Francis J. Bremer in his 2003 biography of John Winthrop, "brought and sent 'fat hogs, kids, venison, poultry, goose, partridges & c.' " The governor himself described the several days around that landing in his usual clipped manner: "There came in her [the *Lyon*] the governor's wife, his eldest son and his wife, and others of his children, and Mr. Eliot, a minister, and other families, being in all about sixty persons, who all arrived in good health, having been about ten weeks at sea, and lost none of their company but two children, whereof one was the governor's daughter Anne, about a year and a half old, which died about a week after they came to sea."

The death of this second child in the exodus from England did not prompt further comment. Instead, the Puritan closed the day's entry there and picked the journal up again later to describe the celebration that attended the ship's unloading. After recording a full list of the bounty offered, John Winthrop remarked such "joy and manifestation of love had never been seen in New England." To him, "It was a great marvel, that so much people, and such store of provisions could be gathered together at so few hours' warning." Despite the loss of his daughter Anne, the day provided major celebration, and a soft landing for John Jr.

Members of the English royalty could hardly have expected more. Once ashore, John Winthrop Jr.'s fortune only grew. Within months he was offered a seat on the Court of Assistants, which functioned as an appeals court and was part of the general governing system. Graced with a good name, a powerful father, an immediate entrée to the halls of governance, and a genial disposition, the charismatic young Winthrop quickly found his place. While he attended to matters of state and business, the mundane but nonetheless demanding details of running a household were delegated to a crew of servants that would shortly swell with the addition of Indian slaves and at least one "neger." Among his human purchases was one made through a Mohegan sachem named Owanico who, surviving records show, "transferred unto master John Winthrop [Jr.] . . . one Indian Squa named Jane . . . to be possessed and enjoyed by him." Owanico signed Jane away with a rounded scrawl that, by a trick of the eye (or an irresistible temptation to perceive a power subdued), can either be seen as a horse balanced unsteadily on two legs, or a whale with blood gushing from its mouth and belly, tail flung high.

It would have been no surprise to New Englanders of the 1600s that young Winthrop owned some slaves. Rather, his brethren might have been more amazed if he did not. Though slaves never made up more than about three percent of the New England population, slave ownership was an integral part of life for those who shaped and ran that culture; and by 1641, John Jr. was unquestionably among those men. In Massachusetts he sat beside his slave-owning father at the Court of Assistants. Theirs was a powerful club. And

5.1 Sachem's mark. Sign of the Indian
Owanico from a deed granting the sale
of a female slave.

though it had its pettiness, its enmities and disagreements, it had
its benefits as well. Members of the court not only feathered their
nests while serving, they found the trees in which to build those
nests and the material to make them strong. Acting quickly in the
court's first years, members granted themselves people (the governor had "leave to keep . . ."); members granted themselves land.

These were men of property. They had their Boston houses, their
country farms, their businesses, their servants and their slaves.
They expected success not only for themselves, but for generations
following. It was the English way. And it was the promise made to
Puritans who agreed to undertake the risks inherent in moving to
a distant land. Tucked neatly within John Winthrop's arguments
for emigration (and contrary to his protestations that this was not
an experiment to be taken up for "worldly" ends) were repeated
assurances of wealth and comfort. In England, well before the exodus, the Puritan complained that overpopulation and an ossified
social system meant that an honest man could not "live comfortably in his profession." Even a large estate would not allow him
"to keep sail with his equal"; while in America ("the Lord's garden," as he sometimes called it), vast tracts of land lay open for the
having, granted to the few.

Members of the court hurried to make the settlers' expectations real. Intermarried, intermingling, they scratched each others' backs. In John Jr.'s first year in government, wrote historian Robert Black, "only a single [land] allotment appears to have been made . . . to a person who was not a member of the Court of Assistants." Black gave the tally as follows: "Two hundred acres went in June to Dudley (deputy governor). Three hundred acres were received by Endecott (assistant) in July. Ludlow (assistant) got 100 acres, and the senior Winthrop (governor) 50 particularly desirable acres in November." John Jr. hardly missed a meeting.

In 1641, however, as the leaves began to turn at Ten Hills Farm, the court gathered in Boston without young Winthrop in his chair. He was sailing into Bristol harbor on the coast of England at the time, fired with the hope and risk of a new enterprise. Not content to merely accept the perquisites that came to him through family ties, he was determined to make a fortune on his own, and experimented ceaselessly. "For the untried, the speculative, the romantically grandiose," explained Black, "he had an insatiable appetite." Failure did not cut his stride. Instead, it seemed to spur him on, and now he rushed ahead with a risky new adventure. All he needed was some backers. With his prospects hardly sure and much hard work ahead, he bowed his head by candlelight while still onboard his ship to write a letter to his wife at Ten Hills Farm. "Remember me," he urged Elizabeth before coming to more important matters, "to all my deare friends, brothers, sisters, cousins. . . ."

By then, second-generation Winthrops stretched across New England and the Caribbean, building ties in a complex weave of power, faith, and property. Soon, the clan would grow again. Early that next spring, John learned Elizabeth had given birth at Ten Hills Farm. Her new baby, the fourth of eight that she would bear him, was a son she christened Wait-Still, a poignant (though perhaps barbed) reminder of her wifely patience. A note from the baby's grandfather, the governor, received about the same time, told John Jr. his wife did well in public, but wept and suffered when alone. He was gone almost a year.

For a woman like Elizabeth, born to wealth and property in England, the farm offered few diversions. Music, art, politics, and even gossip lay a bumpy carriage ride away. Instead of feeling part of the creation of a new society, she found her days taken up with managing a noisy brood. She had a newborn at her breast. Her eldest child, Elizabeth, was only five. Fitz-John (a future governor of Connecticut, like his father before him) was only three, and Lucy just then walking. With four children underfoot and her husband overseas, Elizabeth struggled with depression. John, informed of her complaints, tried to help by securing her a new servant named Mary Gore who signed a contract forbidding her to lounge in taverns or behave promiscuously while in the Winthrops' household. From that he turned to other business, selling off three hundred acres in Ipswich to a tailor based in London. The Agawam experiment, at least, lay firmly in his past. Ten Hills Farm would be the family home, as long as that arrangement worked.

While Elizabeth fretted over her husband's delayed return, the children claimed the land around them. No stories of the raw eviction of a native population troubled their young consciences. No concerns regarding trusts or inheritance, mortgages and deeds, rightful conquest, just wars, King's grants, or *vacuum domicilium* disturbed their play. For them the hills were simply Winthrop land, there before them, certain to be theirs as long as they should wish it. As their father came and went, indulging in one new venture and another over the next few years, the children watched the seasons play and servants hard at work. Crops were planted and put up. Orchards slumped with fruit, and pantry shelves began to creak with the weight of fresh preserves. Fall distracted with a busy kitchen, nuts thumping from the trees, the very air a vibrant blast. Then the snow came, dulling edges, brilliant, white. In winter tools were fixed and cleaned. In spring they did their work again while sheep were sheared and cattle butchered.

Occasionally in fields and meadows to all sides, arrowheads and other remnants of another people boiled from the land. At times there must have been a stranger's face, a whoop and call that sounded in a different tongue. Or perhaps it was a bird. From back inside the house, an urgent voice would call.

Eventually, a certain rhythm held. In summer, children learned the bend and pull of river tides, the secret coves, the rapid currents, the listless wave of weed. At home, they bowed and curtsied for important visitors, bent their heads to tutoring, practiced their good manners, knew endless drills of reading, writing, and arithmetic. After ABCs were done they made their sacred childhood rituals, played hide-and-seek among great oaks, captained tiny homemade ships on bubbling creeks. A sweet parade of strawberries, blueberries, raspberries, and apples marched through pies and cakes and porridge. In the afternoon, the scent of venison, duck, rabbit, lamb, and beef drew them in from endless wanderings. As darkness fell, there often was the whinny of a horse and news from town. From time to time they battled infestations of mice, winters so cold that the fires barely warmed the stone, springs of mud and constant chill. But then the weather changed again, and the children climbed the nearby hills to gaze across great sweeps of green and search the edges of their property. Easy to imagine that there were none.

Then, abruptly, it was finished. John Jr. came home one day, gathered the family together, and announced he saw his future to the south. Connecticut had captured his imagination. He had already secured some land. Shortly, he would own several thousand acres more and rise to the role of governor. And so, with little warning, the family boarded a ship and traveled down the coast toward a new life. By the time the leaves were off the trees at Ten Hills Farm, the Winthrops had unpacked elsewhere.

Happy Instruments to
Enlarge Our Dominions

For thirty years, the farm remained in Winthrop hands, but ever more tenuously. Just six months after John Jr. sailed to Connecticut, a sudden illness sent his stepmother, Margaret Winthrop, to her bed. Frightened and alone, the Puritan knelt and prayed—to no avail. Before the family could gather, she was gone.

It was early summer then. John Jr. was in Connecticut, settling a new estate at Fisher's Island and establishing a complex network of new ties. Samuel had left Harvard and was now in the West Indies, never to return. Stephen was in England. Deane was busy at Pullen Point, today the seaside town of Winthrop, where he managed a farm with a handful of black slaves. Adam did not hear the news in time to make the trip.

For the Puritan it was a terrible loss. Margaret had been his sounding board and friend in those first hard years of settlement. She had borne the hardships stoically and retained, always, a measure of nobility the Puritan admired. "The Governor's wife," John Winthrop wrote toward the end of his long journal, "daughter of Sir John Tyndal, knight," mother of six children, wife of nearly thirty years, "left this world for a better." She was fifty-six, described by her husband as a "woman of singular virtue, prudence, modesty, and piety," all those things he most revered.

In Boston at that time, the economy was booming. Winthrop still had much to do. Houses were built, streets laid, wharves constructed, and major institutions conceived and seeded. English settlements in the Leeward Islands and Barbados had stabilized. Now they began to thrive. George Downing, Emmanuel and Lucy's son, and the Puritan's nephew (later to be knighted, the man for whom London's famous Downing Street is named), stopped in the West Indies for a five-month stay after graduating from Harvard. On his way to England, he wrote a letter to his cousin John Winthrop Jr. in Connecticut to let him know of his impressions. "If you go to Barbados," he advised, "you will see a flourishing island, [with] many able men." It pleased him greatly, and he shared his sense of wonder at the magnitude of trade. "I believe they have bought this year no lesse than a thousand Negroes, and the more they buie, the better able they are to buye, for in a yeare and a halfe they will earne (with gods blessing) as much as they cost."

Enormous profits were at hand. In Antigua, Barbados, and St. Christopher almost every acre soon would sprout with cane. But someone had to feed those workers, provide sheep, horses, cattle, cloth, and other goods as well. Serendipity and logistics favored New England. For just as Massachusetts farmers began to produce a glut, burgeoning slave economies at their back door announced a growing need. "As early as 1647," wrote the historian Bernard Bailyn, "Winthrop had it on good authority that men in Barbados 'are so intent upon planting sugar that they had rather buy foode at very deare rates than produce it by labour, so infinite is the profitt of sugar workes after once accomplished.'" In 1648, the *Welcome* of Boston boarded eighty horses to ship to the Caribbean while a Rhode Island vessel prepared for a long voyage that would move from Bristol to Barbados, to Africa, back to Barbados and Antigua, then to Boston to unload its cargo. "Winthrop and his colleagues looked to the West Indies," wrote Vincent T. Harlow in his *History of Barbados*, "where, as they knew, practically all food supplies had to be imported." What a delicious coincidence, a businessman might gush today. God's signal, the Puritan said then.

Trade with the West Indies, so tenuous just a decade earlier, now spiked. At the very moment that New England farmers needed to secure new markets for their bounty, they found an easy fit. It soon became a crucial one. There was no moral ambiguity here. The hand of Providence seemed clear. By the late 1640s, explained Harlow, "Barbados was suddenly leaping into phenomenal prosperity." In Boston at that time the governor laconically observed the trade "proved gainful" to his fledgling colony. Soon it was routine.

For the Puritan this might have been a time of ease and satisfaction. Instead, with Margaret gone, he found it one of trouble and unease. True, the port was full. Streets were busy. Markets constantly expanded with the arrival of new goods. But the governor longed for somebody to share this triumph. Looking ahead to a life alone with servants left him low. "Age now comes upon me," he wrote glumly in that period, "and infirmities therewithal." Who would care for him as he declined?

By Christmas he had found his match within the circle he knew best. His fourth wife would be Martha Nowell Coytmore, the sister of Increase Nowell, the colony's long-time treasurer and one of the original members of the Court of Assistants. Martha, herself a widow, accepted the invitation. For the Puritan a new chapter began. In the spring of 1648, he was elected to the colony's top office for the twelfth and final time. "The Court of Elections was at Boston," he reported in his journal. "Mr. Winthrop was chosen Governor again." That event was followed by the birth of a new son. Joshua was the last of sixteen children Winthrop sired. The boy would live only to the age of three. Yet his father beat him to the grave.

At sixty-one, John Winthrop remained at the center of colonial affairs, but his fever for the project finally ebbed, and then his health declined. The final pages of Winthrop's journal reflect a heaviness that seemed to sweep the young community. The closing entries of this extraordinary history were not the tales of a rich land bursting with endless promise, or even of the economic bounty that finally seemed at hand, but rather of annoying insults and petty enmities, a "boxe on the eare" suffered by some hapless soul, a shortage of corn, allegations of witchcraft and, more darkly still, the discovery of the bruised and battered body of a woman, her tongue black and swollen, neck broken, "privy partes" swelled "as if she had been muche abused."

The Salem witch trials were almost fifty years off, but there was already talk of the Devil in their midst. Perhaps it was natural

for righteous men who saw a godly power at the helm of their
adventure to also envision evil always lurking at the gunwales. Or
perhaps it was just a time in the life of one man's soul. But in his
last writings, Winthrop seemed preoccupied by the dumb ugliness
of life. As he moved toward his own death, he wrote often of the
morbid, the tragic, and the hauntingly grotesque as though neither
he nor his colony could fully rest. His final journal entry was an account of the mysterious drowning of a five-year-old. Winthrop saw
the Lord's hand there and closed his famous journal with a sober
admonition. It was the Lord, the governor advised, who led the
child in the dark. It was He who pushed her down the well. Winthrop accused the father of shirking his duty to the church. The
man ignored the Sabbath, tending to business instead. In that, said
Winthrop, he acted "against the checks of his own conscience."

With those words, the journal ended.

In February the Puritan caught a cold he could not shake. For
several weeks he languished, "very low," wrote his son Adam,
"weaker than ever I knew him." Then once again the family gathered. This time, all across New England men of power donned their
darkest clothes. In services and speeches, they mourned the passing of a man John Cotton called "friend . . . brother . . . mother"
to the colony. On Boston streets a barrel and a half of gunpowder
was exploded in his honor. Had Winthrop been alive for that loud
passage he might have recalled the words of an old friend, sent to
him by letter many years before. "Out of hard beginnings have
come great matters," the vicar of Great Wenham had advised.
"All plantations were meane at the first yet, . . . when thinges are
come to some perfection, it delighteth people to look back on their
founders, and they glorie in their worthie interprises."

The vicar spoke prophetically. It was always Winthrop's "city
upon the hill," his struggles and his courage, raw determination,
and success, that historians would hold up to the light. Meanwhile,
the Puritan's distribution of slaves, his early embrace of slavery in
the Body of Liberties, his own "leave to keep . . . ," would drift
into great caves of historical amnesia, so much so that centuries
later a distant descendant, a scholar herself and an expert on the
work of the Harlem artist Jacob Lawrence, could say with utter

conviction that one of the things the family always held proud was the fact that there was no slave history there.

For Winthrop, just as the vicar had advised, it was the glory of his worthy enterprises that was carefully preserved and endlessly lauded through the centuries. Even Ronald Reagan identified him as a personal hero. In his Farewell Address to the nation delivered at the White House on January 11, 1989, Reagan spoke of his habit of looking out a particular window at the residence and contemplating what America meant to him.

"The past few days," he told the nation as his second term drew to a close, "when I've been at that window upstairs, I've thought a bit of the 'shining city upon a hill.' The phrase comes from John Winthrop, who wrote it to describe the America he imagined. What he imagined was important because he was an early Pilgrim [*sic*], an early freedom man. He journeyed here on what today we'd call a little wooden boat; and like the other Pilgrims, he was looking for a home that would be free.

"I've spoken of the shining city all my political life," continued Reagan with the simple elegance that was his gift. "I don't know if I ever quite communicated what I saw when I said it. But in my mind it was a tall proud city built on rocks stronger than oceans, wind-swept, God-blessed, and teeming with people of all kinds living in harmony and peace, a city with free ports that hummed with commerce and creativity, and if there had to be city walls, the walls had doors and the doors were open to anyone with the will and the heart to get here. That's how I saw it and see it still."

It is a glorious image. Americans have always held it dear. But of course the story is not wholly real. Winthrop's "city upon a hill" was never "shining" (Reagan added that), the doors were not all open, and that "early freedom man," though free himself, owned slaves, as did his sons, his grandsons, his friends, and many of his fellow founders, a detail later generations apparently found easier to erase than understand.

Whether or not John Winthrop owned Africans will probably never be known. No record shows it. Yet records from the time are incomplete and not always reliable in this regard. The inventory taken after John Winthrop's death, for example, does not note a single Indian in his possession either, and other wills from the period contain similar lapses. Scattered references do show, however, that not only did John Winthrop's eldest son, John Jr., keep at least one "neger" in his household, but his brother Deane, settling in the town known today as Winthrop, operated the farm he inherited from the governor at Pullen Point with the help of a crew of enslaved blacks. A question no historian has answered, though, is whether Deane obtained those Africans through purchase, trade, or with the farm, as part of the wealth his father handed down.

By 1650, with both Margaret and John dead, all responsibilities at Ten Hills Farm now shifted to John Jr. But he had neither the time nor patience for farm management, and new commitments kept him far away. Only his sons Fitz-John and Wait-Still used the property any more, spending occasional holidays there in 1654 while living in Cambridge with a tutor. That arrangement did not last, nor did the tutoring. Fitz-John was turned away by Harvard College for his lack of intellectual fitness. After a year he moved away to find a job under his father's wing. More and more, the emotional hold of the gracious land beside the Mystic lessened.

In Connecticut, meanwhile, John Jr. faced mounting political obligations and business pressures he could not ignore. For him, Ten Hills Farm was useful now only as an investment property and a holding pen for the hundreds of cattle he sometimes shipped north from pastures in Connecticut. Always one to follow the grand vision, perhaps he was overextended. Poor management and bad weather hobbled some of his extensive enterprises. A tide of debt began to rise. Add to that the loss of a ship's cargo to Dutch privateers and a broad crop failure in a difficult season and he was driven, like his father, into debt he could not handle. To meet it, the second owner of Ten Hills Farm took out a sizable loan from a London merchant and used the land he owned in Massachusetts and Connecticut to arrange for a raft of leases, trusts, and mortgages.

In the closed club of Boston politics, that awkward financial tangle was noted with some interest by a few men with good

connections. Hezekiah Usher, the son-in-law of the London merchant who held much of Winthrop's debt, offered the Puritan's
son £2,200 to take Ten Hills Farm off his hands. John Jr. recoiled.
The land was worth at least that much, perhaps much more! He
would not relinquish it. Though the cash would have left him in
the clear, he took another mortgage.

The reason for that choice was almost certainly threefold. Part
was sentimental: His father loved the land and took it first of all
his prizes. Part was practical: Usher's offer was too low. And part
was logical: Here was something solid. Ships might founder, cargoes vanish. Crops could fail. Cattle sometimes froze to death.
Even the Winthrop brothers' "elaborate speculations in sugar" in
Antigua and Barbados, wrote the scholar Robert Black, had gotten
off to a rough start. Those investments "began badly, continued
worse, and yielded . . . little or nothing." In twelve years the Winthrop boys had barely turned a profit in that trade. Yet land was
something else again. And every Winthrop knew it.

Just three decades after their father first helped settle "the Lord's
garden," the best ground was claimed, marked, fenced, mortgaged,
farmed, and spoken for, and pressures for that land began to build.
As Hezekiah Usher's overture so clearly showed, a delicate cov-
etousness emerged among the powerful. Meanwhile, new buyers
jostled in the wings. By the 1660s not only had the colony stabilized and begun to thrive, but the children of families with seven,
eight, nine, twelve, and fourteen offspring were grown and bearing
children now themselves. America's first baby boom clamored for
its share. Now, on sprawling farm lots that stretched all across
New England, this second generation built not "English wigwams"
out of mud and reeds and bark, but substantial homes with great
wood beams and handsome shingle on properties of many acres.
Heating those houses required more wood still. In a startling burst,
farms, cattle pastures, dirt roads, and new towns erased dark alleyways of ancient growth. The constant thud of axes beat the tune
of their voraciousness. John Jr. made a simple calculation: Sell to
Usher? He would not.

Boston by then was a bustling port. Cobblestone streets were
"many and large" observed John Josselyn, that early chronicler of

Samuel Maverick's intention to create a "breed of negroes" who had returned now for a second visit. This time he found wealth and bounty. Shop buildings were substantial edifices made of brick and stone, and they were "handsomely contrived." Three churches held the population's hopes and fears. "The Town is rich and very populous," wrote Josselyn. Many in it, as their fortunes rose, sought a country retreat or land for children and their families. At a time of insecure coinage and tumultuous market fluctuations, real estate became the holy grail.

The land rush of the 1660s alarmed some colonial leaders. Each new town, each tree downed, eroded the power of the church, further dislocated native tribes, and underscored old enmities. In Rhode Island, a powerful sachem known to white men as King Philip sold off six square miles of land (about 3,840 square acres) bordering the towns of Bridgewater, Taunton, and Rehoboth, not for a price anywhere approaching the £2,200 Winthrop rejected as too meager for the six hundred acres he held at Ten Hills Farm, but for the highest price ever paid an Indian, £66. Even taking the proximity to Boston into account, the disparity is glaring. The difference was four-thousand-fold.

Observing such inequities, Rhode Island's founder, Roger Williams, railed against this road the Devil paved. "God Land," he preached, might soon become "as great a God with us English as God Gold was with the Spaniards!" This hardly was a new concern. As far back as the 1630s when Plymouth Colony started stretching north and south with the founding of new towns, William Bradford had expressed a similar worry. This sudden spreading about, the famous Pilgrim sputtered, would inevitably dilute the power of the church and "this, I fear, will be the ruin of New England." Departing settlers, he complained, were only interested in "the enriching of themselves." All of it was greed, he said. And greed did no man good. In time such avariciousness would surely draw "the Lord's displeasure."

This was not the prevalent view. Families like the Winthrops spread themselves across the newly settled land without much sign of guilt or hesitation. Quite the contrary, they steadily expanded their own holdings and did all in their power to carefully preserve the real estate they held. In 1667, citing business concerns, John Winthrop Jr. submitted his resignation as governor of Connecticut so that he could better manage the many properties he owned across New England. It was not his style to trim down. Rather, he wanted to push those lands he did hold toward more consistent profit. The governing officials would not accept his resignation. And just as it had been with his father before him, those leaders not only spared the Puritan's son from the humiliation of landing in a debtors' prison, but rushed to help, granting him an exemption from some taxes, and three years later (when he attempted to resign again) upping his salary and giving him yet more land to add to the many thousands of acres he already counted as his own.

The great tentacles of this massive land boom reached as far as Maine, where the Ryalls by then were firmly established and blessed with a growing family. At Casco Bay, William Ryall finally had his neighbors. The population there might not be as dense as that of Boston or New London, yet fresh faces and the steady sound of hammering were routine and now spreading north and south. In the midst of that expansion, the Immigrant became a figure in local politics and aggressively consolidated his own land claims in North Yarmouth by taking not one but two deeds to his property to better satisfy the several competing bodies then arguing over who in fact controlled that northern turf. Ryall of course never dreamed of claiming possessions on the scale of John Winthrop or his son. But he did well enough. He had Fogg Point, a twenty-acre island just beyond it, and another two hundred acres at the family farm. For a man who had traveled to America with nothing forty years before, it was a proud achievement and something he could pass to seven children.

For all those many years, William Ryall flourished where he was. "A man of honest purpose and practical wisdom," wrote William Hutchinson Rowe in his study of *Ancient North Yarmouth and Yarmouth, Maine.* He became a leader in Lygonia Province, and in 1665 was named clerk of a lesser court. These new roles gave him new confidence; but decades of hard farming left him old. The Immigrant's back ached from years spent twisted at the hoe. His feet were full of bunions, tough as leather. And as he looked ahead it was not the birth of more children and a continued rise in political position he saw for himself, but the inevitable slide toward the end of life. That sense was underscored in 1672 when in a farmhouse busy with the constant traffic of a large and boisterous family William Ryall held a squirming grandson, Isaac, in his arms. Another generation was now pressing for its share. The Immigrant began to think not of how to guard his children but of how his children might protect and care for him. When Isaac celebrated his first birthday, the boy's grandfather deeded all his land holdings in Maine to the boy's father, William, and William's brother John. In exchange, the two men agreed to care for their parents as the couple aged.

Surely the Immigrant must have imagined himself spending his last days in this house he had built with his own hands, where he and Phoebe dreamed their dreams, made love, survived illness, cooked, washed, and nursed sick children, cradled grandchildren, argued, laughed, and shared old stories by the fire, by the sea. But that was not their fate. A second war was coming. This time it would spare no quarter.

Rhode Island was the flash point. Five years before Isaac Ryall was born, the thirty-year-old Indian leader King Philip (father of a son himself) sat with his interpreter to write his will and grant his lands to several heirs. The Indian leader's interpreter, John Sassamon, an anglicized Indian of the Wampanoag tribe who had studied at Harvard and served as translator to the famous "Indian preacher" John Eliot, was fluent in English and trusted by both sides. Yet he did not serve King Philip well. When Sassamon finished the document and read it back to the powerful sachem, everything sounded perfectly in order. Yet soon King Philip learned he had been duped. Penned in English, a language the sachem could not read, the will granted all of Philip's land not to his beloved son and other chosen heirs but to the man who held the pen, John Sassamon, his translator. When Philip understood that double cross, Sassamon ran back to Cambridge and the minister John Eliot while Philip sourly concluded whites had taught his friend too well the ways of Englishmen.

For several years King Philip's bitterness over that betrayal simmered. Meanwhile, new pressures, slights, and manipulations mounted. By the time Isaac Ryall cried his first, the temperature for war had risen. In the summer of 1672, King Philip sold land near the Taunton River for £143. He used the money to buy guns. Now he wanted war. He wanted white men gone.

Employing a logic as simple as it was cold, he reasoned paper deeds and carefully parsed titles imposed according to a scheme devised by whites would be worthless once local tribes reclaimed their land. And so as Isaac Ryall took his first few steps beside the sea in Maine, King Philip got busy in Rhode Island selling every scrap of land he owned except the ground beneath his feet, Mount Hope, his beloved base near Bristol, the famous seat from which he launched his war. It was a risky gamble but the only avenue King Philip then could see. *Forget these white man's deeds*, he told young warriors under his command. Whatever they might claim, bloodshed would erase their power. War would win them back the land—and more.

As King Philip quietly readied a generation of young fighters for an all-out confrontation, John Sassamon got wind of these preparations and set out to betray him for a second time. That January 1675, the Wampanoag translator walked to Plymouth to warn colonial leaders of the sachem's plan. The white men listened, but waved the warning off. Baseless ranting by an overwrought Indian, they sniffed. Local tribes were too weak, too fractured, and too compliant for a war. They could not have been more wrong. Events unfolding over the next months would show their empty hand.

Not long after Sassamon's warning was dismissed the translator's bruised and battered corpse was discovered beneath the ice at Assawompsett Pond, a stop on his way home. Marks on his body were consistent with a violent end. There was no sign of drowning. Murder was the cause. The man was beaten to death, nervous settlers whispered, then left to sink beneath the ice. Suspicion turned immediately to his enemy King Philip. The powerful sachem denied involvement; yet whites produced a witness who claimed to have seen everything from a hiding place behind a tree. *I saw King Philip's men take the man and slam him to the ground*, he told the judge. *I saw those warriors break the man's neck and push his body under water*. After a perfunctory trial complete with plenty of intrigue of its own, the accused were put to death and King Philip's range of options closed.

Having spent nearly five years carefully stirring the coals of war, Philip now faced hundreds of young warriors more than ready for this promised conflagration. Their faces painted, bodies greased, they demanded that the sachem let them loose. By late June, he did. The burn started with a steady drip of provocation as his warriors spread across the region ransacking houses and slaughtering livestock. It sparked when a white boy shot a looter in the face. It caught fire when that boy reacted to news of the warrior's death with the tart rejoinder, well, "no matter." It blazed unstoppably from there. King Philip's men first killed the boy. Then they slew the father. After that they went for every settler they could catch.

Some victims died instantly. Others crawled for hours before succumbing to their wounds. Gruesome stories tell of men and women soaked in blood appearing at a neighbor's house only to die, screaming with agony, on the doorstep of a family too terrified to let them in. Such suffering and chaos suited King Philip's fighting men just fine. This would be a war of terror. It paid no mind to innocence. Across New England, great sweeps of violence cleared whites from isolated settlements, drove Indians from their villages, and cost more lives per capita than any conflict in American history. Among whites, at least one soldier died in ten. For Indians sympathetic to King Philip's cause, the final tally was certainly worse. Not only did countless warriors perish in battle, but those who survived and were captured were sold away as slaves. The devastation that resulted left a scar the length of all New England.

Up in Maine where whites were few, three generations of the Ryall family mobilized. In short order they gathered all they could and fled. Three-year-old Isaac was bundled by his parents. Frantic aunts and uncles gathered bare essentials. In their haste, precious food— insurance for the winter months—was left to go to waste on pantry shelves and down in dark root cellars. Hard-worked fields would ripen through the summer, then rot as seasons turned. Treasured trinkets, furniture, and private keepsakes were abandoned without a backward glance. Yet in those final moments before leaving, cooking fires were carefully extinguished. Surely they'd be back.

Now the Immigrant and several generations of his family traveled not as "courageous pioneers," as so many local histories remember them, but as traumatized refugees clinging to the few goods they could carry. "Intermittent killings and burning by the Indians had [long] been endured," wrote the authors of one early history of the region. This conflict was on a wholly different scale. It "pointed only too clearly to but one thing for them—annihilation." Those few "courageous pioneers" who stayed behind were hunted, tortured, killed, and left to rot in open fields. In less than a year, with brutal efficiency, all of Maine was cleared of whites. At Casco Bay it would be decades before the fields were safe for settlers again.

The Immigrant and his clan rushed south to find shelter in the thriving town of Dorchester, at Boston's southern edge, where the Immigrant's third son, Isaac, had gone to woo a girl named Ruth, then stayed to make a life. Most of the family stopped there, too. But William's brother Joseph broke away from the group in Charlestown and determined he would settle at the foot of Ten Hills Farm. There he prepared to make a new life as a sailmaker outfitting the great vessels of the day. In Dorchester, meanwhile, little Isaac Royall's uncle and namesake got a gun and headed off to be a soldier.

To the people of Dorchester, the cause of this war was intimately understood. Here, as elsewhere, "God Land" lay at the core of old disputes. Officials in the town had played their part and knew the issues well. Five years before, Dorchester selectmen dictated a note to King Philip, "Sachem of Mount Hope," addressing a bitter argument. "It seems," wrote Hopestill Foster, scribbling on the selectmen's behalf in 1670, "there is some difference about the land. . . . We say tis ours already both by grant from our Court and also by agreement with Indians, who say that it was theirs."

That dispute, like so many others of the time, was patched over but never quite repaired. Now it led to war and sent the men of Dorchester off to fight the Wampanoag, while up in Maine, beyond the Ryalls' knowing, all was laid to waste. In North Yarmouth and beyond it houses burned. Livestock starved or fell beneath a knife, or broke free and wandered in the wild. Crops were torched or stolen or left to wither and collapse, humus for another generation. Panicked stragglers were slaughtered in a hundred grisly ways. They died and went to dust alone on that rough shore, no preacher there to give a benediction.

While the Immigrant and his extended family made a new life south of Boston, the town and houses they had built were all destroyed. Across Massachusetts and Connecticut the cost was almost as severe. Over the course of the war fully half of all white settlements were put to the torch and reduced to ash and cinder. So effective and so total was the onslaught that some historians conjecture if native tribes had not already been weakened by famine, disease, and dislocation, whites might have been thrown from Massachusetts, Rhode Island, and Connecticut just as surely as they were pushed from Maine. Instead, just as in the Pequot War, it was those Indians who opposed the whites who took the greater blow.

In Boston, town fathers called all young men to fight and suited up themselves, while the colony's leadership fell into a heated debate about the efficacy of erecting a great wall, eight feet high and built of timber, to keep the "rage and fury of the enimy" at bay. They did not build it. Instead, they moved with fierce precision. No Indian whose will ran counter to their own was safe. Hearty or infirm; young or old; pacifist or warrior; it did not matter. Attitudes of violence were perfectly distilled. The only thing that mattered was the color of a person's skin.

Indians who accepted Christ, studied, worked, and made their beds among their Puritan mentors were no less suspect than those who lived in distant villages having little contact with white settlers. Rounded up and quarantined, Christianized Indians were hustled to isolated spots to spend the war in prison camps without adequate food, heat, or shelter. Fair warning never came.

"When the Indians were hurried away . . . pore souls in terror thei left theire goods, books, bibles," wrote John Eliot, Sassamon's mentor, "apostle to the Indians." Eliot observed with sadness that many westernized Indians were rushed away with less than half an hour's warning. His distress was not broadly shared. In this war no love of a Christian God could save a soul whose veins still pulsed with native blood. Instead, whole clans of Indian converts were sent off to Deer Island (now the site of a massive sewage treatment plant connected by a land bridge to the seaside town of Winthrop), where they were made to stay in a rough internment camp where hardships were so great in that first winter more than half the prisoners perished. There, within sight of the Boston shoreline, thousands of Christianized men, women, and children huddled together with minimal provisions. Visitors described life-threatening conditions. In the December chill, reported one, the camp was "bleak and cold, their wigwams poor and mean, their clothes few and thin." Hundreds of Indians froze to death or starved or died from disease. Yet still no help would come. The people of Boston were informed of the suffering inside those camps. But they did nothing to relieve conditions.

If the Pequot War of 1636 was perceived as brutal beyond imagining by men like William Ryall who lived through it, now that war seemed just faint overture. No check against man's conscience was enough to break the hatred. Instead, each side did its best to annihilate the other. Mass graves were filled. Whole towns became sad funeral pyres.

For a year those fires raged. Then a single gunshot drew the fighting to a close. King Philip, having returned to his base at Mount Hope, was finally hunted down and killed. A soldier presented his corpse to Captain Benjamin Church, who pointed with disgust at the sachem's muddied body and declared that here lay the "great, naked, dirty beast" who started it. Captain Church vowed this "king" who left so many Englishmen to rot in open fields would never know the dignity of a decent burial himself. He ordered the man's body cut to pieces, his head and limbs distributed for grisly trophies. Local church records show the sachem's severed head was carried off to Plymouth, where it was impaled on a spike for all to see. Other body parts were doled out to the favored few. One recipient was the shooter who ended Philip's life. He received a hand and kept that awful relic in a pickle jar and made a profit through the years giving showings—for a fee.

Even as the fighting ended, traumatized and dazed New Englanders faced another crisis. The war had proved almost as expensive as it was deadly. Militias started clamoring for pay. Owners of island prison camps demanded rent. Towns across the region needed rebuilding. Yet local coffers were exhausted. Governing officials settled on an ancient remedy. War provided "gainful pillage," just as Emmanuel Downing had suggested. Prisoners could be sold for profit.

In the summer of 1676, 180 Indians condemned to "Perpetuall Servitude and slavery" in the West Indies were pushed into the hold of the *Seaflower* in Boston Harbor. These prisoners were not the first to sail. According to historian Jill Lepore, hundreds of others had already made the trip. These captives, she argued in *The Name of War,* her elegant study of the conflict, became "rewards . . . distributed in the same manner as relief funds." It was a crude but effective channel of commerce.

There were other compensations, too. In Rhode Island a huge land deal resulted from the war just as surely as "God Land" had been its cause. With King Philip dead, his seven-thousand-acre territory at Mount Hope was finally open for the taking. But who should have it? Mount Hope would be distributed "by right of conquest," explained Wilfred H. Munro in his 1880 history of the town of Bristol. The leaders of Massachusetts, Plymouth, and Rhode Island all laid claim. That prize, Munro wrote with a measure of local pride, "was too tempting to be relinquished without a struggle." To resolve the conflict, the matter was eventually moved to London, where it sat before the king and members of his court.

In England, officials representing Plymouth argued the land should be theirs "because we . . . fought for it and paid for it and many of us bled for it. . . ." In any case, they added, "the profit of war (excepting a few prisoners taken in the latter end thereof) was only land."

After a two-year delay, H. Coventry, a Lord of Trade and Plantations, agreed. "By your Loyalty and good Conduct," he informed the men of Plymouth, "you have been happy Instruments to enlarge our Dominions." As a result, King Philip's seven thousand acres were in "more immediate and perfect Allegiance and Dependence" on the crown. By way of thanks, the king would grant the land to Plymouth.

City leaders divided the windfall. A flurry of quiet deals left four prominent Boston merchants, John Walley, Nathaniel Byfield, Stephen Burton, and Nathaniel Oliver, with title to those acres.

King Philip's plan had failed entirely. The sachem was dead. White men's deeds and titles stood more firmly on that ground than ever. Indian lands would never be reclaimed. Even his beloved Mount Hope was finally lost. A foreign king distributed the land, almost eleven square miles of it, to white men of influence, while the sachem's son and intended heir, a dark-skinned boy and grandson of a tribal chief who years before had saved the Pilgrims from starvation, was sold into slavery, as was his mother; as were many hundreds more.

SLAVERS OF THE NORTH

At war's end, another first son with a lighter complexion and a very different fate, Fitz-John Winthrop, recognized a fine opportunity to press. Having buried his aging father, the governor of Connecticut, at the very climax of that war, Fitz-John, in 1676, inherited vast lands and many responsibilities. That spring it was left to him to resolve the future not only of the six-hundred-acre farm he was raised on north of Boston but that of thousands of other acres, too, in Massachusetts and Connecticut. To settle the old man's affairs, Fitz had to clear considerable debt related to those properties. He also had to face the challenge of splitting his father's holdings in accordance with provisions of the will. With various among his siblings squabbling over what was due, Fitz moved to liquidate some assets. This time Ten Hills Farm would not be spared.

The business of settling the will was sure to be tedious and slow. Fitz dreaded haggling with his relatives and looked for a distraction—and a quick source of funds. He found it in the final days of war. To the victors went the spoils, and Fitz would seek his share.

Like others of his generation, the Puritan's grandson desired "gainful pillage" from the war and sought that gain by selling prisoners for profit. "There was some unpleasantness," the historian Richard Dunn wrote mildly, "over Fitz's receipt of Indian prisoners." The Connecticut council allowed him several captives for his own use; but Fitz had more ambitious plans in mind and "bought ten others from the colony, which he shipped to Barbados to be sold," reported Dunn. And so the third Winthrop to own Ten Hills Farm joined a seamless history upon that ground, and took the history one step further: He not only possessed slaves and endorsed the practice, but sought to make some money by their trade.

Yet now there was a hitch. As war had ripped across New England, the Caribbean market for its prisoners cooled. Fitz would have no easier time selling those ten men than he would resolving the awful tangles of his father's scrambled real estate affairs.

In some measure the shift was due to a miscalculation on the part of Puritans who spent many years vilifying New England's Indians as devious, violent, and headstrong, only to turn around, when it suited them, to try to sell those same people to isolated planters outmuscled by the men they owned. Potential buyers wanted workers they could manage, not rebel warriors fresh from genocidal conflict. On scattered sugar estates a white man's slaves were essential to his safety and to his success. And so the buyers fastened on a simple set of questions: Why purchase men who knew the recent taste of blood? Wasn't it better to buy people baffled by the language, the habits, and the weaknesses of whites? Wasn't it better to buy blacks?

The answer was unanimous, and the trade in slaves rapidly shifted to the east, across the sea.

That change in attitude left New England sellers with "one of their most valuable wartime commodities, Indian slaves, almost entirely unmarketable," explained the author Jill Lepore. This was not a vague adjustment in a point of view. Laws changed, too. In 1676 officials in Barbados banned the further importation of New England's prisoners. Other markets shrank as well. Throughout the Caribbean, though, the need for workers steadily increased. And so across the hemisphere the skin of slavery turned a darker shade. A tide of souls from Africa roared in. Ambitious businessmen prepared to ride it.

Now, on American soil, a new generation came of age: slavers of the North. In Massachusetts, the *Rainbow* and the *Gift of God* had sailed for Africa as early as the 1640s. Since that time hundreds, then thousands of acres in the Caribbean and the American South had been planted with the labor-intensive crops of sugar, indigo, and cotton. The peak of the African trade might still be a century away, but by the 1670s the slave business was already good—and getting better. For ship's captains and the investors who made those voyages happen, dark cargoes turned to gold. The lure—especially to a generation focused more on profit than on God—was irresistible.

In that climate, it was natural for men like Fitz-John Winthrop to be attracted to the trade. But there were major hurdles to surmount. In addition to the dwindling market for prisoners of war, London's Royal African Company held a monopoly on the buying and selling of all Africans. That monopoly (approved in 1672 and not unraveled for a quarter century) would firmly hold until competing merchants, infuriated by their lack of access to such lucre, in 1698 convinced the Parliament to overturn the law. Meanwhile, men like Fitz-John who perceived the lure did better with God Land. And so Fitz refocused his attention on his father's will and resolved to sell the property the Puritan had settled back in 1630: six hundred acres running down the Mystic River's southern bank, the farm where Fitz had ambled as a boy.

Happily, there was a ready buyer. Hezekiah Usher, the wealthy Boston merchant who once expressed an interest in the property, had coveted the land for more than a decade. It was never his to have. He died just as the farm was finally put for sale. Yet the root of that ambition had grown inside his son in all that time, and a year after John Winthrop Jr.'s death, family ties and intersecting fortunes brought that son one step closer to control of the estate. Now it would be a Boston-born merchant and his Caribbean-born wife who would take up residence at Ten Hills Farm.

Ten years before the land was up for sale, Hezekiah Usher's son John married the heir to a considerable fortune built on the trade in American timber. That marriage, like so many of the day, linked two prominent and powerful families, the Ushers and the Lidgetts. Sixteen-year-old Elizabeth Lidgett came to the union with a sizable dowry and an intricate web of social and business connections, coins of gold at a time when personal ties routinely turned the wheels of commerce. John was young himself, just twenty. But he had married well. Elizabeth's father, Peter Lidgett, was a savvy businessman who, after trying his luck in the struggling young colony of Barbados moved the family to New England. There he supervised the cutting of New Hampshire forests to make masts for English vessels. His timing could not have been better. The empire's expansion meant a surge in shipbuilding. A series of wars left the English Navy urgent with demand. Scattered colonies had many goods and thousands of slaves to ship. Yet England herself was deforested while America offered vast territories filled with woodlands breathing and untamed. Peter Lidgett saw his best chance there, and soon the grandest steeples in New Hampshire, giants towering 150 feet and more, came shivering to earth.

By the time of Elizabeth's marriage, her father held contracts with three quarters of London's mast merchants. Eventually the Lidgett name would appear on every important ledger book beside the Thames. This was partly due to Peter Lidgett's considerable business acumen. But it also was the result of an economic system carefully tooled and tweaked to benefit a fellow like him, a man with connections, gumption, and a bit of vision who found a way to fill a yawning need. "The self-sufficiency of the imperial unit was to be maintained," Harvard historian Bernard Bailyn noted dryly. To ensure it, the Crown worked out a simple business maxim: English law should see to it that English goods moved on English ships to English ports for English profit.

Lidgett's business fit that system squarely.

When Peter Lidgett died in 1676 he left his daughter £1,000 and his wife Elizabeth a wealthy widow. John Usher had an inheritance by then, and perhaps the cash for Ten Hills Farm. Instead the prize went to his mother-in-law, Mrs. Lidgett, possessed of a far greater fortune. Still, for the Usher family, years of quiet patience had paid off. What Hezekiah could not buy in 1663, his ambitious son would eventually possess. The land was now within his family's reach.

On May 17, 1677, Ten Hills Farm was sold to Mrs. Elizabeth Lidgett for £3,300. The deed still sits in Middlesex County Courthouse, delivering "all that farm called Ten Hills" to Peter's widow. By then it was a gentle maze, described as "arable pasture and woodland, meadow and marsh." In John Usher's time it was softened and defined by gardens, paths, and fences, as well as multiple structures including all those "tenant or dwelling houses, barns, [and] out houses" lying on the western shoulder of the Mystic River in that season. Almost a half century after John Winthrop first spied that ground, the soil was dug and cleared, planted, shaped, and manicured. The estate would steadily become more buffed, and more coveted, as the eighteenth century dawned.

The selling price was a handsome sum—out of reach for most men then—reflecting both the property's development and its convenient location several miles north of Boston. By contrast, a Boston warehouse and wharf sold by the Winthrops the same year fetched just one tenth the price. Though a bitter dispute over the will would keep the Puritan's descendants haggling over details for another generation, the Winthrop family's tenure at Ten Hills Farm was done. Now another season would begin; and in that season the chains of slavery rattled just as much as they had ever done, and more.

Come Up in the Night
with Them

In Dorchester after King Philip's War, the Royall family was a boisterous clan spanning several generations. The Immigrant did not live to see it grow. Two months before King Philip's body was displayed along the coast, William Ryall died at the height of war on ground he hardly knew. Two years later his wife Phoebe succumbed to illness and was buried at his side.

Far away in Maine the town they built lay charred and empty. North Yarmouth would remain that way—*vacuum domicilium* of another stripe—for another forty years as bellowing accordions of Indian rage three times drove settlers from those shores. Not until the 1720s did Casco Bay become a place where whites could live again in relative tranquility. By then, members of the Royall clan were scattered across Massachusetts and further yet, like seed.

When the Immigrant fled the war in Maine ("trouble with the Indians," so many writers called it), the Immigrant's son Joseph had stopped in Charlestown to make a life. There he gathered all he had to buy a house and wharf and set up shop as a sailmaker not a mile from the docks of Boston. That location and his choice of a trade placed him at the hungry periphery of a world belonging to men like the Ushers and the Lidgetts, merchants with their fortunes cast upon the sea. These men were not newcomers arriving full of dreams or farmers scrabbling at the whim of seasons like his immigrant father, but second- and third-generation Americans already possessed of enviable fortunes and deep roots. "Boston Brahmins,"

generations of their descendants would be called, members of a
newly minted aristocracy that seemed forever on the rise as though
suspended by transparent strings.

Dr. Oliver Wendell Holmes Sr. (father of the great Supreme
Court justice and a member of the caste himself) coined the term
long after the phenomenon was well in place. In an article published by the *Atlantic Monthly* in 1860 he described how well-
bred New England families with deep roots had "grown to be a
caste, not in any odious sense, but, by the repetition of the same
influences, generation after generation." This group he described
as a "harmless, inoffensive, untitled aristocracy. . . ." He christened
them Brahmins, naming them after the highest rung in India's caste
system, and went so far as to describe a typical boy as compared
to a "country boy" of his day. The Brahmin, Holmes wrote, possessed features "of a certain delicacy; his eye is bright and quick;
his lips play over the thought he utters as a pianist's fingers dance
over their music; and his whole air, though it may be timid and
even awkward, has nothing clownish. If you are a teacher, you
know what to expect from each of these young men. . . . [While a
country boy] will be slow at learning; the [Brahmin] will take to
his books as a pointer or a setter to his fieldwork."

Certainly, those contrasts were just as stark two hundred years
before Holmes's article appeared. In his sailmaker's shop at the
foot of Ten Hills Farm, Joseph quickly learned the deep seductions of that other life. He watched these men of privilege come
and go. He knew their drivers and their housemaids, their slaves
in rags and livery. He knew the mansions and the stables and the
gardens strung like lights up Boston's "Merchants Row," and came
to understand the risks and benefits, the losses and the money that
they made. Sailors talk. They talked about what fleets came home
with riches in their holds and who was counting profit. They gos-
siped of great vessels lost at sea and mourned the deaths of hands
on board. They talked about the pirates and the islands of the
Caribbean. They knew which colonies thrived, and why, and which
were deviled by ill winds and evil luck and perhaps the Devil, too.

Joseph never joined that world. A simple tradesman, he was not
invited to their formal gatherings and had no footman at his beck

and call. Instead, he stood forever to one side, observing every detail. Perhaps he shared his stories with his nephew Isaac. Perhaps he gave the boy advice and lay a seed. In any case, certainly the family's devastated home at Casco Bay was not where an ambitious lad might set his sights. The scythe of war had cut so deep the whole of Maine was written off as uninhabitable. Yet while white settlers stayed away, savvy politicians rushed to take advantage. Among them was John Usher, the new owner of Ten Hills Farm, who purchased Maine's sprawling Sagadahoc region as an agent for Massachusetts. Usher knew a buyer's market when he saw one. He paid just £1,250 to secure control of all that land.

Usher's purchase of the Sagadahoc Patent placed the Immigrant's North Yarmouth farm directly under Boston's rule. It also began a vague but important twining of the Usher and the Royall clans that would only increase over time until the Immigrant's grandson Isaac gushingly (but inaccurately) called John Usher kin. Oh how he craved it! Isaac Ryall's highest goal in life would be to join that club of gentlemen. It was a triumph he could almost taste. Ryall—Royall. He could change the name so easily. But how to get in? Young Isaac listened closely as the tradesman told his tales. His uncle Joseph knew which islands minted gold! In time, the two would cast their dreams together.

John Usher, wealthy by inheritance, did not have to wonder how to make his fortune. He was born with one and married well, then used his cash and clout to muscle into the highest echelons of society. And yet for him the salt of life was never found in stuffy drawing rooms but in the rough and tumble of flamboyant schemes and daring exploits. He had his share. The "graceless, grasping son of Hezekiah," as the historian Bernard Bailyn so colorfully described him, would forever be remembered for his sour temperament and aggressive ways. He strode along the Boston docks with a cockatiel's plump pride and left behind the mark of a man who acted boldly with the weight of wealth, social connections, and a scorching temper on his side.

This was a time of alpha men, and they were grabbing all they could. The new master of Ten Hills Farm fit that profile well. He had money enough and political savvy enough to get involved in some of the great land deals of his era. In addition to attaching the vast territory of the Sagadahoc Patent to his home colony of Massachusetts, John Usher helped coordinate the "million-acre purchase" in New Hampshire, a private deal granting a six-mile expanse along the Merrimack River to a select group of investors, most of them related. That territory, almost the size of Rhode Island, was purchased for a pittance from a local tribe. Of course the bitter legacy of that negotiation was many years of war. But Usher and his partners left the resulting violence to other men. The Merchant's goal, and that of every investor in the deal, was not to settle on that dangerous and undeveloped turf but to grab those acres while they could and rip the timber, fur, and other riches from the place.

Theirs was a small club, and it played a high-stakes version of Monopoly across a king-sized board. Among Usher's partners in the million-acre venture were his brother-in-law and business cohort, Charles Lidgett (who knew quite well what riches could be extracted from New England's woods), another in-law, Jonathan Tyng, and Samuel Shrimpton, a former business associate of his father's and now a relative on the Lidgett side. Usher's brother figured in the purchase, too. Though Hezekiah Usher Jr. was not among those who took title to the land, his sweet toehold was the right to mine whatever lay beneath it for the next thousand years.

For all their interest in land, however, the Ushers basically were city folk who held their eyes forever to the sea. Like the Winthrops, they kept their primary home in town, on King Street by the docks. There, John Usher tracked the comings and goings of his vessels, followed shipping news, and felt the pulse of commerce. For him it was an eagle's perch, and he used it well. It was here he cut his deals and scribbled notes in cipher as he aged. It was here he counted up his money, sold his slaves, and maneuvered in the surge of trade down at Long Wharf.

Today in that part of the city, Faneuil Hall draws a crowd, but it is mostly tourists who flock in search of souvenirs and lobster dinners. The docks have been moved back. The clop of horses' hooves is silenced. King Street is now "State" for reasons that are obvious; and where John Usher's house once stood there is instead a glacial cluster of high-rises made of steel and glass. In recent years, a constant mess of gridlock has replaced the shadow of Interstate 93—a span of which soared overhead until the Big Dig threw that traffic underground. Even so, the neighborhood is dark and busy. And though Long Wharf survives in a much-altered form, the place where Usher would have stepped so long ago is now an unforgiving landscape made of asphalt.

Three hundred years ago the neighborhood was just as busy but sat lower to the ground and closer to the water. Roads were narrow (they still are) and cobbled. The air was sharp with horse piss, straw, the umber sag of butchers' meat, the briny smell of seaweed and of smoke. On windy nights a film of salt left clothing dusted. In spring small gardens bloomed. Come fall, migrations swept directly overhead, or settled at the city's edge. Usher thrived in that environment. He loved the constant whisper of politics and gossip and the sense of being at the center of important events; yet when city life began to wear, the family could escape to Medford, where, on a sloping field near Cradock Bridge, they built a house. The dwelling was set back from the riverbank, presiding over field and marsh. Today the edifice survives as just a shadow pressed into the flanks of something grander, added later. Only the outline of the original brick gives the viewer any clue.

Usher's delight in the Medford property stemmed partly from the status it conferred. Most among this growing class of Boston merchants had farms and summer homes beyond the city's doorstep. These rural retreats offered a seal of class as well as respite from the grind of trade. For Usher, owning the old Winthrop farm was a feather in the family cap. There was no better prize. But even if the farm had not come with a governor's cachet, certainly it must have suited the family to sleep upriver on some nights. Living near the docks and looking out across the open sea was well and good when profits flowed. But sometimes that proximity disturbed a family whose fortunes shifted with the vagaries of hurricanes and far-off markets. For unlike their predecessors at Ten Hills Farm, who mostly confined their financial affairs to landlocked matters, this new generation gambled its future on the water, the weather, and the distant needs and tastes of empire. That fact put the Ushers at the epicenter of an international system built on slavery. Historian Barbara Solow describes it well in her introduction to the 1994 volume, *Slavery and the Rise of the Atlantic System*: "What moved in the Atlantic in those centuries was predominantly slaves, the output of slaves, the inputs to slave societies, and the goods and services purchased with the earnings on slave products," she observed.

John Usher's three-hundred-year-old ship inventories prove her point. Though the Merchant is often identified as a Boston stationer in histories (he wrangled a lucrative contract allowing him to print all Massachusetts laws and codes), the description obscures a rather more complex reality; for it was his life as a trader, not a simple bookseller, that consumed most of his attention, and it was there he made his fortune. In this respect he perfectly exemplified the pattern Solow captures: He moved the "output of slaves" in the form of sugar, molasses, and rum. He shipped "inputs to slave societies" in stocks of fish, corn, pork, wheat, cattle, boards, and nails. He even handled staves and barrel hoops to make the goods that *held* the goods those slaves produced. Indeed, there was no aspect of the trade he did not know, and touch.

That pattern was set well before John Usher's birth. Hezekiah Usher early on had aimed the family business toward Antigua and St. Christopher, slave islands yielding storms of riches in his time. The result was a handsome inheritance for his children and a solid network of business and shipping ties young John could press to his advantage. Upon his death, Hezekiah divided a £15,000 fortune among his heirs (a staggering sum for the time), and willed a "negroe woman" (unnamed) to his "dear wife to be at her dispose."

These were men and women who never had to cook a meal, plant a seed, mend a gown, or fix a shingle. Yet despite such comforts and advantage, John Usher found his own life not without its worry. Ships were costly to procure, outfit, man, and load; and until a ship came home it was only the occasional letter back that signaled if a merchant's fortune had moved up or down. Inevitably, some voyages brought heartstopping news. And there were personal concerns as well for a man whose wife and daughter were anxious to explore the world beyond their shore. Some of the mightiest vessels in the sea never made it home again. Perhaps that fact alone would send a man upriver to find peace.

Not long after Elizabeth Lidgett bought Ten Hills Farm, Usher would have needed peace. Early in 1679 he and seven coinvestors received sobering news in a letter from Cadiz. A fleet of ships dispatched to Spain was struggling in every way. For Usher and his partners it was a time of considerable risk. Now it was a time of worry, too. Captains of the fleet had done the best they could, the venture's leader wrote, yet all the news was bad. One ship lost her sails and rigging. Stocks of corn were left unsold. For want of buyers, captains were left waiting idle in the harbor, and some among them finally tossed their cargo overboard. Other of the merchants' ships, "having layn 4 months in the bay" without a good result, were headed home "halfe freighted." What little corn the fleet *could* sell was deemed fit only for livestock—and priced accordingly. Spaniards disparaged the stuff as of a "small inferior graine." Hundreds of bushels rotted in the heat of dripping wooden holds. Tobacco was another disappointment. Much was damaged. Buyers slicing into clumps of leaves too often found them "rotten at the heart." Bundles that survived the journey were often rejected as of poor quality. Spanish merchants, reported Commander Benjamin Price, want "a large substantial browne leafe," but the fleet had only a "small thin dry leafe of noe substance." Price considered it "the worst parcel entered into the bay for some time," and reported that it sold for just a fraction the price expected—and even then "with no small difficultie."

By the time his letter reached Ten Hills Farm and the drawing rooms of other investors back in Boston, conditions were so dire one ship was abandoned at the docks "until we . . . raise some money," came the woeful news. And there was more pain yet to come. Raisins, figs, and anchovies—all those delicacies the merchants were so anxious to import—were nowhere to be found along those docks in Spain. Only olives were plentiful and of high quality that season. That meant losses coming and going, and no profits to be tallied at either end.

In Boston's polished chambers news of all these troubles hit the merchants like a thunderclap: A broken ship. A rotted cargo.

Ships returning home half full? A glut of this, and none of that! How could they recover? Friends and relatives, all of a tight group, talked into the night as they weighed that awful crisis. Close, intermarried, interdependent, they functioned as a unit, strode shoulder to shoulder as pallbearers at important funerals, watched the courtships of their sons and daughters, shared the gossip of the city, followed shipping news with shared concern. Like a "single interrelated family," Bailyn called them. And they were.

In that season of disappointment the Boston merchants tried to look ahead. Sails could be replaced, at least. John Usher and his brother-in-law, Charles Lidgett, knew just the man for it. They knocked on Joseph Ryall's door. In a year of ugly weather the sailmaker was busy. Usher and his partners signed him on and paid young Isaac's uncle £9 18s. 4d. for 119 yards of canvas. Other contracts followed.

Joseph's pay, of course, was a pittance compared to the enormous profits a man like John Usher could expect in better times. Even in that season of crisis they had ample monies yet to draw on. Maybe Joseph told his nephew that. Maybe he told Isaac men like these were born into the life. Luck of the draw. A twist of fate. Nothing to be done for it. No son of a poor carpenter could ever expect this! Perhaps a certain envy showed. Surely young Isaac's sense of wonder grew. What was a farm in Maine compared to this? Or a life spent in clouds of sawdust? Good canvas for the sea? Isaac wanted something more.

Usher's clan was restless, too. But their restlessness was of a different sort. Financial failure ripped them like a saw. It set a few to thinking: Why should we risk everything for slender margins on inferior corn when merchants of the Royal African Company, trading in slaves, hold a monopoly on that potential lucre? Why are we not there? What right has a distant king to block us from this trade?

A time of whispers started. Perhaps it might be best to bend some rules. The monopoly granted the Royal African Company in the trade of slaves from Africa began to chafe. Men like Usher wanted in on that business. And why not? These were not religious men or political leaders dedicated to a great experiment. They were businessmen intoxicated by the swell of empire. In a time of grand ambition they found their way to wealth by maximizing their advantages. But now as they faced huge losses, London's bindings pinched, and a system that was designed ultimately more for England's benefit than for their own sat unwelcome on their shoulders. Slaves were what the market wanted. Slaves were where the money was. Let the men of Boston undermine the Crown's oppressive dictates from afar. Let them move illicit cargo in defiance of the law. And so a habit that began with war and the sailing of the ship *Desire* now expanded.

Usher was the sort of man for it. At thirty-two he had the energy and confidence of a younger man who had never known a great defeat. Laws and nervous words of caution did not slow him down. Instead, he was like a pit bull when he found something he wanted. And in that moment what he wanted was some slaves.

Maybe it was inevitable. Usher and his fellow merchants stood at the mouth of a great flood. In Usher's century, "300,000 Englishmen swarmed across the Atlantic . . . with more than half of them making for the Caribbean," wrote Nuala Zahedieh, a scholar of economic and social history at the University of Edinburgh who has published widely on the British Atlantic economy of the seventeenth and eighteenth centuries. Those whites needed workers, and increasingly, as the colonies were settled, those workers came from Africa. By the late 1600s, the color of many Caribbean islands and in parts of the American South would tip from white to black. The deluge had begun. Now it started to intensify. Indeed, the rush of slave importation was so furious that although countless Africans would die in the Atlantic passage, of thirst in flat-backed fields of cane, in childbirth, of disease, suicide, choked by the hangman's rope, or beaten by a master, still the ratios tipped. In Barbados (where by 1680 almost every acre had been cleared for sugar), there were almost seventy thousand slaves working the fields by the new century. More and more would come, until there were ten black faces to every white. "In terms of immigration alone," historian David Eltis wrote with memorable simplicity in 1983, "America was an extension of Africa rather than Europe until late in the nineteenth century."

From the planters' perspective the economics were nothing but convincing: Slaves, though they cost two or three times the price of white servants to procure, worked for life, added children to the system, and made a good return on those investments. For traders, the lure was simple, too: Demand was sure. Great profit may lie waiting.

With that as a draw, two men with deep connections to Ten Hills Farm concocted a bold scheme. What the government would not allow, they would do in secret.

John Usher would be there. With him was his new father-in-law, John Saffin, a powerful and wealthy merchant who had recently married the widow Elizabeth Lidgett. Pompous, bewigged, rich, and unapologetically convinced the sale of slaves would make him richer still, Saffin along with several associates embarked upon a plan to smuggle slaves into New England directly from the coast of Africa. In a series of private meetings, five men agreed to join the venture. They would be John Usher, his father-in-law John Saffin, Edward Shippen, James Whetcombe, and Andrew Belcher, respected merchants all.

Throughout the spring, they sketched a plan. Smuggling a cargo of black slaves directly into New England in defiance of the Royal African Company's monopoly was a daring gamble, to be sure, but the payoff might be riches corn would never give. By summer they were ready. Pooling their resources, they hired a ship and a man to captain her. They swore an oath as partners. What English courts would not allow, they would do in secret. The *Elizabeth* would go with Captain William Warren at her helm. His orders were to sail for Africa. He left in 1680.

In the many months the ship was gone, people started talking. News of the *Elizabeth*'s mission eventually found its way to the ears of Rhode Island officials who, incensed by this attempt to circumvent the law, announced they would capture the vessel and punish every merchant in the deal. In Boston, John Saffin called an urgent meeting. If the *Elizabeth* were stopped at sea, he warned, her cargo would be confiscated and each among them might be called to stand before a judge. It was certainly too dangerous to simply wait for Captain Warren to return. Instead, they must go to

him, inform him of the danger, and take his Africans away before
the king's men in Rhode Island were any the wiser.

And so a game of cat and mouse began. In June 1681, the Boston partners hired a second ship and instructed her captain, William Welstead, to intercept the first. A copy of his instructions sits
in Boston in the files of the Massachusetts Historical Society. It
says this: "We did the last year send out William Warren, master of
the ship *Elizabeth* for Guinea & at his returne ordered him to put
into Swansy for intelligence from us how to proceed further." Now
that plan was foiled, and the merchants wanted Welstead to find
the vessel and take her smuggled cargo before she ever came near
shore. *Lie in wait*, the letter ordered, either fishing or engaging in
some other likely activity until the *Elizabeth*'s sails were sighted.
Then go to her and take her slaves and send the first ship off again.
As for the Africans, "Come up in the night with them . . . giving us
notice whereof with what privacy you can, & we shall take care
for there landing."

Darkness would conceal. Secrecy was paramount. Anxious buyers
waited.

Well aware that any leak could foil the mission, the merchants
now took extra steps on shore to conceal their intent. Not one
among them spoke. The captain's orders, penned in a careful script
and conveyed in a sealed letter, were explicit on the need for sub-
terfuge. "Keepe your men ignorant of your designe," Welstead was
instructed. Only the captain was to know the purpose of their sailing. Let his crew think they were merely fishing or employed in
some other innocent task so long as that activity in no way proved
"prejudiciall to our mayne designe."

William Warren, sailing back from Africa with a crowd of captives in his hold, learned of the new plan only when Welstead
came aboard. The two captains shared a greeting, then Welstead
produced a sealed message which he offered to his fellow sea-
man. Warren broke the seal and read the following: "Mr. William
Warren," instructed his employers, "When you went hence we
gave you our orders at your return to put into Swansy & stay there
for farther advice from us; which, our intentions the Governor of
Roade Island Understanding, doth as we are Credibly informed

intend to Ceise you. . . ." To avoid that grievous end Warren was ordered to transfer all his slaves to Welstead's ship and sail discreetly out of sight until he could devise some sort of alibi for his long absence. "Deliver your Negroes" the letter said. Stay mum if you are questioned.

The plan succeeded brilliantly. Though the details of the slaves' transfer have been lost, by that August Usher's ledgers show him counting up the costs and profits of the mission. To William Welstead, captain of the second ship, the sum of two pounds, eight shillings was paid "for passage of 6 negroes." Other entries show cash spent for "rum and provisions for said negros." These notes were followed by a careful tabulation of the prices paid for men and women. The average was £25. Joseph Rainer bought a woman for that amount. Another buyer received a £2 discount for buying in bulk. He paid £73 for a man and two women. A third client, Joseph Fordham, would only pay once he knew he liked the girl he'd bought. He was given a money-back guarantee and two months' grace before the bill for her came due.

There the story ends. Just as it was with Josselyn writing about a rape forty years before, there was no followup or other particular interest in these people's fate. Did they work in fields or kitchens? Did they sweat in rum distilleries, or tend to infants in the house? Did they cook or sew or stoke a blacksmith's fire? Or did they bend to hard labor at the docks, hauling cargo and unloading ships? Did they make bricks? Did they plant seed? Did they rock a noisy child late at night? Did they marry? Did they make a family or ever find their way to freedom? The records do not say.

Unlike whites of influence who left extensive details regarding christenings, marriages, deaths, church memberships, elegant portraits of their winks and frowns, trinkets passed through generations, silhouettes, ephemera, account books, inventories, wills, even letters and diaries holding clues to their most private longings, unlike them—with all that literacy and sense of self—the lives of these slaves and hundreds of their kind were easily erased. Today at Ten Hills Farm it takes a team of archaeologists digging in the dirt to find just the smallest shard to show a slave's experience. From 1999 to 2002, a team of scholars from Boston University led

8.1 Slave game pieces recovered at the Royall House, Medford, Massachusetts. Courtesy Alexandra A. Chan.

by Dr. Ricardo Elia and Dr. Alexandra Chan conducted a formal dig at the old house. Month by month they sifted through the earth at Ten Hills Farm to find small remnants of another time. Some of these were homemade marbles, brown and slightly uneven, made of local clay and left to roast in the embers of the kitchen fire. A broken piece of china (sanded down to form a square) salvaged from the master's trash became a game piece rescued and remade. In those three years the team unearthed 65,000 shards of history. But even so, there was not much there to tell of lives of slaves. What they did find offered precious insights, if precious few.

What is clear despite this void is that these Africans whom Usher and his friends imported joined a community of several hundred slaves already settled on that northern shore. And what manner of slavery was it? Historians until recently granted Massachusetts (and almost all New England for that matter) something of a pass, describing a mild, essentially paternalistic form of bondage more like father-child relations than those of master-slave. Scattered bits of evidence, however, gesture at less comfortable realities. In and around Ten Hills Farm and among the small and close-knit group of families that made up the upper ranks of the elite, slave suicides were sometimes recorded; and there were crimes that spoke to a deep hatred.

On the very day John Usher tallied up his profits from the voyage of the *Elizabeth*, three criminals were put to death in Boston. One was a white man convicted of a rape. Two were blacks charged with setting fires. Jack, a slave from Weathersfield, was hung, then burned. Another slave named Maria, charged with killing her master's child by burning down his house, was sentenced to "a burning for a burning," in the parlance of the time. Hers was the first burning at the stake in New England. It would not be the last. As the fire crackled, Jack was cut down from the gallows and thrown into the flames as well. Perhaps John Usher smelled the stench. Certainly he knew the punishment. And yet for him that grisly odor would have only been a footnote in an otherwise rich life.

You May Own Negroes
and Negresses

◆

Slavery in Massachusetts by this time was common, so accepted, in fact, masters sometimes joked about the agonies of men they owned. One surviving letter from the Winthrop family shows Wait-Still, the Puritan's grandson born at Ten Hills Farm, writing to his brother Fitz in Connecticut, making fun of his slave "Black Tom" whom he was sending south. In the letter, which accompanied the slave's delivery, Wait told his older brother the man was of negligible value and had a troublesome habit of giving visitors a shock. "He used to make a show of hangeing himselfe" when strangers came to pay a call, Wait quipped, but "is not very nimble about it when he is alone." Fitz accepted the gift and perhaps his younger brother's advice, too: "Have an eye to him," Wait cautioned, and "and [if] you think it not worthwhile to keep him [either], sell him or send him to Virginia or the Barbadoes" and be done with it.

As more and more slaves arrived in Massachusetts, they chafed against their fate in many ways. But merchants rising on the strings of trade found it easy to ignore their pain. John Usher, for one, put his mind to other things, for after the *Elizabeth* came safely home his wealth increased and his schemes only grew in scope. In 1686 he was named treasurer and receiver general of New England. That same year he helped arrange the "million-acre purchase," securing a vast New Hampshire territory for himself and a few friends and a brother who would have the right to mine for a millennium.

Other profits ripened on a more familiar tree. Records from the late 1600s show Usher and his circle running goods between Boston, Nevis, Barbados, Jamaica, Antigua, Spain, and London in a nearly constant loop. An inventory on file at the Massachusetts Historical Society shows one of their ships leaving port low to her waterline, weighed down with "nails, fish, pork, makrill, boards, staves, shingles, pease, 1 horse, hay, water, Indian corn, hoops, light money and corn," in short, anything (even water for those parched Antiguans) those men could find a buyer for, the seaborne Wal-Mart of their day.

While Usher busied himself with matters of business, his wife and daughter left for England, traveling with the family slave, Sarah, whom John had bought on credit from his mother-in-law, the wealthy dowager Elizabeth Lidgett. Despite that slave's constant attention, the Usher women were not happy on their voyage and not long after they landed they wanted to be home. They were homesick, Elisa Usher complained to her husband in New England. They were lonely and quite ill. They missed Boston and the farm. Money worries dogged their every move. Londoners seemed less than welcoming. Friends back in America did not write. Perhaps they did not care. To top things off, just as the women were packing to go home, Sarah ran away and Elisa could find nobody to help her track the woman down.

"Dearest Love," Elisa wrote to her husband back at Ten Hills Farm, "I am forced to abide here, although nothing [could be] more tedious to me." The journey, meant to bring such pleasure, instead left her "continually labouring under continual pain, both of the body and minde." In a rounded, graceful hand that could not have been more different than her husband's cramped, untidy scratchings, Elisa complained that friends abandoned her and even "my nearest ones are more concerned with other matters, witness every letter I have had. . . ." Both Elisa and her daughter had contracted smallpox and suffered terribly with the disease. Betty Usher nearly died of it, and medical costs were mounting. Now the £100 advanced by the Belcher family was running thin, "not with riotous living," Elisa hastened to explain, "but bare necessity (and scarce that), all things excessive deer, especialy for strangers."

When she tried to hire a white maid, she found those alabaster-skinned girls "so difficult, and so cost[ly] to go for New England that I must be forced to keep Sarah with all her bad honors." She informed her husband of her slave's sudden disappearance on the eve of sailing.

Sarah "should have gone on board 2 days agone," Elisa allowed with some vexation. Instead, she took off "with all her cloaths, as farr as highgate." No one in London would "avise me what to doe," the matron grumbled. And so John Usher's absent wife took a coach, she told him, and went to find the runaway herself. By the time the two women returned, the ship had sailed. Elisa sent her letter by another captain. "Pray," she wrote, "let my master know my heart is with him often although he may so esily forget me . . . give my love to all my friends if I have any. I must bide thee fare-well, my dear, and remain thine," Elisa Usher. They would book another passage and be home before too long.

In Massachusetts, whether at Ten Hills Farm or at the family mansion down in Boston, at that time Sarah could not even dream of running off. A visitor from France explained the situation clearly. "You may . . . own Negroes and Negresses," she wrote. "There is not a House in Boston, however small may be its Means, that has not one or two. There are those that have five or six," and runaways were invariably returned by helpful neighbors. All you have to do is ask, the visitor reported, and the matter would be done. Perhaps an unscrupulous ship's captain might try to sell a fugitive, she wrote, but such an outcome was unlikely, since "that is open Larceny and would be rigorously punished." Sarah would be long dead before any enslaved black woman could find safe haven in New England. In her day, there was no underground railroad, no talk of abolition, no argument of moral purpose or religious imperative as it might concern a slave. Indeed, so extensive was the practice that "an imaginary 'hemispheric traveler' would have seen black slaves in every colony from Canada and New England all the way south to Spanish Peru and Chile," explains the scholar David Brion Davis in the opening to his study of slavery in the New World.

For Elisa and Betty Usher, the homecoming was sweet. Within a year Betty would be married. Her husband was a gentleman cut of the same cloth, a merchant and sometime slave trader whose family settled in a mansion down by Winthrop Creek. For the Ushers then it was a golden day, a time for seizing all life's pleasure. And they did—and with such gusto that several weeks before Betty's wedding, the Boston judge Samuel Sewall made a note in his diary that the bride's uncle, Charles Lidgett, and his friend and business partner, the fabulously wealthy Samuel Shrimpton, had begun their celebrations prematurely. "Mr. Shrimpton, Capt. Lidget and others," Sewall complained, "come in a coach from Roxbury about 9 aclock or past, singing as they come, being inflamed with drink. At Justice Morgan's they stop and drink healths, curse, swear, talk profanely and baudily to the great disturbance of the town and grief of good people. Such high-handed wickedness has hardly been heard before in Boston."

Perhaps. But it would be heard again. The winds of great new fortunes were then rising. They brought with them a tide of excess that would grow unchecked among the merchant class for several generations more. Gambling, drink, and self-indulgence would pummel the weaker members of the class even as they entertained the rest. In the end, the lure of these diversions was so great it took the frightening upheaval of a revolution to bring those revelers to ground.

For slaves like Sarah all that entertainment only meant more work. And there was no end to it. When Sarah's owner Elizabeth Lidgett (now Elizabeth Saffin) died, Sarah did not go free. Instead, she stayed with the Ushers, from whom she had once run. The old woman's will was clear on that point. Elisa Usher now received all her mother's treasure, to include any "wearing Apparill, and all my Rings, Bodkins, Jewills and Orniments whatsoever, and my nigro woman named Sarah, which Nigro Woman my Sonne-in-Law John Usher stand indibted for on my Book of Accounts." She was also granted the bulk of her mother's estate, £5,500 of a £7,000 fortune.

To the slave, Sarah, Elizabeth Saffin gave £20—not enough to buy her freedom.

John Usher and his wife at that time were securely in the upper class. They could have bought as many slaves as they wanted. For not only had John Usher's wife just inherited a fantastic sum, but his own star kept rising, too, and he took every advantage. As the years clicked by he became lieutenant governor of New Hampshire and used that new footing to push his way through yet more doors of power. When his wife Elisa died, he waited only six months before marrying the governor's daughter, thereby adding to his wealth and influence again.

By 1700, with his mother-in-law dead, his first wife buried, and her brother Charles Lidgett off to England, there was no one else to claim the land. It had taken fifty years, but the broad expanse of Ten Hills Farm was finally—and firmly—in John Usher's hands. He would live there and die there having realized one of his life's deepest ambitions. As the new century dawned, the "graceless, grasping son of Hezekiah" was master of all he surveyed.

In Bristol around the same time, John Saffin, Usher's father-in-law and smuggling partner, also remarried, also rose in power, and also continued with his schemes. Though this frequent visitor to Ten Hills Farm would later be recalled in local histories as one of the richest merchants of his time, in fact his more dramatic legacy lay in his racist thinking. That thinking was made clear in the first major debate over the morality of slavery to take place in North America, a debate led, on one side, by John Saffin, and on the other, by the straitlaced Boston judge Samuel Sewall, who earlier had objected to the wild revelry this group indulged in on the eve of Betty's wedding.

Sewall and Saffin lived at opposite poles of a moral landscape. Unlike Saffin, who had delighted in his smuggling scheme, Sewall was "dissatisfied with the Trade of fetching Negros from Guinea . . ." but stopped short of speaking out against the trade until 1700. That year, John Saffin's betrayal of a slave in his control —promising the man's release, then reneging on that promise— inspired the younger judge to take a public stance. Sewall produced an angry pamphlet titled "The Selling of Joseph." In it, using biblical analogies, he took aim at Saffin personally and made an argument for slavery's end. "Originally, and Naturally, there is no such thing as Slavery," Sewall chided. No argument, however facile, should ever equate "Twenty Pieces of Silver, and LIBERTY." Anyone who thought so, Sewall cautioned, jeopardized "his own claim to Humanity."

Saffin would not stand for this. He knew the words were meant for him, and he replied some months later with a pamphlet of his own. In "A Brief and Candid Answer to a late Printed Sheet, Entituled, The Selling of Joseph," Saffin employed twenty separate justifications for the system that had made him rich. "God hath set different Orders and Degrees of Men in the World," he asserted, ranking blacks lowest among them. In verse, he described their character as "prone to revenge," full of hate, with "mischief and murder in their very eyes, libidinous, deceitful, false and rude," and worse. For months the matter of slavery was debated in fancy drawing rooms and the occasional printed text. But in the end, slavery won. It would remain the norm at Ten Hills Farm and well beyond for almost another century.

With the first debate over slavery resolved in favor of the masters, there were few checks—moral or otherwise—on the expansion of that system, and the next decades would see a burst in importation. At the start of the eighteenth century, the black population in Massachusetts—though never to rise above three percent of the colony's population as a whole—quintupled, and laws controlling that minority were made more severe. In 1703, Massachusetts passed a law making it illegal to set any slave like Sarah free. The impetus for the legislation was at once racial and economic. Older slaves were sometimes dumped on township poorhouses when they grew too old to work. That put a strain on small-town finances. Local leaders saw through the ruse, rejected the burden, and closed the door on such releases. Interracial marriage was also outlawed. "Prone to revenge," full of hate, with "mischief and murder in their very eyes, libidinous, deceitful, false and rude. . . ." The first debate on slavery was done. A racist portrait had its hold, and its effect.

Facing that defeat, Judge Sewall chose to publish one last salvo. In it, he argued slavery's damage could never be undone. "Purchase them (for Toyes and Baubles) perhaps you may," he wrote sourly, but do not call it moral. And beware: If a later generation should determine "we have done those poor Wretches any wrong," he wrote, "We can never make them Restitution."

Those words, arresting today, stopped nothing then. Instead, importation spiked and the number of slaves doubled, then tripled and quadrupled in ensuing decades. Up at Ten Hills Farm more slaves would come, so many slaves, in fact, a separate house was built for them.

Part III

The
Master

ANTIGUA

◆

A bend of turquoise drew him. He must have stood on salty ground there, out by Beggars Point, chatting or standing with his back to the warm sea, pausing in the moment that always comes before a great decision, a furious sun pulsing overhead, one hand in his pocket as he pondered a sizable investment for a man of twenty-eight.

He would have weighed the distance to the nearest harbor, four miles down a white sand road, slow by horse and cart, but close enough for trade. He would have considered the prevailing breezes, enough to blow the creaking, thumping sails of a stone windmill. He would have touched the thin Antiguan topsoil, good enough for cane, and wondered at the cost and availability of slaves, those "likely" men and women advertised for sale. He must have walked the land and let his mind envision it transformed: rum bubbling in his distillery, molasses stacked up by the barrel, slaves bustling with their orders, coachmen waiting for his call. In his mind's eye, perhaps someone winsome stood nearby to fan him during dinner, while other men and women labored out of sight to cook for him, to clean his house, to nurse and tend his children. Perhaps he imagined a garden marked off by a line of waving palms, colorful blooms twining in a fragrant hideaway.

Or maybe he thought only about ledger books and money and the risk of losing everything. Whatever the particulars, he had a plan when he stepped off the boat from Boston. Grandson of a simple immigrant, son of a poor carpenter, Isaac Royall wanted what the men before him did not have. He was hungry for a fortune and he wanted to be master. For forty years and more, he was. The "Colonel of Antigua," he would call himself. It was a splendid game of reinvention. Acquaintances found him pompous, fancy, and thin-skinned, a dandy with a grand estate. But of course all that came later. First the island of Antigua (pronounced An-TEE-ga with a Spanish lilt) had to rise inside the circles of Atlantic trade, and Isaac Royall with it.

❖ ❖ ❖ ❖ ❖

Discovered and just as quickly abandoned by Christopher Columbus in 1493, Antigua was just a brown line in blue water to the famous explorer and his restless crew, something to be passed without much thought. Columbus dismissed it with a sneer, not even bothering to stop. Short scrub and twisted pine were not the spice and bounty he was seeking. He let the scraggly island shrink to nothing in his wake, just a disappearing bump in a hurricane-swept sea. As the ship sailed off, a sailor made an inkblot on a piece of parchment. Columbus named it after the miracle worker of Seville, Santa Maria la Antigua.

Back on shore, Carib warriors dropped their spears into the sand. The danger passed. The giant ship had sailed away. But this was only a reprieve. English merchants unpacked with a commanding hold on the territory in 1632. A rudimentary administration loyal to King Charles took hold. These men would gradually remake the land—almost every inch of it—and take advantage of the weather and Europe's growing taste for sugar to build an efficient engine of great wealth. What they needed, though, was just what Henry Winthrop had needed in Barbados several years before: workers to clear the fields, plant and cook, and serve these settlers in a hundred ways.

To men with expansionist tastes in foggy enclaves back in London, rounding up the locals seemed a capital idea. A ready workforce was at hand. And so in their first weeks ashore, men with guns moved about the island with single-minded intent—to track down every man, woman, and child they could—and press them into service. Oh, but those honey-skinned Caribs were not so easily subdued. Flexible and fierce, they knew each cove and hiding place the island had to offer. Having taken the island by force themselves from the more peaceful Arawaks, they were proud warriors and savvy fighters who did not shrink from battle. With a violent push they drove the first men off. Then more English came, and more guns, too, and gradually the power tipped. For years the island was a dangerous place and full of lethal shock. Hundreds of Caribs were slaughtered. Others fled. Scores sickened. Some were captured and enslaved. Some committed suicide. A few escaped across that gleaming turquoise water and resolved to fight. Still the English stayed, and thrived. Frustrated with these "troublesome Caribs," they began importing Africans instead to do their work, and turned with murderous energy against inhabitants whom they earlier had hoped to bind to service. Eventually, a formal policy of genocide evolved.

Settlers in Antigua were given "great encouragement," one nineteenth-century author remarked, to kill the Indians and steal their property. Records show it. Today in St. John's a musty volume published in London in 1734 and held now in the Antigua and Barbuda National Archives building describes *Acts of Assembly, Passed in the Charibbee Leeward Islands from 1690 to 1730.* The volume makes for dry reading until the full meaning of the language sinks in. One page shows legislators tending to some last-minute business shortly before the Christmas holiday of 1693. On December 21 that year they passed *"An Act to encourage the destroying the* Indians, *and taking their Periagoes"* or large canoes. Other atrocities would come. Good bureaucrats, the English tallied all of them.

Even with the official embrace of genocide, the island's troubles were not done. Antigua would be hauntingly unsafe for blacks, whites, and Indians for another century at least. Surviving Caribs with little left to lose launched fearsome raids from nearby islands. The French were warlike, too, and came in ships to try to pry the island from England's grip or at the least strip residents of whatever wealth they had. Like the English, they were hungry to expand their turf. And so the bloodshed repeated in bitter cycles of attack and retribution with no easy end. English soldiers from Antigua played their part. In one raid that sounds today like a ramped-up game of "capture the flag" played for keeps with cannons, muskets, knives, and fire, three hundred soldiers from Antigua sailed to a nearby island, "beat the Inhabitants into the Woods, burnt their Town, nailed down their Guns, demolished their Fort, and returned back to Antego with the Plunder," wrote the Antiguan genealogist and historian Vere Oliver, whose three-volume history of the island published in 1898 stands even now as the best resource on the island's past.

On and on it went. Only when the French and English joined forces to go against the Indians together did they finally break Carib resistance. Yet truce between those mighty, far-off powers was short-lived. Once rid of "these troublesome savages," Vere Oliver explained, old enmities resurfaced and the French and English turned their guns against each other with renewed vengeance.

In the midst of all that slaughter came waves of drought, sickness, and devastating hurricanes. Tobacco crops were often disappointing. The hoped-for riches were, at first, elusive. But then a well-connected gentleman with a major pedigree and flowing auburn curls arrived intent on a new venture. His experiment, launched in the mid-1600s, would revolutionize the life of islanders. As King Philip's War scorched across New England, Colonel Christopher Codrington quietly spread sugarcane across his 725-acre estate, called Betty's Hope. Here, he thought, was a crop to make Antigua worth his while. The experiment met with staggering success. Other planters followed suit, and soon waves of cane replaced tobacco as the favored crop. Everyone was growing it.

Sugar proved a hungry mistress. Its cultivation took the work of many hands. And so a noisy call went out for slaves. As the calendar of centuries turned, terrified new workers were unloaded by the boatful. Disoriented, fearful, sick, and far from home, hundreds—then thousands—of men, women, and children, young and old, fit and feeble, stood shackled, humbled at the docks, while dealers drank their rum, inspected merchandise, and shouted orders in the din. Day by day, ship by laden ship, the lives of generations were twisted into agonized new forms in that ugly seaside marketplace.

Between 1673 and 1711, the Royal African Company delivered sixty thousand black slaves, mostly men, to the West Indies. Antigua got its share. Independent traders transported more, illegally at first, then, after 1698, with the blessing of the English government. Island records show the power of that change: In the final year of the Royal African Company's monopoly a lone independent trader landed eighteen slaves on Antiguan soil. Seven months later—with the monopoly now lifted—another ship brought 212 people for sale. Among them, those too ill, too weak, or too old to fetch the highest prices were sold as "refuse," at a discount. Wealthy planters would not touch them. More would come. Demand was high, and traders rushed to meet it as fast as wind could push their sails.

In 1701 almost sixteen hundred slaves were tossed ashore by independent traders. The next year the tally rose again. All the while the Royal African Company still churned those waters. At rowdy portside auctions planters sealed the fates of thousands. For an island the size of Martha's Vineyard, 108 square miles, the surge in importation was fantastic, disruptive, and intense. And it continued. Long after Colonel Codrington was laid in his grave, his heirs still bought their slaves in bunches: "30 or 40 I shou'd think full enough for a first purchase," a descendant once instructed his attorney. The result was that by the time of the American Revolution nine of ten of Antiguans traced their ancestry to Africa.

Throughout this time white planters engorged with the promise of great wealth expanded their investments and took rough measures to ensure their safety. They passed new laws, secured and cleared more land, and set many thousands of dark hands to work. The money flowed, yet at the cost of a serious imbalance that would forever pester the elite: How could a small minority of whites control so many blacks in bondage?

An aggressive slave code was devised. It restricted workers' movements, limited family life, and choked back speech as well as any effort to foster independence. If a slave in Antigua grew so much as a cassava to sell for profit, he was punished. If he spoke disrespectfully to a white man, woman, or child of even the lowest class, he faced torture to the point of death. Extended and updated at various junctures in the island's history, the slave code was hardened until almost any infraction called for a slave to be whipped, disfigured, killed by public hanging, burnt to death, or broken on the wheel.

Many tried to run. But they were tracked by bounty hunters with few stops on their behavior. Countless chases ended only when a corpse was dragged behind the hunter's horse. Runaways who came home in one piece, still breathing, were submitted to public whipping and torture as a warning to the others.

Today in Antigua that history is buffed and sweetened. There is a Runaway Bay on the island's northern coast, full of tamarind trees and brilliantly colored sailboats and a hotel and lounge, too, bearing the name, which most tourists mistake as a reference to their own running off from obligations back at home, so lighthearted is the signage. Then again, how does one deal with such a past? In Antigua it is sometimes everywhere and nowhere all at once, hiding in plain sight.

For wealthy planters back in Isaac Royall's time, the most important aspect of the island's laws was that whites who lost their slaves to a public hanging or a rough hunter's treatment almost always recouped their investment in the form of a payment by the state. If a bounty hunter went after a runaway and the slave was returned, all to the good. If that slave was caught and killed in the taking—compensation to the owner. If he was tried, found guilty of some crime, and condemned to death by an action of the court—compensation to the owner. If he was found guilty of fomenting a revolt or otherwise disturbing the island's tender balance—compensation to the owner. The fundamental premise of the system was nothing if not simple: Win-win for whites. Lose-lose for slaves.

As slave unrest grew, a cage, pillory, stocks, whipping-post, and ducking-stool sprouted in St. John's. Yet always there were those few who managed to get free. Some men and women dodged their owners, then their hunters, and joined a small population of fugitive blacks who established a defiant culture in the hills. These

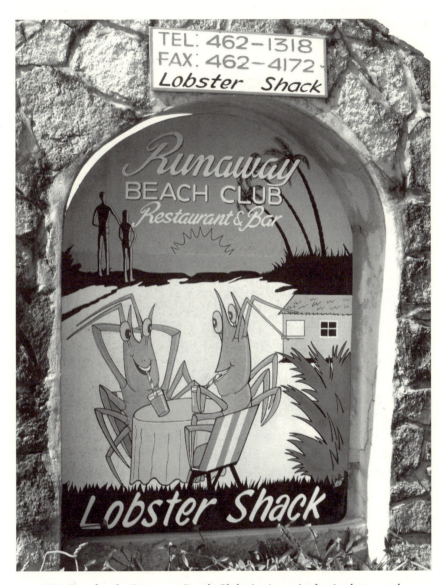

10.1 Sign for the Runaway Beach Club, Antigua. Author's photograph.

people, called *maroons* (a term perhaps derived from a bastardiza-
tion of the Spanish *cimarron*, for "wild and untamed"), terrorized
whites for generations, dropping down from their sanctuaries in
the hills to stage midnight raids to steal, plunder, and talk others
into fleeing.

Frightened members of the ruling class, desperate to maintain
their hold, strained to get more whites to come. If only the balance were kept, they argued, they might live their lives in peace.
And so as the 1600s closed, the English government ordered fifty
female convicts from England sent to the Leeward Islands to provide an influx of white mates and mothers. They would boost the
population! Elsewhere, other attempts were made to attract new
settlers ready for a great adventure. One pamphlet distributed in
New England and New York around that time invited whites to
come and make a life.

In St. John's, meantime, plans were hatched to give every soldier
who retired from His Majesty's service on the island a plot of land
and a store of basic goods to make a start. Poor whites did not
have much to hold them otherwise; and plenty of ships set sail
with able-bodied white men leaving, never to return. Those soldiers knew the risks and knew the deck was stacked against them
as poor whites. But for many young men in the infant colonies
of North America, there was an extraordinary pull to that warm
shore. Part was economic. Part was pure romance. Newspapers
from Boston to Charleston, South Carolina, in that day told a constant tale of adventure and success, tracking the movements of
wealthy Caribbean merchants as though following the peregrina-
tions of a much-admired royal class: This gentleman off to Barbados, another to Jamaica, the Leeward Islands, the West Indies. This
ship just arriving, bulging with its cargo. When ships returned,
pineapples were lashed to fence posts at sea captains' gates to announce a safe arrival and an open invitation. So important and so
profitable was the Caribbean trade (and so expensive those rough
pineapples!) that in Isaac's day the fruit became a favorite symbol
of riches, reproduced in gold and silver, porcelain, fine stenciling,
in architectural adornments and gateposts made of wood and iron.
The fruit itself was often placed at the pinnacle of huge displays of

10.2 Pineapple gate adornment. The Royall House, Medford,
Massachusetts. Author's photograph.

food at fancy feasts. Its thorny sweetness spoke to great success, good rum, and plenty of engaging stories from afar.

To young white New Englanders just starting out in life, the message was inescapable, the lure tremendous. What great adventure lay in store! Like ambitious youths of another generation watching Internet moguls from Google, Yahoo!, Apple, Facebook rise to fame and riches, this generation looked south to scattered islands and thought, *Well, why not me?* What power and what riches might lie waiting! Many felt the urge to go, and from 1700 to 1724 Antigua's population of white settlers almost doubled.

Isaac Royall was among the first in that new wave, setting sail in 1700. For him, there was precedent. Seventy years before, his grandfather had abandoned everything he knew to make a new start on a distant soil. Isaac did the same. But even without that family history, he might have gone. To him it was easy enough to see that the gathering of great wealth was not the work of busy hands in rocky soil, or ever to be found in the skillful wielding of a hammer, chisel, mallet, gimlet, froe and plane, but rather (as John Usher so well knew) a matter of the timely exploitation of unfair advantage. Perhaps Isaac's uncle Joseph, the sailmaker in Boston, told him that. Perhaps he breathed it in the very air. In any case, New England could not hold him.

As a youth, Isaac had ingratiated himself with the Boston gentry. He studied commerce and accounting and began to spell the family name with an oversized flourish that took up inches on the page. *He* would not be Isaac Rial or Ryall, as records of his forebears had styled the name, but Isaac *Royall*, with a peacock's long-tailed "I" sweeping gently to the left for Isaac, and ski-jump "R" for Royall with a swooping flourish protruding to the right. Every Royall afterward would keep the "o" (if not the flourish), and Isaac, as patriarch and protector of the clan, would ensure that the name stuck.

It was a long way up from being the son of a poor carpenter to a man so affluent that he one day would buy John Usher's Ten Hills Farm and make it into "one of the most pretentious and elegant residences of the time within the suburbs of Boston," as one nineteenth-century writer put it. But that would be his arc in life. The eldest of nine, heir to almost nothing, he hungered to be part of a newly minted aristocracy and sought to make a mark that would last beyond his time. Let his younger brother Jacob spend his days tending to the mechanics of business down by Boston's docks. Isaac had a grander vision. He sought not only a respected name, but wealth and power worthy of that name. And so he left bruised thumbs, straight cuts, and dovetail joints to his father. He left the grind of ledger books and small-bore negotiations to his younger brother. He left the mending and sewing of canvas to his uncle Joseph. Real success, Isaac wagered, would require of him daring, gumption, wit, a proper marriage, a strong stomach, a curious nature, and good start.

Of course, it took a nest egg to begin with. Isaac found it in his first marriage, when at the age of twenty-five he wed Elizabeth Eliot, daughter of Asaph, great niece to the Preacher of the Indians, and widow from a powerful family with branches in Antigua and New England. Elizabeth Eliot was a teenager then, recently widowed, not yet in her twenties. In May 1699, a son was born. His grave was dug that summer. Little Asaph's mother hardly lasted longer. By fall two new headstones were in place, and Isaac found himself alone, a widower with a small inheritance, a fresh set of extended kin, suddenly a man of property. At twenty-eight he had no obligations that could weigh him down, no ties to bind. And so he sold some land and booked his passage, and turned his fate toward slaves and sugarcane on island soil. For him it would be creaking bulkheads, island insurrections, and the world of international intrigue, over a life forever bound ashore.

It was 1,800 miles from Boston to Antigua, but for Isaac the journey ended with the sight of land and the hope of a large fortune. In time, he settled on the northern coast, with a small inlet to call his own (today a part of Hodges Bay) and a view to Prickle Pear Island. It was a harsh country, waterless and hot, but increasingly prettied up according to English custom and colonial taste. Isaac would design one northern corner of it to his liking. But first he had to learn to function in a chaotic world marked by mutinies at sea, turf battles on land, violent uprisings by slaves, and the slightly more mundane but no less urgent depredations of drought, hurricanes, earthquakes, and yellow fever. As if that catalogue of woes were not enough, dysentery, heat, humidity, and infestations of mosquitoes rounded out the newcomer's experience.

For all of that, ambitious traders who came to understand the vagaries of harvest, the mercilessness of market demand, the mechanisms of slave control, and the delicate science of producing rum had much to gain. The most successful planters knew a brutal and effective driver in the fields was crucial; so was a good "boiler," a talented and trusted slave who came to know the cane, "how it had been raised and treated, the kind of soil in which it grew, whether that soil had been richly or slightly manured, the age of the cane, its species, whether it had been topped short or long in the cutting, and whether it had been arrowed, bored or rat-eaten." It was a complex business fraught with risk. A firm hand, a quick mind, an ample workforce, and a solid network of connections were the tickets to success. Isaac Royall had all that, and a brother and an uncle back in Boston, too, pulling at the strings of commerce there.

When Isaac arrived in Antigua, the island was already a place of bacchanalian indulgence for the few, one of foul dislocation for the rest. Among these slaves' descendants is Jamaica Kincaid, author of the bitter volume, *A Small Place*, in which she describes her black Antiguan brethren as "the millions of people, of whom I am just one, made orphans." For those who came in chains (or were born to those who came in chains) Antigua offered, in Kincaid's words, "no motherland, no fatherland, no gods, no mounds of earth for holy ground." No hope of gorgeous destiny awaited them. No gentle replication of the things they left behind would help define their new and foreign home. Instead, their fate would be the theft of language, naming, custom, past and future, freedom, choice, even of the food they knew.

To Isaac, of course, the fields of cane awaiting him were not a bitter crop, and he was certainly no orphan. Instead, he quickly joined a group of men intent on molding their small playground to a soothing and familiar design. Acre by acre, the land was cleared and made anew as drivers commanded sweating gangs to strip the ground of brush, clear the tangled flora, chop down trees, and then replace the whole of it with tidy fields, large mansions, and fine gardens.

In 1700, only half the island was under cultivation. Fifty years later, it was completely reinvented, most of the native vegetation torn away, replaced with sweeps of cane and neatly tended gardens designed to suit the ladies of the house. During the years that Isaac Royall and his family called the island home, it was "improved to the utmost," even to the mountaintops, so it was "fit for Sugar Canes and other necessary Produce." Dotting that landscape were also dozens of municipal ponds that served to slake the thirst of a people who had settled on an island with a dearth of water. But even that was sometimes not enough, and droughts would take an awful toll.

Overseeing all of this was a pampered class sequestered in great mansions crowded with elegant furniture, expensive silver, crystal, tapestries, and heavy drapes quite out of place for that environment. For them, the island's hardships were neatly kept at bay. For them, on the best of days, heaven could not come down closer. The result would charm white visitors for centuries.

"The prettiest little harbour I ever saw," no less an observer than Samuel Taylor Coleridge said upon first landing in Antigua. "The neatness of the docks, the busy village which has grown up in their vicinity, the range of hills of various shapes and colours" provide "such a combination of tropical beauty, and English style and spirit, as I never saw." Echoing Henry Winthrop's words upon arriving in Barbados long before, Coleridge pronounced himself "very pleasantly surprised" with all he saw.

Others would be too, including an Irishwoman who reported on her trip in some detail. Though she unpacked in a different century, her arrival must have echoed Isaac's own. She rushed to the deck as land drew near. There, a bleak vista and the desperate squawking of a seabird caught the night before stopped her in her tracks. Antigua, she reported, seemed "dull and dreary" at first glance; but by the time the ship reached shore the ground had done its magic. Up close, drifts of green replaced the brown, and distant hills presented not the "barren, sunburnt" look the author first complained of, but a "blending of a thousand dyes" any painter might enjoy. It was harvest time. Workers climbed the hills, their bodies steaming from the heat, doubled with the weight of cane. In fields of green, "white sails of the various mills glittered in the sunbeams," the author wrote enthusiastically. She found it quaint and to her liking. Above the fields, she spied a "great house," elegant and commanding, that "looked down upon its little hamlet of negro huts, picturesquely embosomed in trees."

Her heart lifted. "On we glided," she wrote giddily, "the merry breeze piping in our ears." At the dock, passengers were met by "plenty of black boys, to grin and chatter, and get all the biscuit and beef they could." When she looked away from them, great waves of beauty caught her.

The beach is just the beginning, a popular tourist slogan crows today. Even the long-exiled Kincaid, whose loathing for the island's history is raw and certainly well-earned, cannot resist a burst of pleasure: "No real seawater could strike that many shades of blue at once," the author writes, "no real cloud could be that white and float just that way in that blue sky." And yet for her, as for so many others whose personal story did not include a seat at great house tables, there always was that history pounding. It prompted islanders to see those gawking, pink-faced tourists as forever greedy, rough, and ignorant, nothing but "an ugly, empty thing, a stupid thing, a piece of rubbish pausing here and there to gaze at this and taste that," their eyes forever wandering and their white bellies overfull.

Such bitterness is centuries old, and Isaac Royall helped create it. Home for him was an elegant mansion surrounded by poverty so deep that workers moved about in tattered rags and sometimes died for lack of water like neglected cattle during times of drought. In this distant, desolate, riverless place, Isaac made his fortune. He stayed for forty years, always keeping one foot in New England, since he could, and since he needed it.

By 1703, Isaac Royall was listed as co-owner of the sloop *May-flower* with his uncle Joseph, the sailmaker to whom John Usher turned in a bad year. After a quarter century, Joseph had risen steadily in society and that year completed a stint as "clerk of the market," a position that brought him ever closer to the beating heart of Boston's trading life. He knew the men of Merchants Row. He lived and worked among them, building up his business carefully. Though Joseph had arrived in Charlestown with nothing in a time of war, by the year Isaac sailed for the West Indies, his fifty-five-year-old uncle was more than ready to expand his role. As the *Mayflower* plied the waters back and forth, the sailmaker's own wealth increased. Upon his death in Boston at the age of eighty-three, Joseph left a will that carefully outlined a comfortable estate. An inventory still on file in crumbling Massachusetts records counts three houses, a Negro girl, a silver tankard, and a feather bed as his most valuable possessions. The girl, worth £75, was valued less than the real estate, but twice as much as the tankard.

Isaac's brother Jacob, born in Dorchester when Isaac was just turning ten, became another ally, serving Isaac's interests in almost perfect symbiosis, by opening a dry goods shop down by the Boston docks, selling Isaac's rum and sugar for the best prices he could fetch and acting as middleman in everything from the purchase of fine real estate to the private sale of slaves. In some negotiations, Jacob arranged to deliver "seasoned" men and women to the elite. Among the buyers was Massachusetts governor Jonathan Belcher, the son of the Boston trader of that name, Andrew Belcher, who several decades earlier had smuggled Africans into New England in collusion with John Usher, John Saffin, and several other men.

Andrew Belcher's son was trained to lead, and he lived up to lofty expectations. A graduate of Harvard, he won his master's degree there in 1702 while Isaac was still busy establishing himself at Popeshead District in Antigua. Before long, the needs and interests of these two men would intersect. While Isaac Royall created a life as sugar baron, master, and slave trader, Jonathan Belcher won a reputation as a man of unusual political finesse. After serving as governor of Massachusetts, he would move on to New Jersey, where he took up the mantle of governor again and also helped secure the future of Princeton University, whose trustees in 1755 would laud him as "founder, patron, and benefactor" of a school that might have died without his help and backing.

During Belcher's years in Boston, Isaac Royall was the governor's "go-to" man for slaves. The Master in Antigua and the governor of Massachusetts would be friends across that watery divide, trading slaves, sharing letters and advice. The phrasing of one letter speaks both to an ongoing correspondence and a series of sales on Isaac Royall's part. "I must ask your pardon," the Massachusetts governor wrote the Master, "for the trouble of sending me one more." This one should be young, he told the Master, and pliant, "not less than 16 & not exceeding 20 years of Age."

Trades like these were gentlemanly affairs, neither advertised nor recorded in official records of the day. Instead they were the stuff of a handshake or a letter and a knock upon the door. Isaac's brother Jacob helped with such things and was not above sometimes using the connections they afforded to advance his own ends. When Isaac considered buying a house in Boston, Jacob went to see the governor. Might Mister Belcher consider selling his *own* house at Hanover Street? Yes, the governor was willing. Life and politics seemed to call him elsewhere then; but the deal did not go through. Isaac had set his heart on something bigger, grander, better.

His brother Jacob, meanwhile, moved rapidly to take advantage of an opportunity. As the Master backed away, the shopkeeper stepped forward, negotiating on his own behalf to win the deed to another Belcher house, this one adjacent to the governor's mansion, three stories high and finished with a fine garden. It would be Jacob's home until his death, a dwelling fine enough to suit both his rising station in life and his second wife, Rebecca Winthrop Adams Royall. The daughter of John Winthrop's sixth son, Deane, Rebecca had come of age attended to by slaves at Pullen Point, a farm gracing the northern edge of Boston Harbor, now the town of Winthrop. Among families such as these, selling either men or mansions was accomplished in congenial privacy. A buyer's word and social station counted just as much as any contract.

Of course much other business having to do with the sale of Africans was conducted in the more open glare of public life. "Negroes,

Males and Females . . . for Cash, good Bonds or six or nine months credit" read a newspaper advertisement bearing Jacob's name and likely involving his brother Isaac's merchandise. "A Likely Negro Man about 20 Years of Age, and also a Negro Woman about 35 Years Old, fit for Town or Country To be sold by Mr. Jacob Royall, in Boston," read another. Decade after decade Jacob hawked his goods in the *Boston Evening-Post* and the *Boston Gazette,* offering buyers in the general public "Choice Barrel Alewives," "All sorts of Dutch Stone, and Delf ware . . ." good West India rum, sugar, molasses, ladies' gloves, ribbons, buttons, people.

Far off in Antigua, meanwhile, the Master's effort to penetrate Boston's elite was bearing fruit. He was not a shopkeeper destined to serve another man's whim but a fellow merchant who would rise to equality or higher on the social scale. Not only had he befriended the governor, but by 1706 he was already well enough situated to write a letter to John Usher at Ten Hills Farm using the somewhat mystifying address "Dear Kinsman," though no clear line of kinship emerges from either family tree. In that letter Isaac Royall repeatedly called the older man "dear friend," and in his characteristic flowing hand detailed a life made of seaborne trade, a pesky island intrigue, a fellow merchant's "barbarous" behavior, and a raid at the nearby island of Nevis. Toward the letter's close he could not help but add a bit of shameless self-promotion and a boast of his new wealth. "Amongst my troubles and misfortunes [let me] inform you as my friend of my *good* fortune," the Master wrote. He had amassed, he said, "above six thousand pounds!" It was a huge sum, and the bumptious Royall wanted the whole world to know it. He had joined the club.

In 1707, at the age of thirty-five, Isaac married for a second time. This match was with Elizabeth Brown, a widow from a neighboring estate who was a woman of property with a broad network of connections. She came into the marriage with a four-year-old named Ann, who would always stay in Isaac Royall's life. Ann Brown (she kept her father's name) would grow up to marry a

10.3 Elmwood, 2008. Author's photograph.

wealthy Antiguan planter named Robert Oliver and give birth to a boy named Thomas who later gained notoriety as lieutenant governor of Massachusetts in a time of war. Master of a sprawling estate called Elmwood, Isaac Royall's grandson Thomas would live beside the Charles River near Harvard College with his wife and many slaves at a mansion that today, its grounds much diminished in scope, remains important as the gracious home of Harvard presidents. The massive yellow dwelling, set off a Cambridge side street bearing the mansion's name, is attended by a cheerful cluster of small outbuildings, softened by the shade of ancient trees.

For now, though, Ann Brown was just a four-year-old adjusting to life in a new family. In 1707 she moved with her mother to a hundred-acre estate set back from the water on Antigua's northern tip. There, from her bedroom, she could look across great waves of cane and beyond it to the sea. A towering windmill made her lullaby, its flapping sails a gentle metronome. Out in the fields,

10.4 Contemporary remnants of the Royall Estate, Antigua.
Manager's house (refurbished) and mill, 2008. Author's photograph.

men and women with skin as dark as the molasses they produced bent to endless labors in the sun. Ann might watch them from the harbor of the "big house," a two-story mansion sweetened with sea breezes and the cooling touch of stone. That house, set on a slight rise, was complemented by the manager's quarters, a stone dwelling fifty paces off, a cane press, a still, a cistern, the busy mill, a stable for the Royalls' horses, and a huddle of simple mud and thatch huts that housed the family's slaves.

Theirs was a classic Caribbean sugar estate, graced with all the appurtenances any landowner of means required. Spread across those rolling acres, it lolled gently by a bay that bore the family's name. Today, most Antiguans in that island neighborhood do not know the Royalls' history, or even that the family lived on this old ground; but old maps do show it, and a middle-class housing development on the property carries the Royall name in blue across its stucco gates. In that tiny, isolated place, so much of the

old history is lost. Who would want to cling to it? A large hotel, the Sunsail Club Colonna, now stands at Royall's Bay. The
staff inside—black and white—has not heard of Isaac Royall or
his private bay, though they sit beside it day by day. Inland a short
drive, the Royalls' main house is gone (dragged off stone by stone
over the years). On the site where it once stood, the dwelling is
replaced by a small veterinary clinic with a fenced kennel out
in back. The towering hulk of the family's single sugar mill still
stands, though it has long since been stripped of all its thundering machinery. The manager's house survives as well. Renovated,
the old stone dwelling features a fantastic ocean view interrupted
today by taller growth than cane.

Down at the Sunsail Club Colonna, a two-star waterfront resort
owned by an Italian consortium, tourists drink in an open-air bar
and watch the sun traverse an endless sweep of water. The hotel
offers rooms averaging $400 a night and hosts loud visitors who
come for water sports and respite from the winter months. As a
gimmick, the lobby is built around the sturdy circumference of a
sugar mill, refurbished in recent years and made to house a business center with its several gleaming new computers, a half-dozen
chairs, a telephone.

It was from this perch on the island's northern tip that Isaac
Royall and his family found their way into Antigua's humming
social life. There they hosted parties, traded secrets, attended to
the pressing requirements of a small society. In his counting room,
Isaac supervised a growing fortune, tallied up his profits, penned
letters to the Codringtons and other wealthy traders, and watched
the flow of trade. Isaac loved the life and shortly found a role
in government. Each year, he cemented his position further. His
record, though, would be an odd one; for he proved himself a nervous conservative in a time of violent change and chose to back a
politician so reviled that the man was set upon by an angry mob at
the culmination of several years of petty conflict. It was a hideous
island drama that captured the attention of a generation.

II

CRIME, PUNISHMENT, AND COMPENSATION

◆

Not long after Isaac Royall settled in Antigua, Daniel Parke, a foppish Virginian with a well-earned reputation for philandering, arrived to serve as governor and captain general of the Leeward Islands, a string of volcanic bumps rising haphazardly between Puerto Rico and Martinique, whose capital, St. John's, lay roughly at the center. The new governor was welcomed with a lavish party. Antigua is a small place, and small things can sometimes rock it. Daniel Parke was no small thing. He stepped into St. John's brandishing his royal appointment papers and a personal memento from Queen Anne—a portrait of the queen set in a jeweled frame. In their titillation and their hope, island leaders cheered him on and ordered a great mansion built, something fit to house this stunning gentleman. Parke would live in happy splendor for a time. Then his welcome chilled.

Selfish, pompous, and unconcerned with the sensibilities of the men he needed most, Parke quickly alienated the elite. Within a year island leaders asked for his removal. Yet Isaac Royall supported the man and stood faithfully at the governor's side while others turned their backs in raw disfavor and distrust. Week by week the situation worsened. Opponents charged the governor with bribery, the unjust imprisonment of personal enemies, the mismanagement of public funds, and the private use of public servants. They asked the queen to make him leave. Parke brushed off his critics, seduced the wife of one of the wealthiest traders on the island, then arrested his mistress's husband on charges the man was plotting a coup d'état. Outraged legislators went on strike. Government business ground to a halt. The signs of crisis deepened.

One year after Isaac Royall's wedding, in the fall of 1708, Parke was riding his horse beside a cane field when he was shot in the leg by a slave apparently acting on the orders of his master. "As he was riding along the high road," one author related, "leading from St. John's to English Harbour, a negro, named 'Sandy,' fired at him from a piece of canes belonging to the plantation of the Honourable Otto Baijer," a man dead-set against Parke's continued rule. The outraged Parke survived the injury but ignored the warning. Instead of giving up, he drafted a 103-page letter to the queen, whining of his unfair treatment. Months passed as bits of correspondence moved across the sea. Then at last an order came from London: The planters won. Parke's appointment was rescinded. But even then he did not quit. Instead, he isolated himself in the governor's mansion with a band of soldiers and clung to power for another year.

Finally, the boil burst. On the morning of December 7, 1710, Parke awoke to find five hundred men positioned on a hill above his St. John's mansion. They were organized into military units and well armed. Inside the residence, frantic soldiers checked and raised their weapons. Several shots were fired. Still the figures came. As Parke struggled with his buttons, a wave of men fell on the house. They found the governor half dressed and cowering in a bedroom. A shot blasted through the wall. Another took the governor in the leg. A storm of hands closed in. The governor collapsed and was carried roughly to the street. Outside, the mob bore down, while back inside the governor's residence someone lit a fire and the fire quickly spread.

What happened next is still disputed. By some accounts, hundreds of enraged islanders set upon the man like dogs, tearing at his flesh with such fury that an arm was pulled away, and then a leg, and finally his head, until at last the blood lust died and the governor's shredded and dismembered body lay baking in the sun. In a starkly different version, sober islanders testified the victim was taken to the street, where he was protected from the mob by guards, carried gently to a nearby house, and tended in his final moments by a nurse and surgeon.

After weeks of gritty courtroom drama, the tamer version won. A steady parade of witnesses described the initial assault as an unfortunate yet necessary act of self-defense. Parke, these witnesses hotly informed the court, had instructed his soldiers to fire into the assembly! Innocent lives were in jeopardy. The island's future was at risk! If anything, one witness argued after the next, the group had acted with admirable self-restraint. A surgeon tended to the wounded governor. A nurse assisted. Yet still they could not save the victim from himself. The man had thrashed so violently, the surgeon coolly testified, his blood flow would not stop.

Wherever the truth lay, the crisis was done and a time of bitterness was purged. With the house burned to the ground and all possessions in it charred and ruined, there was nothing left to remind Antiguans of the governor's arrogance, his pompous ways, and his adultery. All that remained was to tidy up the matter of his money. And that was no small matter. There was a lot of it, so much, in fact, that the distribution of Parke's wealth would one day help to shape another nation's destiny.

The money trail was roughly this: In 1757, when Daniel Parke Custis, the slain governor's grandson and heir, died suddenly at the age of forty-six, he left a fortune to his widow, twenty-six-year-old Martha Dandridge Custis. That inheritance made Martha one of the wealthiest people in the colonies ("very, very rich," said Henry Wiencek, the author of *An Imperfect God*, "with an estate worth more than £40,000, as well as some 18,000 acres. . . ."). Nine months later, a tall and charismatic soldier came to call at her plantation. The visit was successful. George Washington had found his wife. "The month after they met," wrote Wiencek, "both George and Martha were firing off orders to their London agents for something gay to wear." Washington wanted a blue velvet suit including a "coat, waistcoat and breeches for a tall man." Martha, heir to this great fortune, equally smitten, was "thinking *way* ahead," smiled Wiencek, and "sent her favorite nightgown out to be dyed a 'fashionable' color."

The marriage was sealed and consummated. With it came a life-long bonding as well as wealth beyond George Washington's imagining, an influential set of relatives, and at least eighty-four "dower slaves" whose fates Martha controlled throughout the couple's marriage and beyond her husband's death. So great was the effect of that dowry, mused Wiencek, that "had Martha not entered the picture," America's legendary first president "might have returned to the militia to pursue another dream." But here we rush ahead of our own story.

In Antigua in the months after Parke's death, political ripples were felt by all. In the restructuring that followed the governor's assassination, Isaac Royall was elected to the island's governing council. It was a surprising outcome given that Royall had sided with Parke. But the Master always made his own political bed well. He survived a bitter challenge and by December 1711 was filing expenses for his government work. In 1712 the new governor, Walter Hamilton, granted the family six more acres of prime land in Popeshead District.

For the Royalls, the next few years would be a time of success in public life, profit in business affairs, and enormous changes at home. For in the midst of Parke's long crisis, Elizabeth had given birth to a daughter, then a son, to join her daughter Ann. These children were born into a town by then only one-third white, according to the 1712 census. Many of those whites were children. In 1719 a second son was born. He would take his father's name and be Isaac Royall Jr. Five years later came a girl, Penelope, another sister. Yet the Master's family would not be large. Antigua in the early 1700s was full of illness, drought, and sudden death, and within the decade disease would claim first the eldest daughter, then the eldest son. When Penelope was born in 1726 her sister was long-since buried, and her fifteen-year-old brother John had just been laid into the sand. Penelope and her half-sister, Ann Brown, would be the only siblings Isaac Jr. carried forward into life.

Ann, Isaac, and Penne thrived, however, and spent their early years in pomp and luxury. "My little estate there," Isaac Jr. would call the plantation in Antigua all his life. Indeed, in many ways the island would always feel like home to them, the place his family ran to when there was trouble, the place they keened for during cold New England winters. And what a home it was. If the children needed a glass of water in the night, a slave would run fetch it. If they felt a chill or received a minor cut, a slave would come and tend. If they combed their hair or required help fastening a garment, an attendant would bow low. That was what they knew.

In 1726, just after the death of his older brother, seven-year-old Isaac was sent to Boston for his schooling, with his uncle Jacob for a tutor. The shift in circumstance was partly a matter of health (two little graves attested to the island's dangers), partly an issue of good breeding. The family required a certain level of sophistication the island of Antigua never did afford. To see to the young boy's every need, two slaves, Cuff and Peter, traveled with him and stayed in Boston as his servants. In Jacob Royall's household perhaps they worked alongside John, a "Negroe Servant to Mr. Jacob Royall, Esq." whose baptism was recorded at Boston's Christ Church. Or maybe John came later, after Cuff and Peter had already moved along. Early records do not say. In any case the tutoring arrangement lasted until young Isaac turned sixteen and ran away aboard a ship bound for home, his birthplace in Antigua. Jacob and his wife undoubtedly welcomed the lad's escape. That boy was wild and untrainable, the shopkeeper sputtered in a letter to his older brother. He was no proper Boston lad but an island savage spoiled beyond reason. For his part, Isaac Royall Jr. complained these northern relatives were humorless, harsh, and unforgiving. No love was lost on either side.

In the years of Isaac Jr.'s absence, the Master continued developing his plantation and took on new, if limited, political duties in both the Leeward Islands and New England. These appointments helped oil links to men of mighty rank and ensured at least one trip north each year. More and more those trips came to seem a pleasant respite from an island culture in a process of rapid disintegration. By the 1720s everything felt tenuous. For many planters a single twist of fate could threaten a life's work. And twists did come. In some seasons, crops failed entirely, plagues of insects swarmed, and out beyond the richest families' cushioned parlors slaves and livestock perished in the heat for lack of water.

Always a good businessman, Isaac Royall started hedging his bets. He bought properties in Rhode Island and Massachusetts. During annual visits to New England, he collected friends and new associates enough to ensure himself and his family a stable community in that home away from home. He was a man who knew his vulnerabilities well and realized they were growing. When he served as pond warden for St. John's in 1723, an assignment that meant looking after the scant water supply provided by slave-dug ponds dotting that northern district, he gained sickening insight into the precariousness of life in a dry land. Even rainfall now was changing. Half a century of clear cutting had altered the ground's ecology. With the hills denuded and almost all arable acres given over to sugarcane, drought and erosion hammered at the fragile soil. Efforts to replant were launched; but they were haphazard, and too small-scale to make a difference. The sad result was that three decades after his first landing, Isaac Royall's home remained a wild frontier, prettied up for sure, and made into a staggering engine of great wealth for the favored few, but no safer and certainly no more sustainable than it had ever been. If anything, hazards were constantly magnified, as were attempts by the upper classes to drown those hazards out in play, in drink, in revelry.

Elaborately staged feasts, weekend gambling orgies, and a steady drama of luxury and ostentation came to dominate the lives of wealthy whites, who moved like dancers in a crystal ball in which the sun was always shining and the sea was always blue. When they were not impressing one another over meals and tea, planters and their families whiled away whole days in gambling and drink, so many diversions, in fact, the "little difficulties" of which Isaac sometimes complained seemed to vanish in a rising tide of entertainment.

For all of those distractions, however, planters understood they were living on the knife edge of disaster. "Antigua is in a most deplorable Condition from the Dry weather, which has Continued for Eight Months past," Antigua's governor wrote in an anguished missive from that time. A passing squall provided a fleeting illusion of relief. But it came in a blink and left as fast, only littering false hope. For several years in succession, rich harvests were the stuff of memory. Wells and ponds lay dry. Ships that came to fill their holds with rum sailed off again with only ballast for a cargo. Sugar crops were counted as a total loss for two years running. Only drinking and gaming seemed to thrive. So desperate was the situation, warned the governor, water imported from Guadeloupe and Montserrat "sold at fifteen shillings a Hogshead."

Rum was cheaper.

Few could afford water at such prices, and many masters left their slaves to fend for themselves, which most often meant choking in the dust or bending double for a drip of morning dew. Increasingly, workers faltered in the fields and did not rise again. The hardship was so great, the governor complained, it had already "occasioned the loss of many of the Cattle and Negroes." Yet still the number of slaves increased, as did their rage.

A time of escalating social chaos prompted changes in the law. Here again, the musty volume held in Antigua's modern, air-conditioned archives gives ample clue to what the island's leaders were then thinking. On February 1, 1722, legislators passed a bill intended to lighten the slaves' burdens. Harsh existing codes, the legislation said, proved "highly inconvenient . . . [for] instead of answering the good Ends proposed" they seeded tension and "Disorders between White Men and Negro Slaves, and in a great Measure rendered our Slaves prey to idle and ill disposed Persons."

These very "idle and ill disposed persons" were the legislators' next target. With the passage of Act 175, "*An Act against deceitful, excessive, and disorderly Gaming,*" lawmakers turned their ire against irresponsible and predatory whites and aimed to punish those involved in devious gambling schemes and other disruptive behavior. This legislation was designed to put a stop to "Fraud, Shift, Cousenage, Circumvention, Deceit, or unlawful Device or ill Practice whatsoever . . ." indulged in on that island by men who cheated at a vast array of amusements including "Cards, Dice, Billiards, Tables, Tennis, Bowls, Skittles, Shovel-board, Nine-pins . . . Cock Fighting, Horse Races, Dog Matches, or Foot Races, or other Pastime . . . whatsoever. . . ." By lifting some of the most draconian burdens off of slaves and clamping down on the ugliest behavior of whites, those legislators reasoned, perhaps a measure of stability and even refinement might return to island life.

The plan failed. Slaves—given a taste of leniency—wanted more. Many ran to the hills. The maroon population swelled. Their raids on the great sugar plantations did not stop. Whites, meanwhile, were outraged by this new limit to their fun and pronounced themselves shocked at the slaves' utter lack of gratitude. They urged legislators to bring the hammer down again. And so within a year, the old was new again. Next on the books was Act 176, passed in December 1723. That act—second in length only to the act that established the outline of the island's court system—encompassed forty-one provisions imposing stringent controls on everything from crime to slaves' freedom of moment. Among a few of the more vivid rules were these:

> Item VIII: allowing that any person who killed a runaway while "in pursuit, shall receive Three pounds lawful Money of this Island for every Slave so killed, and Six Pounds for every Negro so taken alive."

> Item IX: allowing the owner of any slave so killed to be given compensation for his loss to be paid "out of the Publick Treasury of this Island, the full Value of the Slave. . . ."

> Item XVIII: allowing that any slave found guilty of a crime in which "the Life of any White Person shall be *endangered*, or *attempted*, or Dwelling-house or Out-house belonging to any White Person shall be burnt, or *attempted to be burnt*," shall be put to death. [italics added] Negro informants in such cases would receive a £3 reward for ratting on the miscreant.

Whites, meanwhile, faced new limits on their behavior, too. For one thing, they could not any longer "kill, destroy or dismember" slaves just for fun:

> Item XL: allowing that "cruel Persons [who], to gratify their own Humours, against the Laws of God and Humanity, frequently kill, destroy, or dismember their own and other Persons Slaves, and have hitherto gone unpunished . . ." shall be punished. If prosecuted and found guilty [two *big* "ifs" in that environment] offending whites would be fined from £20 to £100.

This seesaw to extreme repression only stoked the slaves' despair. Rebellion would come next. In 1728, the pressure spiked. Rumors of a slave revolt sparked from house to house. Maroons up in the hills were armed with a simple and yet deadly plan. They had the support of thousands of slaves. All along the coast, at the Codrington's estate at Betty's Hope, down by Royall's Bay, in the fields, and in the houses, slaves were past their breaking point. Everyone could feel it.

Isaac Royall in this moment started to wonder if he hadn't had enough, *made* enough, to go. The Master by then was well into middle age, and his fortune was greater than he might have dreamed. His son Isaac Jr. was almost ten and would someday rise to take the family business. The Master himself, in his late fifties then, was young enough to start again; old enough to want some peace. If the family returned to New England they could settle in the comfort of the ruling class. Money, family ties, and business associations assured it. All around, many planters were already pulling out. Most left for England, where they bought enormous mansions and fancy titles, too. But Isaac thought of home, which for him was Massachusetts.

Antigua's white population peaked in 1724, observed the historian David Barry Gaspar in his classic study of the island's slave system. After that, whites began to leave and the numbers dropped. Some whites bailed as soon as they tired of the climate and the stress. Others hung on longer but finally succumbed to the steady drumbeat of "disease, drought, inability to pay taxes, indebtedness, land engrossment by the wealthy few, fear of war, and the hiring out and training of black tradesmen," explained Gaspar.

Poor whites had few prospects and many legitimate complaints. Wealthy whites realized the risks increasingly outweighed the benefits of island life. Even some of the richest planters started to find the situation too hair-raising to endure. Absentee landlordism increasingly became the norm. After peaking at 5,200 souls in 1724, the number of whites who called the island home began an inexorable decline. Yet still more boatloads of chained workers came. In Africa, of course, one small island's struggles were hardly a footnote in a booming trade. Slavers did not stop their depredations. Even in Antigua business was still good. In the year the white population peaked, more than 1,500 Africans were dropped into that island's markets. One year later, as whites began to leave, another 1,600 disoriented Africans stood unsteadily beside the docks. As a result, although slaves had a high mortality rate and low birth numbers, the black population continued to grow even as white numbers fell, pushing the ratio of blacks to whites from four to one in the year Penelope Royall was born to nine to one by the time she turned fifty. Still then the gap was widening.

Among the newcomers in that time must have been a black girl not yet in her teens who was walking, she said later, by the Volta River near the coast of what is now Ghana when the men with moon-white faces came. That girl would end her days at Ten Hills Farm. But until the day of her death she would recall a single misty morning of her youth. She was with her parents praying to the god Orisa, she explained in an account of her life penned half a century later, when strangers roughly pushed their way into the clearing. The girl was caught and dragged across the ground. As the rich and loamy forest closed behind her, the siren of her parents' wailing rose, then fell away. That keening song of loss would always be her final memory of home.

The Master bought such people by the score. One day he bought her. As a slave she went by the name Belinda and served the Master's family fifty years, becoming one of only several dozen slaves who were brought into the Royalls' lives to stay. Hundreds of others were used, sold, buried, discarded, or simply left behind. According to the calculations of archeologist Alexandra A. Chan, whose work at Ten Hills Farm became a book called *Slavery in the Age of Reason: Archeology at a New England Farm*, the Master sold at least 274 slaves in two decades, and made such a profit in the business it exceeded the entire cost of Ten Hills Farm and accounted for more income, in total, than his sales of sugar and molasses combined.

Though the slave trade still was booming when Belinda was first captured, it was clear by the early 1730s that the glory days were done for the Master in Antigua. Isaac Royall slowly turned his thoughts to a new venture. He must have sat across a polished table then and raised the prospect with his wife. But Elizabeth would not be budged. Antigua suited her, she said. It was her home. Her friends were there. Her life! Her eldest daughter Ann was married now. Ann lived on a neighboring estate with the wealthy planter Robert Oliver. No. She would not go.

HOMECOMING

Over the next few years Isaac Royall did not let the prospect of a move to Massachusetts drop. Instead, on one of his trips north he stopped at Ten Hills Farm. Isaac's friend, his "kinsman" John Usher, had died six years before, leaving a sloppy legal tangle in his wake. By 1732 the tangle was resolved and the estate was up for sale. Usher's heir, Betty Jeffries, had married a successful merchant by then. She was a mother, too, whose son had joined the family trade and dealt in all the goods that moved across the seas ("send me in your schooner a handsome likely young negro not exceeding twenty years of age," one customer urged Betty's son). Betty knew the sprawling farm of her inheritance was much too big for them. What her family needed instead was a fine house close to Boston and the docks.

For herself and her family, Betty Usher Jeffries took one hundred acres at the southern tip of Ten Hills Farm near Winter Hill. It was enough for them, she knew, and prime ground, too. They would sell the rest. And so, for the third time in a century another family came to Ten Hills Farm. The Master was the buyer. The farm was his way home. New deeds were drawn. Reduced in size to five hundred acres now, that gracious property fetched £10,300.

As he contemplated this latest purchase, Isaac Royall must have stood beside John Usher's small brick house near Cradock Bridge and weighed the move. His wife opposed it. His children were Antiguan born. And yet the island was unsafe and Isaac Royall wished to look ahead. As he walked the grounds he would have seen the Mystic River in the distance, cows munching in the open pasture lands between. Maybe it was a sight to warm his heart after all these decades gone. But there were problems, too, that any man of taste could see.

How rough and unfinished those Medford acres must have seemed to a gentleman accustomed to the manicure of island properties maintained by scores of slaves. The Master gazed off toward the water and imagined a great sweep of verdant grass. To replace the rough and tangle of a working farm he would make a vista fine enough to suit a king. His brother Jacob oversaw the job. Jacob had the salt marsh dammed, the meadow plowed, the last few trees cut down, the earth turned, manure spread, and after several years, the whole of it "[laid] down with grass seeds," just as Isaac had instructed in a letter from the time that has survived. Then at last this simple farm might have the pleasing aspect familiar fields of cane provided.

Isaac Royall next considered the house. It was situated well, with open views. But it required a total overhaul. The structure John Usher had built, though sound, was cramped. It hardly fit the Master's needs, much less his aspirations. All around, the grounds required landscaping. Isaac's mind raced. The small brick house could be expanded. He could make it something worthy of himself, a replica of the great mansions in St. John's, perhaps! Of course a slave house must be built. Slaves would stay in the main house with his family just as they had always done. But so many would come! Field hands, too. They must have quarters somewhere. Where should he put that structure? And then there must be a carriage house, some other outbuildings, a barn or two. He mulled the matter over. John Winthrop had stood here. The land itself had pedigree!

Before the Master closed the deal, he sat in more familiar environs in Antigua to write a letter to a friend. Did Governor Belcher know the property? Did *he* believe it could be made fit to suit a man of the best taste? Jonathan Belcher was not convinced.

"If you were here," the governor cautioned, "I am perswaded you would not be so fond as you have been." Yet after some consideration, Belcher's attitude would soften. Oh, it was a fine place, he conceded at last, but much in need of work. If the family could just wait a bit, and make a plan. . . .

In correspondence through the year, Jonathan Belcher mixed real estate advice with political observations and concerns of a more private nature. He thanked the Master, in a letter now held in the Massachusetts Historical Society, for providing him "the negroe boy, which you will be pleased to send me by the first good opportunity this spring." In that same correspondence Belcher allowed that Isaac's brother Jacob had concluded the business of purchasing the Medford farm. The deed and documents were all in order. Ten Hills Farm belonged to the Master now in every hill and detail. "It's a good estate," the governor smoothly reassured his distant friend. True, renovations would be costly. But the end result would suit the Master well. Oh, and there was one more thing. If Isaac planned on bringing slaves, he should surely make a budget. There was, the governor advised, "a duty here of £4 a head on negroes, laid many years since."

When the time came to pay that duty, Isaac would petition the court for leniency. The twenty-seven slaves he brought with him from Antigua, he explained, were imported for his family's use exclusively.

From 1732, when Isaac Royall bought the farm, until 1737, when the renovations were complete, work on the house and all around it progressed at a furious pace. Teams of the best craftsmen constructed a grand manor, adding on to the small brick house that Usher used and devising a wood façade that was cut to look like stone—the material Isaac Royall was more familiar with. Field workers created gracious views. A formal drive was laid and lined with elms. Garden paths were softened with the low green trim of imported boxwood. A two-story brick slave quarters was built in anticipation of the influx Isaac Royall would soon bring, and a gazebo was placed atop a two-tiered mound and so cleverly designed that ice stored down beneath the floorboards ensured that even the most delicate of strollers might find cool respite on the hottest day. The marsh beyond the house was drained. Now it lay neat and open, sweeping to the water in a formal, grassy green.

Still, Elizabeth Royall would not move. She preferred tropical breezes to northern winters full of snow, and argued with her husband. The Master complained about the woman's reluctance in a letter to the governor. Jonathan Belcher merely winked this latest problem off. "Let Madame Royall know we have plenty of good wood," he coached, ensuring that winter fires would always keep the family warm. "She must therefore not entertain a thought of staying behind." If she did, "you may tell her," the governor teased cheerfully, "the governor and council here have the power of divorces, and I would not have her run the hazard of losing so good a husband for want of paying him due honour and respect. . . . At least she must come and try one winter and I have no doubt she'll [have] as good health as Antigua ever gave her."

Jonathan Belcher closed that letter saying the Master's brother Jacob had inquired after the Belchers' property at Hanover Street. That deal seemed fine. Business between friends was best, he wrote. "I told him I should rather you should have it than any other man. It is certainly the most of a gentleman's seat of anything in this country." Yet it was Jacob, by then a wealthy man himself ("Boston's most active slave trader," historian Robert E. Desrochers Jr. dubbed him after studying newspapers from the era), who would seal the deal, this time on his own behalf. Jacob and his wife moved in shortly afterward and from that perch orchestrated the sale of Isaac's slaves and the completion of his brother's sprawling project to the north. For five years Jacob commuted between Boston and Medford, overseeing the transformation of the house and grounds. By the end of it the property was an elegant escape supervised by the Roman god of trade, a nearly human-scale figure of Mercury carved out of wood and perched at the gazebo's top to gaze across the property and lend his blessing to the family business. Might commerce bless them there just as surely as it kissed them in Antigua. Oh, and it would.

As the renovations lumbered forward, Isaac Royall gradually prepared his family to quit the life they knew. Next door, Elizabeth's daughter Ann and her husband Robert Oliver were also packing. The island was a mess. They had their son Thomas with them now. They wished to keep him safe. And so they moved to Dorchester with a crowd of their own slaves while the Royalls settled at the new estate in Medford with their twenty-seven.

In Boston while those families packed, Jacob Royall was unusually busy, juggling jobs and selling off new merchandise. Not only was there Isaac's work to do, but the exodus of whites from the West Indies came in tandem with a surge in demand for slaves along the streets of Boston. From 1725 to 1736 Boston's white population increased by roughly a third, while the number of slaves to serve them increased almost fourfold. Seeing this spike in demand, families like the Royalls and the Olivers kept their island plantations but likely sold off excess workers to the North and to relations in the Carolinas and Virginia, then left their tropical planations—and the rest of their many slaves—under the whip of a new master, someone who would tend to business in the planters' absence. Some ships in that era came into Boston's port with twenty slaves and more for sale, a high number for that town. Jacob stood firmly in this powerful new tide. For a time he advertised slaves not one by one but by the "parcel," large lots of them described in the language of the time as "likely negroes," "seasoned" by their time in the West Indies, acquainted with the English language, trained in the ways of whites.

Of course not all who came were sold. In Popeshead District as the time for sailing neared, Isaac Royall and his son-in-law, Robert Oliver, called scores of workers to their sides and informed them that their lives were soon to change. They were moving north. And so those men and women said goodbyes and packed their meager things and sailed into another place they did not know.

During those years there was a buzz down at the docks in St. John's. With so many families pulling out, it was a bustling, busy time. Ships were packed heavy with trunks, furniture, oil paintings, fine draperies, silver, crystal, and the like. It was an exodus of spirit and of stuff. At his estate beside the sea, the Master's fancy carriage was broken down for export. His horses likely went north, too, as would the men who trained them. Month by month, boxes and parcels of all sorts were packed and thumped in mountains at the wharves. The frenzy of departure grew. The Master, like so many others then, had amassed his treasures by the ton. Now he shipped them north to Jacob's care, so he might recreate the life he knew.

While the Royalls and other planter families prepared for their sailing, conditions all around them worsened. A year after the purchase of Ten Hills Farm was finalized, a powerful hurricane crashed ashore, doing just what hurricanes do. Earthquakes shook the island two years later. Then drought sank its heavy teeth into the land. "We are so dry in some Parts of the Island at present," one writer exclaimed, "we have hardly any Water for Man or Beast, and the poorest Prospect of the next Crop that ever I knew in my Life." Even wealthy whites sequestered in their great estates and addled by a constant flow of claret and good rum could not remain aloof. In August 1736, Isaac wrote a friend in Boston that he might be forced to distill seawater for his slaves to drink "if it not please God to send us rain within eight or ten days." Then, as that long dry spell continued, the sudden shock of a slave plot threw even the most determined revelers to their knees. By October it was clear no individual of any race or station could ignore the deepening crisis.

"This Island is in a very great Confusion at present," one terrified white resident wrote in late October. Three slaves that day were "rack'd to Death in the Market Place," he wrote, three others "burnt alive." More executions were anticipated. And they would come in waves. Throughout that difficult time, daily executions commanded everyone's attention. "We are in a great deal of trouble in this Island," one planter reported with a heavy heart. To him, much of the barbarity seemed pointless. The "Burning of Negroes, hanging them on Gibbets alive, Racking them upon the wheel, & c." cost the lives of "many sensible Negroe Men, most of them Tradesmen, and Carpenters, Masons, and Coopers. I am almost dead with watching . . . as are many more."

Among the dead and exiled were two slaves belonging to the Master's plantation.

By the end of March 1737, eighty-eight slaves had been executed. The final tally, meticulously recorded in Antiguan records, was as follows: Five broken on the wheel. Six gibbeted. Seventy-seven burned to death.

The plan, investigators said, was simple: Kill all the whites.

The bloodshed was scheduled to begin at a lavish party held to commemorate the anniversary of the coronation of King George. On that night, as festivities reached their noisy peak, a rebel was to ignite a barrel of gunpowder hidden underneath the ballroom floor. The initial explosion would kill scores. A raging fire would take the lives of others. Anyone who survived that double punch and ran screaming for the exits would be slaughtered by rebels stationed at the building's doors. In that first blow, most of the island's elite would perish. But the plan did not end there. The sound of the explosion was intended as a signal. Twelve hundred rebel soldiers stood prepared to fight, each with an assignment. They would fan out across the island and massacre every white they found. Bonfires built on nearby hills would spark and send the message well beyond the reach of sound. The rebels would not rest until the land was theirs. Even children were not safe. Only color mattered.

It might have worked. Simple plans are best. But at the last minute the governor's son died, and the ball was postponed to allow a time of mourning. Tension flared among the plotters. Then someone talked; and executions started.

A gaudy, semi-fictionalized account of the crisis appears in Mrs. Lanaghan's 1844 history of Antigua in the guise of the "Legend of the Ravine." In that story (penned more than a century after the plot was exposed and two decades after Antiguan slaves were freed), a deaf-mute eight-year-old hero named Julio, loyal slave to his master's beautiful and spoiled daughter, chances across the plotters, wrestles with his conscience, and finally turns against his own people. Julio in this account is a prepubescent slave dressed up like a doll, or perhaps a grinder's monkey, in a "white tunic embroidered with crimson, and a broad belt of gilded leather, with tassels of buillion gathered in folds around his slender waist." To complete the outfit, "Smart silk stockings encased his legs, and white leather shoes, ornamented with gold, graced his little feet." Only when he ventured out was that extravagant outfit complete: On those occasions he wore "a small crimson cap, in which was placed a single ostrich feather . . . its snowy plume strangely contrasting with his ebon complexion."

In Mrs. Lanaghan's tale, Julio is the perfect slave, a docile boy so devoted and well trained that he anticipates his child-mistress's every pout and whim. Her "slightest action," wrote Mrs. Lanaghan, "was noticed by him, and her every wish granted, if possible. Did a shade pass over her brow, he flew for her lute, or arranged her books at the spinet; did a smile illuminate her face, Julio jumped for joy. It was his task to gather for her the sweetest fruits," and all the fairest flowers. And yet one day the boy grew fearful. While out walking in the countryside he had seen the plotters gather. An Obeah sorcerer was with them, "some object," wrote Mrs. Lanaghan, "which could scarcely be pronounced human," white-haired and "puckered up in a thousand wrinkles." Her skin was light. Her cackle could be heard for miles. She bent her head to speak with the king of the Africans, a powerful man who made a fearsome sight, his complexion of the "deepest jet . . . his large black eye [shining] with the fierceness of a firebrand." In his lap lay a club and pistol.

The boy cowered in fear and fascination. This African was no innocent dressed up like a doll but a man of dangerous capabilities and ferocious will. In fact he was the boy's father, a slave so proud he had banished his own wife when she called him not by his chosen name, but by the name his master used. During her exile, the king's wife had given birth. She named the child Julio. It was her dying wish that he should never know his father. As Julio cowered in the shadows he still thought himself an orphan. But it was his father whom he watched with silent terror and incomprehension. And it was his father whom he would betray.

When the coronation ball was put off, some among the plotters said the plan should be retooled, but not delayed. Others spoke of caution and the benefit of patience. The plan was good, they argued; best for them to stay with it. While they argued, Julio found his voice, wrote Mrs. Lanaghan, now merging fact and fantasy. "By gestures and passionate mutterings," she wrote, the deaf-mute shared his story. Julio's owners knew the gathering could only mean one thing. When the plotters met again, white soldiers were there waiting. Then the executions started.

Those executions were all too real. Newspapers in North America and England reported on the plot and its grisly aftermath.

But Vere Oliver's spare account of those events, folded in a dusty, leather-bound, three-volume *History of the Island of Antigua* published in 1895, is perhaps as good as any:

> November 18: Four Justices sign a warrant for seven negros to be burnt at the stake at Otto's pasture for conspiracy, one to be hung up alive in chains, there to die of famine.
>
> November 29: Eight more negros to be burnt.
>
> December 20. Twelve more negros condemned to death.
>
> 1736–7, January 8. A negro who stabbed himself after his conviction had to be broken on the wheel, and ten more were sentenced to death. . . . From various depositions from eye-witnesses and informants it appears . . . had the plot succeeded all the whites on the Island would have been massacred. The slaves used to meet in the woods, and over 2000 of them were present when one of their number was crowned king. . . . By the Island laws all slaves executed were paid for by the public, their owners being recompensed the full value, so that in the present instance the carrying out of justice was a great expense to the tax-payers.

Isaac Royall was among those granted compensation. Island records show his driver, Hector, charged with conspiracy and burned to death on February 18. The Master was awarded £70 for loss of property. Another Royall slave named Quaco was banished to Hispaniola. And so it went for months: Death, banishment, and compensation. It was an ugly, fearful time. For Isaac, the joy of island life was done. That July he packed his family on a ship and headed north, for Massachusetts Bay. Twenty-seven slaves went with him. Ann and Robert Oliver would go to Dorchester, and slaves with them, as well.

As always, the coming and goings of such men were recorded in newspapers of the day. The Master's arrival was no exception. "On Wednesday last arrived here the Ship *Unity*, Michael Dalton commander, from the island of Antigua, who brought here passengers Col. Royal and his family . . . ," reported the *Boston Gazette*. The ship had made it safely through a storm. The travelers were

12.1 Royall House and slave quarters, Medford, Massachusetts, 2008. Author's photograph.

welcomed in a surge of friends and family. Ann was married and traveling with her family. The Master's two surviving children, Isaac and Penelope, known as Penne by her mother, were seventeen and twelve. Their lives would start again on ground the Winthrop children once had walked. Like those children before them, the young Royalls owned everything they saw. And there was more than that. Elsewhere in New England the family already owned another 882 acres and at least thirteen slaves on various farms in Stoughton and Freetown (now Walpole, Massachusetts, and Bristol, Rhode Island, respectively).

Another chapter of the Master's life unfolded. The house at Ten Hills Farm was finally complete. Its rippled windows looked across soft acres of orchards, gardens, woods, walkways, and fancy arbors heavy with new grapes. On that ground the wealthy Royalls and their servants would make new patterns from old habits. For sixty-five-year-old Isaac and his wife, the climate was different and some of the customs strange, but they were able to easily replay familiar patterns in a life of privilege.

The Royalls' slaves gradually adjusted. But their transition was profoundly different. For them there was no longer hope of a revolt. There were no maroons plotting in the hills, no secret gatherings to crown a king, no flirting and finding soulmates in the busy press of market day. They were no longer part of a vibrant, if oppressed, majority, but isolated members of a class of men that never grew above three percent of the Massachusetts population. Living away from the more crowded centers of Boston and Cambridge, the Royalls' slaves must have cherished those few times they could connect with the nascent community of free blacks living by the docks in Boston's North End, or other slaves from other families outside of their own small group. Such opportunities were rare, though, and mostly they had just each other. Friends and family left behind in Antigua were never seen again. Life for them closed in.

For the Master, life opened in a final act. It would be brief. In his second year upon that ground, death would catch him suddenly. But first, there was a wedding.

THE BENEFACTOR

◆

Not a year after the Royalls returned to Massachusetts, a slow parade of carriages pulled up at the entrance to the Master's elegant estate in Medford. Thirteen-year-old Penne, dressed in fine imported silk, met them at the door and curtsied to arriving guests as slaves retrieved their coats. There was nothing like a party to pave one's way within the gentry; and what a party it must have been, a heavy feast of oysters, roasted meat, filleted fish, and crisp-skinned fowl all washed down with rum and punch, inside a loud balloon of festive noise. For the Master and his children in that moment, the nectar of life at Ten Hills Farm must have tasted just as sweet as it ever did in Popeshead District. Money, privilege, and position softened everything they touched.

Inside the thrumming din of conversation on that day, young Isaac Royall and his bride, both still short of twenty then, danced into the polished core of Boston's gentry. Here was the place where they would stay. From the farm's gracious perch beside the Mystic, long before he came upon his first gray hairs, young Royall would help define the culture of his time. Like other prominent men, he soon could boast a complex web of influence, many slaves and properties, varied social duties, and occasional other obligations reserved for people at the pinnacle of colonial wealth and culture. But on that chilly night in early spring 1738 the far-off knell of leadership was hard to hear. Instead the sound of laughter, fiddle music, and excited gossip filled his ears. And so Isaac and his bride,

a dark-haired, broad-boned Scottish heiress named Elizabeth Mc-
Intosh, began their journey with light hearts and perhaps very little
thought ahead.

For Elizabeth McIntosh the wedding at King's Chapel was
surely a happy turn after several early traumas. Her father, a young
merchant (proud descendant of a Scottish queen), drowned at sea
while she was still a toddler. Her mother died before Elizabeth's
fifteenth birthday. Orphaned at that early age and next in line
for a considerable Old World fortune, Elizabeth, with her sister
Mary, moved from Bristol, Rhode Island, to Boston, where they
lived with a gentleman named Job Lewis, his wife, and her young
brother, Thomas Palmer. There the girls might have enjoyed a quiet
passage through their teens. But news of their inheritance brought
trouble. A greedy uncle came to town, petitioned the governor
to become their guardian, and said he wished to bring his nieces
"home" (where they had never been) to Scotland, where he could
mind their riches.

Governor Jonathan Belcher refused the man's petition. It was an
unambiguous ruling, but Shawn McIntosh did not give up so easily. Having sailed the Atlantic to lay his claim, he hatched a plan to
steal his nieces from their keepers and invited them for dinner with
their guardians the night before he sailed. The dinner was unevent-
ful and it ended early. But the evening was far from over. Just after
nine that night, as the girls and their several chaperones made their
way down Boston streets, they were set upon by a dozen men. In
the darkness and confusion, rough hands and the element of surprise won out. Elizabeth and Mary were pushed along a narrow
alley, then dragged onboard their uncle's ship to sail at the first
light. Thomas Palmer, shaken but uninjured in the attack, dusted
himself off and raced to the governor's house, where he breath-
lessly explained the assault, obtained a warrant, and was given
Jonathan Belcher's permission to gather up a posse. By sunup on
that Sunday morning, Palmer's group was armed and ready.

Any ship's captain facing ten men bearing guns would have
done what that ship's captain did. He let the posse board. The girls
were freed. Their uncle was captured and put under guard. But
while the posse did its work aboard that swaying vessel, news of

the kidnappings rippled from pew to pew in Sunday services. By the time Shawn McIntosh appeared, held tight by guards escorting him through town, an angry crowd had gathered. Scores of jeering citizens squeezed close and tried to touch the prisoner, to spit on him and roughly tear his clothes. Shawn barely made it to the jail.

In hushed conversations over the next months one thing seemed quite clear: Those girls needed to marry. Only then would their fortunes (and perhaps their very lives, some said) be safe. And so when Isaac Royall Jr., then nineteen, began to set his sights and make his bid, young Elizabeth was receptive and her guardians relieved. Isaac's proposal was accepted, and a wedding date was set. What would follow was the marriage not just of two young people but of their fortunes, too, to make a weave of family and business ties that stretched from Ten Hills Farm to Rhode Island, then across the water to the Caribbean and beyond. Before long, Isaac and Elizabeth would supervise an extended clan—and an impressive fortune—typical of the devastatingly efficient ruling class to which they now belonged. At a time when cousins married cousins (and money married money), the resulting stew of blood and business became so thick it could confound the most tenacious genealogist. Theirs would be a small world, and one that floated gently across every one of life's advantages.

Isaac's greatest test in life would be a war. But on the day of his marriage, he and his young bride could not see ahead to that. Not yet humbled by the awful swords of life, they only sensed great things ahead. And well they might. On each side, inheritances were richly seeded; and sooner than they might have thought, death would yield astounding bounty.

On July 27, 1739, one year after the wedding and two years almost to the day after the Royalls came ashore in Boston, the Master died at Ten Hills Farm. He was sixty-seven. Having spent a lifetime accumulating wealth and his last decade building an estate he considered worthy of that wealth, he was able to enjoy his new role as a country gentleman in retirement only for two years. A stonecutter in Dorchester bent to chisel out his lengthy epitaph, and all of it was done. Ten Hills Farm went to the Master's son and namesake, Isaac Royall Jr., who settled in those freshly polished quarters with his mother, his sister, his teenage wife, and a score of slaves.

After the Master was laid inside his tomb in Dorchester, beneath a newly minted family seal consisting of three sheaves of wheat (it should have been cane!), a sign of plenty, Isaac Jr. examined the extent of all he owned. The estate was considerable. There was the property in Antigua, now managed by overseers but still in the family's hands; the primary residence at Ten Hills Farm, with its many acres and outbuildings. Another farm lay twenty miles to the south in the town of Stoughton, a short day's ride by carriage. A slightly longer day on dusty roads landed Isaac and Elizabeth home yet again, this time on a third farm in Rhode Island, just outside the busy port of Bristol. From there they could go by ship to Isaac's "little estate" in Popeshead District, in Antigua.

On Elizabeth's side there was more property still, and many more slaves, too. Through her grandfather, Henry McIntosh, Elizabeth would inherit half of Fairfield Plantation in Surinam, and all the slaves who worked on it. Elizabeth also won land in Bristol with a storied past. Her grandfather had bought it for a song from Nathaniel Byfield. Known as Mount Hope Farm, it sat beside Narragansett Bay, stretching in a fertile arc down to a rocky shore. This had been King Philip's land, Mount Hope, his seat of power willed to his young son. But now the war was done; the sachem dead; the son enslaved. The land had been doled out. Nathaniel Byfield got his piece. His son-in-law, Elizabeth Royall's grandfather, Henry McIntosh, willed it to his granddaughters, Elizabeth and Mary. And so between them the Royalls owned six homes, and slaves at every one.

Eventually, Isaac and Elizabeth would own yet more property than even that, so much, in fact, that when Isaac died his wealth laid the foundation for one of America's most revered institutions, Harvard Law School. The bequest to Harvard was not of any of these six properties but rather of investment lands in Worcester County, where even today the town of Royalston (named after the Benefactor) is a Massachusetts backwater so remote it is disturbed only by the rare whine of a Harley Davidson on summer nights,

13.1 Harvard Law School seal.
Trademark, President and Fellows
of Harvard College.

and depicted in a whimsical local T-shirt as "Conveniently located in the middle of nowhere."

Harvard received that land and other acres in Granby, Massachusetts, in 1786, and sold the real estate off in three parcels over the next thirteen years. In 1815 the school used the money to endow the Royall Professorship of Law. Two years later, the law school was established; and to this day it uses the Benefactor's signature three sheaves of wheat as its trademarked seal.

It was a generous gift. But it might as well have been a blade of grass in a great lawn. The land represented just a fraction of Isaac Royall Jr.'s holdings at the time he died. Even at the age of twenty, the Master's son already had sufficient wealth to stand among the giants of his time. He enjoyed the fact and, like his father before him, moved to fix and frame it every way he could. In 1741, not long after the birth of his first child, he commissioned a portrait. The artist was Robert Feke, a dark-haired and pale-complexioned thirty-six-year-old just coming into his prime. Today Feke's massive canvas showing the Law School's benefactor and his family hangs in Harvard's Law Library in the fourth-floor Casperson Room, a place so forbidding and obscure it seldom sees a visitor. There, on a wall immediately to the left behind a heavy set of clean glass doors, the Benefactor, young Isaac, looks down on cases full of legal memorabilia and freshly polished bookcases crowded with portentous tomes. A circular visitor's desk sits idle on a winter afternoon, but offers postcards of the Royalls to random passers-by who must step back—and look up—to gaze into the Benefactor's face.

13.2 Isaac Royall Jr. and his family, 1741. Robert Feke.
Courtesy Special Collections Department, Harvard Law School Library.

What meets that viewer's eye, art historians have taken some pains to explain, is one of the first portraits of the period to show not just a man of some stature and inheritance, or even that man and his wife, as increasingly became the style, but an image of extended family. In fact, everyone close to the Benefactor at that time is there except his mother (who, when her turn came, would also distance herself from him by cutting her son completely from her will).

At the painting's right is twenty-two-year-old Isaac, his left elbow pushing up against the gilded frame, his right leg bent to show a hint of stocking poking out beneath red breeches. He is the only figure standing, the only one with legs, a book, a pose and attitude of power. On his face he wears an imperious expression, one eyebrow almost imperceptibly lifted as though taking the measure of his portraitist mid-stroke and wondering at his skills. On his head he wears a powdered wig that flows in curls behind his shoulders.

His scarlet coat and gold-trimmed vest are interrupted with white ruffles designed to soften and impress. He is undeniably the painting's hero, towering confidently above his women, straight-backed and cocky, one hand resting on a golden pocket at his hip.

Beside Isaac—all in a row like bobbins—sit his women. His wife Elizabeth is there, immediately to his right, dressed in blue with ruffles. Then nineteen, she comes across as a solid figure, someone who might have thrived just as well carrying pails of milk and churning butter. Here, though, she wears not the attire of a Scottish farm girl but the wardrobe and demeanor of a lady of society, a satin dress cut low to expose a stretch of porcelain skin, and on her face a look entirely drained of spontaneity. Her auburn hair is fastened back. Her bones are strong. One arm cups a daughter (her namesake who will live only two days past the age of seven), standing awkwardly in a fancy gown, gripping a red coral fetish (something to ward off the Evil Eye, tradition said, or perhaps the more mundane disturbance of disease) finished with a finely tooled gold handle.

Isaac's sister-in-law Mary McIntosh is next. She is Mary Palmer now, having wed her savior by the time the artist showed up with his paints. Sweet-faced and unfocused, she tilts toward the child and smiles vaguely into space. Mary seems a more sympathetic figure than the others, but she comes across as fragile, too, as though life might come and knock her down. She is the only figure smiling.

Seated at the end of a small table covered with a richly patterned oriental carpet is Penelope, coheir to the Master's fortune. She tilts away, staring coolly at the viewer. Unlike her brother Isaac, who seems to own that painting in every sense, she exudes detachment, as though she only deigns to sit at her brother's insistence. Her expression is otherwise impossible to read.

Behind the group two large windows frame a sylvan scene. It is mid-September as Feke puts the final touches on his painting. The leaves outside are full. The clouds hang low and heavy, anchoring the image with great billows of white. It might be rural England past the glass. Feke keeps the vista open, representing the window's slim wood muntins only in the barest trace of paint. With no hard grill to stop the eye, the landscape spills into the dark interior of the mansion as though the grounds, the house, and these young people in it all are one.

Though the painting was hailed by the Law School's founding curator of manuscripts and archives, Erika Chadbourn, as "one of our Law School's most prized possessions," and is identified today by curators who call Feke "arguably the most influential colonial portraitist," few people ever see the painting of the Benefactor and his women. It takes a Harvard ID to get past the library turnstile and a certain amount of curiosity to find those double doors. For those who take the trouble, the massive portrait presents a stunning ode to opulence: too big to store, too much of a bother to move, rich in every detail, hiding in plain sight. Isaac Royall (whom one contemporary described as a man who delighted to display his riches) would have loved the solemnity of the Harvard chamber where the painting rests, but certainly his ghost must long for more foot traffic!

Feke's portrait fixes the family in its wealth but gives no hint as to its origin. Not a brushstroke creates the shadow of a slave. No painterly symbol—not even a pineapple—alludes to the hundreds of workers in the West Indies whose labor made the family rich. No sly clue implies the family's trade in human beings. Instead it is a whitewash, and the first of many, that celebrates arrival even as it disinfects the family's path to riches. Fine living and refinement are presented here as absolutes, a happy accident of life, perhaps, and just as much worth crowing about as the Master's giddy news from decades earlier that he did not care to boast, but friends might want to know: He was rich! That was what mattered, what was memorialized and kept, as though luxury was destiny for a generation bred to rule. Certainly it seemed so for this new band of men and women. No one in the painting was over twenty-two.

Documents about the painting kept on file at the Harvard Law School Library show several references to the Royalls' sugar operations in Antigua and at least one to Isaac Sr.'s slave trading. But more is made in those pages of the Benefactor's public role and generosity in death. Almost every author notes that Isaac Jr. won a position on the Governor's Council and adds that late in life he was the first man in North America awarded the title Brigadier

General. But as to the family business, vague euphemisms abound. One historian describes Isaac Sr. as a man who "made a great fortune in the mercantile trade." Another sheaf of papers in the Law School Library's file describes Isaac Jr. only as a "Massachusetts magnate" before listing his multiple accomplishments.

Of more interest than slavery to those writers apparently was the web of personal connections that placed the painter in the house. Here it is possible to discover that Feke's grandfather married Henry Winthrop's widow, Elizabeth Fones, not long after Henry Winthrop drowned. The Fekes therefore had always known the farm. Too, the artist was related to the Palmer family, and so to Mary McIntosh, the sweet-faced girl to Penne's left. Perhaps that was his entrée, one writer conjectures. Or maybe, considers another, it was the painter's friendship with the artist John Smibert that won him the commission. Smibert had painted the Master not long before he died. But Smibert was ill himself in 1741 and probably tossed the job off to his friend. These questions seem to merit scholarly concern.

However he got there, what Robert Feke did once he was inside the house was to immortalize a moment that was quickly fading. The child held by Elizabeth would die. Other children would be born. Mary Palmer moved on. Even Penne would be at the dining table less and less. Not long after Feke's paint was dry, it was her turn at the altar. In 1742 she married Henry Vassall, the fourteenth of eighteen children born to a wealthy sugar planter in Jamaica. Like Penne, Henry Vassall was an island child, born on a Christmas morning into a Caribbean house with many slaves. Fine-boned and handsome, he arrived in Boston at the age of twenty, following his brothers' path. Two of the older Vassall boys attended Harvard. Penne's husband was not so favored, and he failed to win a place. Still, family ties would serve him well throughout his life, and these would bind the Royall and the Vassall families in a scrim so dense those families seemed to almost fuse.

As Henry Vassall prepared to marry into the Royall family, he bought a seven-acre property in Cambridge from his elder brother John. The land, like the family, was blessed with good connections and many ties to Ten Hills Farm. The old Boston merchant

Andrew Belcher had purchased it the same year he counted up his profit from his slave smuggling venture with John Usher. The trader willed it to his son Jonathan (early supporter of Princeton, governor of Massachusetts and New Jersey), who bought his slaves from Isaac Royall while the Master was still living in Antigua. Later it went to Jamaican-born John Vassall, who sold it to his brother Henry just a month before his marriage.

The couple's house today is a slightly dowdy clapboard structure discreetly divided into condominiums. Situated at 94 Brattle Street, surveying one of the most famous avenues in Cambridge, it is dwarfed by neighbors and outshone by more complicated architectural fantasies up and down the block. Like a stern aunt appearing at a fancy party in a tattered dress, the ancient gray dwelling gives off a solid air of history, but a rather unwelcoming aspect from the curb. The façade is stern and boxy. Though a bright blue plaque details the building's provenance, pedestrians are more apt to stop next door to stare at the Stoughton House, a more commanding shingle structure built by celebrated Boston architect Henry Hobson Richardson in 1882; or wander up and across Brattle Street to gaze at the Longfellow National Historic Site (a crusty relic that welcomes visitors with a formal garden filled with plantings from another era), the mansion another Vassall (this one Henry's nephew, John Vassall Jr.) built with his inheritance fifteen years after his father vacated the house at No. 94.

Back in Penelope's day, Brattle Street was a perfect example of how great fortunes made through slavery were transferred to New England almost whole. In Cambridge wealth built on the uncertain sands of sugar was preserved within a dizzying array of kinship ties and new enterprises in New England. Masters along the street were relatives and friends. Many knew Antigua well and had some slaves from there. As a result, slaves along Brattle Street had their ties, too, and slave weddings, births, and sales made a second webbing at the far end of the social scale.

White and black, up and down the street, those lives were intertwined. This was the world the Master once had craved to join, the world his son and daughter inherited, married into, and would help perpetuate. Indeed, by the mid-1700s Isaac and Penelope were so fully of that world it was hard to locate anyone from their circle who stood *outside* an exquisite honeycomb of intermarriage; almost as hard as sorting through the headache-inducing crisscross of connections that resulted from those links. For Penelope Royall the strands of DNA strung down Brattle Street were roughly these:

> When Penne married Henry Vassall and moved to No. 94 she became sister-in-law to John Vassall,
>
> whose son, John Jr., built the mansion up the street at No. 105 (the Longfellow House),
>
> which meant Penne was a stone's throw from her husband's nephew, John Vassal Jr.
>
> who married Penelope's niece through her half sister, Ann Brown,
>
> who grew up with the Royalls in Antigua
>
> when her widowed mother (Elizabeth Brown) married Isaac Royall back in 1707.

But there was more.

> About the time Henry's nephew married Penelope's niece,
>
> Henry's niece, Elizabeth Vassall, married a man named Thomas Oliver,
>
> Ann Brown's eldest son through her marriage to the Antiguan planter Robert Oliver,
>
> and thus Penelope's nephew by her half-sister.

Thomas Oliver was heir to two fortunes made in slaves and sugar. As he came of age, wealth from the Brown and Oliver families of Antigua enabled him to buy one hundred acres in Cambridge, just upriver from Henry and Penelope at No. 94 and his sister and brother-in-law at No. 105. On a gently sloping hill pitched above a sweeping marsh, the heir to those great fortunes developed the grand estate called Elmwood, the home of Harvard presidents.

The equally complex family circles that existed among blacks are considerably harder to trace. Basic records were rarely kept, and those that did exist were often poorly handled, which left them vulnerable to every archivist's nightmare from creeping mold to ravaging insects, or an unwitting toss into the trash as the centuries clicked by. What is clear, though, is that at least some of the slaves on Brattle Street first knew each other in Antigua, then worked

together again at Ten Hills Farm before being dispersed by the
provisions of the Master's will.

In that will, the Master gave his wife Elizabeth "2 negros, my
chariot & horses . . ." to keep with her at Ten Hills Farm or attend
her as she traveled.

He gave his stepdaughter Ann and her husband Robert Oliver
a dozen blacks, "two negros and their 10 children," to go to
Dorchester to serve along with those Antiguan slaves the family
already had imported.

Penelope received "2 negros & their 6 children," who moved
with her to Cambridge. Among them were a girl named Present,
and a woman named Abba and her children Robin, Cuba, Walker,
Nuba, Trace, and Tobey.

Eighteen more enslaved men, women, and children would stay
with Isaac at the farm.

As this will shows, there was an effort made to keep these slave
families intact. Nonetheless, with the Master's death a close and
interdependent slave community that had been transferred from
Antigua to Ten Hills Farm was torn asunder. Families dispersed,
then drew close again when weddings between various generations of the Royalls, Vassalls, and Olivers brought those white
families—and their slaves—within strolling distance of each other
down along the banks of the Charles River. Other Antiguan slaves
who stayed behind at Ten Hills Farm would have seen these people
rarely. Four miles was a great distance to a slave with little time
off and no means to travel. Yet when the Royalls moved by coach
their coachmen, at least, could pick up bits of news when they
went down to Brattle Street and saw old friends and kin.

And kin there were: aunts and uncles, sisters, brothers, cousins,
nephews, and perhaps half siblings and others, too, slave children
with white fathers who did not own up to that illicit tie. This fact
would have made the weave complete. For if the pattern of sexual
relations so routinely documented in households of the South also
found expression in those families of Antigua and the North, the
kinship circle on Brattle Street and up in Medford would have
closed just that much tighter, closed seamlessly, in fact, in unac-
knowledged blood relations.

Even without such racial mixing, family connections among blacks on Brattle Street shortly became more complicated yet, as slaves were sold, willed, or traded house to house between white families. At Henry Vassall's house, for instance, a slave named Tony, Henry's coachman from Jamaica, married Cuba, Penne's housemaid from Antigua, and they had several children of their own. That family did not stay intact. For when hard times came, Penne sold the couple's children down the block to serve her husband's nephew, John Vassall Jr., while Penne kept the father, Tony, for herself.

A separation of 150 paces was not the tragedy so many other slave families endured. But the absence of control was no less real. And that fact, like so many others, was searingly familiar whether a parent lived in Massachusetts or Antigua.

Countless aspects of slave life—including an owner's ability to rip black families apart at whim—were repeated in perfect echo in Antigua, then in Massachusetts. The mansion at Ten Hills Farm was designed to replicate a big house in Antigua. A carriage ride from the Medford farm to Brattle Street took roughly the same time as a trot from the Royalls' estate at Popeshead District to the docks down in St. John's. The carriage was the same carriage that had been shipped ahead; and the man who drove that carriage was most likely the same liveried man in bondage who once drove the Master down Antigua's roads. All he had to do was memorize another route: glide beneath the elms at Ten Hills Farm, turn right at the tall gate, right again at Two Penny Brook, loop to the southeast, then turn again on Brattle Street, where more big houses held the mirror up.

In Antigua the Master could travel a short distance to see his younger sister Wait-Still, who lived with her husband, Captain John Haddon, in St. John's. A generation later, the Master's son could travel roughly the same distance to see his own sister down in Cambridge. Those roads were already well worn. It was the same trip the Puritan might have made a century before when he moved between the farm and Cambridge. Two things had changed in the intervening century, however. When the Master's son rode down those roads his slaves were Africans, not Indians, and the destination was sought after not because it was a center of mind and spirit but because it was the heart of family and the home of lavish entertainment.

Once their owners were distracted in those elegant Brattle Street residences, slaves who made the trip from Ten Hills Farm could visit folk they knew as kin and neighbors in Antigua years before. For all of them, the work would have been similar, too. Slaves picked to make the journey north—and kept within the family all those years—were hardly anonymous field hands bending in the sun but favored servants who spoke English, cooked meals and served at parties, spun and sewed, fed and cared for children. These men and women kept the silver polished and the pewter shining and the household running. Outside, they made sure the family's fine horses were well fed and brushed. They were maids in uniform, coachmen who wore livery, skilled craftsmen in the art of carpentry, disciplined individuals all, with intelligence and a deft sense of survival. The traits each shared, the traits they had been picked for, were the wit and temperament required to keep the grandest mansions running smoothly. These men and women had their masters' trust. That fact alone made them members of a small elite.

This matter of station has consistently and perhaps conveniently been confused with ideas about the supposedly "gentle" culture of slavery as it evolved in the North. Yet that assumption breaks down with even the scantiest analysis. The great shibboleth of northern slavery is that it was somehow "benign," softer than its southern cousin, even vaguely "familial" in some way, as though all could gather happily around a kitchen table, a master at the head. Yet the reality for these slaves could not have been more at odds with that fine fantasy. For them, the most fundamental truth was this: Whites who ruled their lives at Ten Hills Farm and in the big houses along Brattle Street were, in many cases, the very *same* men and women who had ruled their lives on warmer shores.

How then could these slaves whose enslavement did not end say the institution was in some essential way transformed? Why would simply sailing north change the underlying dynamic between a master and the men and women whom he owned? It is a torturous exercise to even think it. Rather, to those Africans plucked first from their homes, then taken from Antigua for a journey up to Boston, it must have seemed the only thing that really changed for them was weather. Even the decision to sail was not their own.

Perhaps "kindly and paternal" relationships sometimes did emerge as slaves and their masters worked in these close domestic quarters. This, at least, is what Samuel Batchelder suggested more than a century later when he wrote his history of Cambridge while living at Penne's house at 94 Brattle Street. But more likely it was comfortable for Batchelder to think so while surrounded by those ghosts. To anyone who first was bought and jumped to orders in Antigua, then moved and jumped again for the *same* master in New England, the notion would more likely seem obscene.

And *still* these men were buying men. And the people they already owned knew it—from working side by side with these new imports, or hearing of the purchases from brethren owned by other families, or through gossip shared with the growing population of free blacks residing then in Boston. By 1700, there were more than four hundred slaves counted in the colony. Thirty-five years later, when the Master bought Ten Hills Farm, the number was six times as great, and the total would continue growing. In 1754, when Massachusetts officials made their first formal tally of black slaves, 4,489 were included in the count. The second census, completed in 1765, showed the number growing still—up by more than one thousand to a total of 5,779 black men, women, and children without freedom.

In the midst of that influx, one of Brattle Street's most distinguished gentlemen, John Oliver Jr. (another Royall relative), bought two black men by mistake who were not slaves at all, but free men sold under false pretenses. Oliver sued the ship's captain who brokered the deal, but lost in court. Still the buying continued. One year later, during one of their many trips to check on sugar operations in Antigua, Penne's nephew, Thomas Oliver, and her husband, Henry Vassall, attended an auction in Antigua at the estate of a wealthy planter. At that sale they bought everything from crockery to cooks. Henry, struggling financially, bid only on a mahogany shaving stand he fancied that was valued at four pounds. His nephew, the wealthier Thomas Oliver, master of Elmwood, spent more freely, shelling out £900 for silver, slaves, and art that afternoon. To him the sum was nothing.

As it was in Antigua, so it was at Ten Hills Farm and in the mansions along Brattle Street. The buying and selling continued. The lives of privilege and of constant sacrifice continued. The system, moved up north, continued.

This was as the Master had intended; what he wanted. He left behind "a SON & DAUGHTER," the inscription on his tomb advised, "To inherit a plentifull Fortune . . . [and] an Exemplary Pattern for Their Imitation."

Imitate him they did; though they began with more than bootstraps.

LUXURY ON THE GRANDEST SCALE

Up at Ten Hills Farm in the mid-1700s, Isaac Royall Jr. lost no time cementing his position and ensuring that his legacy would last. While Penne and her husband Henry Vassall established themselves at 94 Brattle Street in Cambridge (enjoying their extensive gardens and a view that stretched one thousand feet to the Charles River), and Ann and Robert Oliver began the construction of a grand mansion several miles to the south in Dorchester, Isaac Jr. and his family continued with the transformation of the house and grounds in Medford. For all three siblings, it was a time for luxury on the grandest scale. Soon it was a time of many christenings as well; for though the Master lived only to see his stepdaughter give birth to Thomas in Antigua, his widow, Elizabeth Royall, would be a grandmother time and time again. And each of her three children, Ann, Isaac, and Penelope, would name a child after her, or more than one, if that first infant died.

Penelope gave birth in her first year of marriage. Her Elizabeth was born just before Christmas. A second daughter, Penelope, came one year later but did not live. In Medford, meanwhile, Isaac's Elizabeth was joined by a second daughter, Mary, who was born in January 1744. Three years later, Isaac Jr. buried his firstborn (the wobbly-kneed infant from the Feke painting) and welcomed a new baby (a second Elizabeth) with a christening at Christ Church Boston where he kept a pew.

These two children, Mary and Elizabeth, would survive into adulthood, making the Royalls a family of four. Penne's Elizabeth thrived as well, making the Vassalls a family of three. Ann and Robert Oliver produced more cousins still. As Thomas turned four, the infants Isaac, Elizabeth, and Richard Oliver followed in succession, wailing their first in the clear air of Dorchester not far from the sea. The network and the binding grew.

Isaac Royall Jr. was busy in that time. A new father with grand expectations of success, he was not satisfied with the mansion at Ten Hills Farm alone and ordered an elegant residence built on what once had been King Philip's land beside the sea in Bristol, Rhode Island. Known then and now as Mount Hope Farm, today this fragment of Elizabeth Royall's vast inheritance is operated as a bed-and-breakfast (named "editor's choice" by *Yankee Magazine* in 2008), and touted as a "perfect location for weddings, corporate events, retreats, strategic planning sessions, seminars, reunions, rehearsal dinners and outings . . . [with] a multitude of spectacular settings for your special day." There, where once a powerful sachem planned a war and met his death, guests can rest in the "Isaac Royall Library," an elegant wood-paneled room on the first floor, before retiring upstairs to the DeWolfe chamber, named after Captain James DeWolfe, a leading Rhode Island slave-trader.

The Royall history regarding slavery is never mentioned on the inn's website. The DeWolfes do not get off so easily. The source of their great fortune is noted, if briefly. But there is plenty more not pretty enough to fit on any brochure that hopes to lure new customers. Captain James DeWolfe, after whom that upstairs bedroom is named, was charged with murder once for binding and gagging an ailing slave aboard his ship, the *Polly*, lashing her to a chair, then heaving the seat and its terrified occupant over the gunwale and into the sea to her death. A Caribbean court would dismiss the case and accept the captain's explanation that this was a mercy killing done for the health of other slaves and crew, since she was ill. Charges were dismissed. But there must be something else. For at a time when such heinous acts were not altogether uncommon, almost all the *Polly's* crew refused to execute the captain's orders. Thus the charges. Thus the trial.

For the Royall and Vassall families at that time business in New
England and Antigua proved consuming. This was not the heyday
the Master had experienced. Yet Isaac Jr. and his brother-in-law
did the best they could. Together they expanded the Royalls' estate
outside St. John's by leasing an adjoining property from Ann and
Robert Oliver, their neighbors in both Antigua and Massachusetts,
their kin. With this attended to, Isaac looked north. With his fortune assured, his hunger now ran to politics and his ambition to
the title governor. Oh, here was a venture even more sweeping
than his father might have tried! Already serving then as a representative to the Massachusetts General Court, Isaac Royall Jr. in
the 1740s tried to move a step higher on the political ladder. At
the urging of friends he agreed to fund a plot to oust the governor.

The scheme was Jonathan Belcher's. Isaac was the banker and
the presumptive winner of the seat. In letters from the time he declared himself prepared to spend "five hundred pounds sterling" in
this attempted coup. His only reluctance, he allowed, might come
in quitting his beloved Ten Hills Farm ("Royalville," as he renamed
it), his "Beautiful situation" in Medford where he spent whatever
was required "to render life easy & agreeable" to him.

The intrigue in New Hampshire dragged on for several seasons.
The sitting governor proved more resilient than expected, however,
and the plan eventually collapsed. By the time Isaac Jr.'s political
ambitions were dashed he was poorer by a thousand pounds. He
was also far less welcome at his sister's house in Cambridge.

Relations in the family became strained after Elizabeth Royall
died in April 1747. In her will the old woman left £11,000 to be
divided between her two daughters, Ann Oliver and Penne Royall,
and the three granddaughters who bore her name: Elizabeth
Oliver (born to Ann), Elizabeth Royall (born to Isaac), and Elizabeth Vassall (born to Penne). Outraged over his exclusion from
his mother's will, Isaac Jr. filed suit and became entangled in a
lengthy fight with Henry Vassall. The conflict dragged on for years
and culminated with Isaac Jr.'s defeat in court. Penne and Isaac
drew apart. The family began to splinter. Defeated in politics and
defeated in the court, he turned his attention more and more to
material things, things that would not let him down.

Of course there were other strains, too. Henry was gambling and drinking heavily by then. He held Isaac in contempt for selling their Antiguan sugar at a loss to fund his vague political ambitions. Sourly, Henry ground his family into debt. As that debt grew he borrowed from friends and mortgaged everything he had to maintain the lifestyle he was born with, the lifestyle he knew best. He ran through Penne's considerable inheritance. He ran through what little money he had of his own. Still, month by month the debt increased, and though it may not have been apparent looking at that gracious home beside the Charles, Penne's family struggled to get by. Despite scores of fine paintings on the walls, elegant furniture, formal gardens, a stable overflowing with fancy horses, chariots for every occasion, and enough slaves to do their bidding in an instant, despite all that—the family now was poor.

Isaac, meanwhile, seemed to move from riches to more riches. The fracturing of family ties was of no paralyzing concern to him. He had other things to think about. The business in Antigua demanded his attention. He often traveled to his boyhood home to oversee the operations there. When at home at Ten Hills Farm, he dabbled in community affairs in Boston and Medford and kept busy forever polishing his reputation as a man of style, discriminating taste, and conspicuous consumption. The house at Ten Hills Farm was quickly filling up with art. John Singleton Copley was a frequent visitor. He came to put his brushes to the Benefactor's features and his daughters' dimples. While the walls grew tight with paintings, outside the mansion every barn and outbuilding began to bulge with the great harvest of Isaac Royall Jr.'s avarice.

When Isaac needed new horses for his carriage he saw to the matter personally. For him, no middling hag would do. "WANTED," blared one newspaper advertisement bearing his name, "Two Pair of handsome well made Coach Horses (Geldings) fourteen hands an a half high or more, of a good Breed, either Black, Sorrel, Bay or Brown, from three to six Years old, that Trott all, and are exactly match'd as to size, colour and marks." He found a pair, then was back in the newspaper again looking for two more "*to match*. . . . N.B. They must be black, with a white Spot on their Foreheads, fifteen Hands high, trot all, not above six, nor less than four Years old." In addition, advised the ad, the gentleman wanted a new "Coachman that can be well recommended, and understands the driving of a Coach and Four. . . ."

What a sight his carriage must have been, with its matching geldings and its fancy driver wheeling underneath that gracious line of elms at Ten Hills Farm. Today a mural above a fireplace in a second-story bedroom shows the scene. It is a fantasy of wealth and leisure painted much after the fact, an artist's rendering of a time of almost unimaginable luxury.

Matching horses certainly were not all Isaac Royall Jr. wanted. In the same newspaper advertisement, in yet larger type, the Benefactor sought a new slave from "Any Person that has a negro fellow to dispose of, between 16 and 25 Years of Age, that is sober, honest and healthy and understands the farming business." He promised a good price.

The buying and selling of such human property would continue to consume him. Yet there were problems that demanded his attention, too. A year after Isaac Royall Jr. advertised for this new "negro fellow" to help out at his farm, he found himself on the other end of a transaction with "A Likely Negro Wench to dispose of, who understands Household Business, and something of cookery: Also Four of said Wench's Children, viz. three Girls and one Boy."

In that day Boston owners were sometimes known to give black children away for free, to any who would have them. Royall, however, put them up for sale "for no other Reason," he noted carefully, "but Want of Employ." Perhaps he was not being wholly candid. In the same ad that ran in the *Boston Evening-Post* in April 1762, Isaac Royall Jr. also sought a man to help about the farm, someone savvy in "the Management of Negroes. . . ." For even in New England, where slave communities were small, some men rose against their bondage any way they could.

Throughout the Benefactor's time at Ten Hills Farm, court records and newspapers were dotted with reports of runaways, thefts, and the occasional serious crime. "In base return for their humane treatment," tut-tutted Samuel Batchelder in a talk written at his historic home at 94 Brattle Street and presented to the Cambridge

Historical Society in 1915, "the slaves sometimes displayed rank ingratitude and treachery."

In Isaac Royall Jr.'s time that "rank ingratitude and treachery" found expression in a daring theft. On the eve of the wedding of William Brattle's daughter, Penne's slave Robin joined forces with a laborer named William Healy to steal a heavy box of coins and silver intended for the bride. The haul—a significant dowry for the daughter of a major family—amounted to a small fortune any slave could only dream of:

> Six hundred and three Spanish Milld Dollars,
> one half of a Dollar,
> and one Eighth of a Dollar,
> One hundred and Seventy Pieces of Eight,
> One large Silver Cup,
> Two Silver Chafing dishes,
> One Silver Sauce Pan,
> Three Silver Tankards,
> Nine Silver Porringers,
> thirteen Large Silver Spoons,
> One Silver Punch Ladle,
> Twelve Silver Tea Spoons,
> One pair of Silver Tea tongs,
> One Silver Pepper Box,
> four Silver Salt Salvers,
> One Large Silver Plate,
> Two Silver Cans,
> Two Silver Candle-Sticks,
> One pair of Silver Snuffers and Snuff dish,
> two Silver Sweet Meat Spoons,
> One Silver Spout Cup,
> One Hundred and thirty three Small pieces of Silver Coin,
> Two hundred and Eighty Six Copper half pence &
> Eight Small Bags. . . .

Penne's slave Robin pleaded guilty to the crime and told a lengthy story of how he and William Healy snuck into the barn, took out the metal box, and hid the loot beneath his master's house at No.

94. "Our design," Robin told the court, "was to go to Cape Breton & from thence to France," and freedom.

Instead, the two men ended up at a public whipping-post, where each was given "twenty Stripes upon his naked back." Punishment did not stop there. The thieves were told to pay the father of the bride *three times* the value of the stolen goods or be sold into servitude for twenty years in the freeman's case, or away to another owner for "the Term of his natural life" for Robin. The court put the total of the stolen goods at £786. It was an impossible amount, worth many times more than the value of the men themselves, and the verdict meant no end to hardship. For Robin it meant a move away from family and everything he knew.

Up at Ten Hills Farm news of that sorry end touched the slave community at its core. All those slaves knew Robin from his early childhood. He was among the six children willed to Penne Royall by the Master thirteen years before. With his sister Cuba and four other siblings he had moved from Ten Hills Farm to Brattle Street upon their owner's marriage. It was under Penne's feet—under the floorboards at No. 94—that Robin hid the treasure. In this he was helped by Henry Vassall's coachman Tony, Cuba's husband; so many of those slaves were kin.

Tony seems to have escaped serious punishment; but even so, Cuba felt the jolt and surely sent those shockwaves back to friends and family who still resided at the two-story brick slave quarters at the Royall House in Medford. The message of that verdict was quite clear: Keep busy. Stay out of trouble. Do your work. And there was plenty of it. On a normal day there were over forty mouths to feed at Royall's farm, and fields to hoe, crops to plant and weed, horses to shoe, and other duties to attend to. Luxury was not easy to maintain.

While Isaac Royall's slaves whispered about the theft and the punishment that followed, the Benefactor continued headlong with his various pursuits, burnishing his reputation as a man of consequence and ordering the finest goods money could then buy. The dining table at Ten Hills Farm was set with silver commissioned from the master craftsmen Paul Revere and Zachariah Brigden. Shelves inside the mansion sat heavy with imported china. Drawers bulged with yards of silk. Books, artwork, and fine furniture crammed every corner of the place.

Isaac did enjoy his toys. Not only did he have his dandy carriage at his beck and call, but beside it sat one of America's first fire engines. Henry Vassall, not to be outdone, had another and stabled it beside ten horses at his Cambridge home. These were men who loved to shop, consummate materialists attracted to every bauble, every benefit, a gentleman could get.

That habit wound seamlessly through the generations. In a portrait from 1758, John Singleton Copley portrayed the Royall girls, Mary and Elizabeth, as dainty princesses floating in a sea of silk. Seated with their shoulders touching, the two were trussed in folds of blue and yellow and set against a field of red like two silk lanterns glowing. In that painting Elizabeth extends one hand, palm up, toward the viewer. There a hummingbird (perhaps hinting at the family's deep foundations in the tropics) rests gently on her fingertips. On Mary's lap a King Charles spaniel tilts his head in adoration. Folds of fabric soften the environment around them. Everything is in its proper place. Even the sky seems to cooperate. The blue outside the window appears incapable of rain, broken only by the most unthreatening of clouds. This painting "is less a presentation of character," observed Carol Troyen in a 1995 article published in the magazine *Antiques,* "than an expression of Isaac Royall's materialism. The Royall sisters are presented as the offspring of a grandee."

Well, of course. That was the whole point. If you had it—you had to show it. There was nothing wrong with ostentation. But as to slaves who made such riches and such pampering possible, they are invisible, or nearly so. Slaves were one possession a family of great fortunes did not boast. Rather, here it is only the hummingbird resting on a child's hand that may provide a clue.

Somewhere out of sight, however, as many as seventy slaves toiled for that family on its various New England properties. Scores more worked for the Royalls in Antigua. At Ten Hills Farm there was Belinda and her daughter Prine, and George, a slave who slit his throat rather than be sold. There, too, there were children peeking around corners, Robin's nieces, nephews,

14.1 Mary and Elizabeth Royall, 1758. John Singleton Copley.
Photograph © 2010 Museum of Fine Arts, Boston.

whole passels of relations examining a life they knew they'd never
live. At Ten Hills Farm, just as it was in the great plantations
of Virginia, South Carolina, Jamaica, and Antigua, those parents
watched children whom they knew they could not protect; hus-
bands lived with wives who could be sold away; generations lived
with parents and with children who would die without a breath
of freedom, as would they.

For these slaves at Ten Hills Farm, a treasured item was not an imported whimsy brought from Europe, not a fire engine or a dress that cost as much as a small house or a bit of silver worked with delicate simplicity, but a rough clay pipe and those fragments of broken crockery painstakingly fashioned into game pieces for a competition in the dust. A slave child's marbles were not colored glass but clay.

Alexandra Chan, the archeologist who spent years digging through soil near the Royall House in search of such treasured clues, believes there may have been more slaves working at that property than surviving records show. "There was a tax," she said. "I've always thought how easy it would be for Isaac to just move some [slaves] down to [the family farm at] Stoughton right before the tax man came." Though wills and inventories show at least sixty-nine slaves in Isaac Royall's service at one time or another, Chan believes the real number might be twice that high, counting all the family's New England properties. Of course there were more men and women in Antigua, too, and at those vast, family-owned operations further south in Surinam, as well. Everywhere—opulence—and all the work required to keep the standards up.

By mid-century, partly due to the labors of these slaves, Ten Hills Farm boasted four barns, a pigeon house, a corn house, coach house and stable, and the slave quarters with its massive fireplace, busy all year round. Among the slaves there was someone who must do the laundry, tend the fires, light small lanterns to keep back the night. Out on sloping fields there was a formal garden to tend, wood to cut, and crops to harvest. Elsewhere there were candles to be dipped, wool to spin, lard to become soap, clothes to wash, beds to make, chamber pots to empty, chickens to feed, sheep to shear, and meat to smoke. The list went on. And when the Royalls entertained, as they so often did, there was more work still.

When the day was done the attic in the main house filled. Up there, slaves slept on thin bedding on the floor. They slept on the second story of the main house, too, within calling of the master's chamber; and in the kitchen down below. A bedroll on the floor was the best that they could do. Slaves in the "out kitching" (now called the slave quarters) constructed slim partitions for a precious veil of privacy.

How stark those contrasts were. Yet how consistent. When the Benefactor's coachman took his master down to Brattle Street he must have marveled at those ten horses Henry Vassall stabled, and run his hands along the polished sides of the gentleman's "coach, the chariot, the chaise, the curricle, the old curricle," and other vehicles Henry's inventory carefully described, all sheltered in the coach house then. Perhaps he walked along those graceful pebble paths that lay between neat rows of boxwood and meandered near the marsh, or slipped inside to study the *150* paintings that adorned the "blue room," the "best room," the "marble chamber," the "green chamber," and the "cedar chamber" in Penne Vassall's house, rooms of which that later resident, the Cambridge historian Samuel Batchelder, would later write with pride. So what if all of it was mortgaged to the hilt? Let other generations deal with that.

Henry's house was often noisy with a game of cards. Like the planters in Antigua, he lived for his diversions. Yet he had little luck with them. As Penne's husband reached middle age, he dug himself a cavern of debt so deep even faithful relatives could no longer pull him out. To make ends meet, he mortgaged the house at No. 94 not once, but time and time again. Yet still the losses came, and sometimes rages, too, an anger so intense that many years after his death, one of his old slaves, a man named Darby, recalled Penne's husband as bitter, hard-drinking, and dissolute, a "wicked man," whom Darby and his friends believed might be the very Devil come to life.

"He was a gamester," Darby said, a "severe and tart master to his people" so unloved that on the day that he lay dying when he pleaded with his servants to please pray for his soul, "they answered that he might pray for himself."

Samuel Batchelder, reconstructing this story many generations later in his 1930 history of Cambridge, hesitated to take that condemnation at face value. Rather, he added a broad caveat: "Biased and overdrawn as we may hope this description to be," Batchelder sniffed, it certainly did prove at least *one* bit of gross injustice. Henry Vassall was the youngest son in a large family and struggled with that disadvantage through his life. At his wealthy father's death, Henry received just £3,000 in Jamaican currency, not the spectacular fortune he enjoyed in youth, not the fortune he may have always considered as his due. What man could rise from a disability so severe as that?

True, three thousand pounds Jamaican was a paltry sum for a man of Henry's breeding. Samuel Batchelder explained it probably sealed the young man's choice of Boston for a home. There, the author observed, Henry could mine a "well-stocked matrimonial market" flush with eligible ladies of good income. Penne was such a woman. And sure enough, Henry's visits to Ten Hills Farm had begun not long after Penelope Royall came into her own inheritance. The wedding followed rapidly from there. And then a birth. And yet the money did not last, and neither did it save the man from his own weaknesses. Instead he squandered Penne's inheritance and his own and died young, in 1769, leaving Penne a widow at the age of forty-four, alone amidst the rising talk of revolution.

PART IV

THE
PETITIONER

WE SHALL NOT BE SLAVES

By the time Isaac Royall Jr. reached the age of forty, he knew almost everyone in power and was not without some clout himself. A signal of his popularity came with his promotion, in 1761, to the post of brigadier general in the governor's horse guards. It was a largely ceremonial position, yet as the first American awarded the rank it was an honor he cherished. Not everyone was so impressed. The promotion came at a time when all across the colonies a serious period of reappraisal had begun. Increasingly, as the decade wore on, a citizenry born and bred in North America wondered whether British rule was what they wanted, or what they deserved. In heated conversations they entertained a series of difficult questions: Who was this distant king to them? Wasn't it their labor and their ingenuity that made the new world thrive? Why should Britain be their master? Americans could rule themselves.

Some among the Benefactor's political circle began to call for freedom. In doing so, they often used a powerful metaphor to make the case. *We shall not be slaves to Britain,* they advised.

To Isaac Royall Jr. all this talk of freedom was a tedious distraction. He only wanted what he had already. And so as others looked across the sea and began to think America should be her own nation under her own flag, Isaac Royall tried to steer a middle course. As a member of the government he was expected to speak, and so he did, urging calm and calling for mutual respect.

The "valiant Brigadier Royall is . . . become a great orator," the Loyalist Thomas Hutchinson wrote approvingly in a letter to a friend. Yet eloquent as the Benefactor may have been on this point, history would soon sweep him off the stage. He did not believe America could win a war against the world's greatest military force. He did not seek a revolution. And so as the hum of conflict gradually intensified, Isaac Royall ducked by calling on Britain to be more sympathetic to American interests, and Americans to remain faithful to their leaders from afar. His was a measured position at a time of rage and passion, yet finely parsed as his lectures may have been, they won few converts. This was no time for cautious compromise. Upheavals of the moment demanded fierce conviction and unreasonable hope. The Master's son had neither. When the most difficult debates came up before the council he was often marked as absent. While he prevaricated, the thunder of approaching war began. It was a storm from which he found no shelter.

After the Stamp Act was passed in 1765, requiring the payment of a tax on every piece of printed paper used within the colonies, British tax collectors were hung in effigy on a tree at the south end of Boston. This protest was mild compared to what was coming. In August a group of Patriots gathered on King Street not far from John Usher's former residence. After being riled by a series of speeches, the crowd stormed the house of a government official, wrote John Boyle in his *Journal of Occurrences in Boston*, "and destroyed almost every article therein." Boycotts and mass action kept the tension high. The Stamp Act proved impossible to enforce.

Ruling at an ocean's distance, Britain's top officials had critically misread the mood. The Massachusetts economy was stalled. The population was stagnant, too. A series of new taxes was only gas on that fire.

Even Isaac Royall felt the pinch. He turned his mind toward domestic matters and focused his attention on a tavern and thirty-acre parcel of farmland he rented out beside the Medford bridge, both of which stood empty that spring season. In the *Boston Evening-Post* he advertised "choice Land." It certainly was that. Positioned by the main road connecting Boston with points north, the farm and tavern satisfied the classic realtors' mantra of "location, location,

location." Isaac wanted the matter settled. Fallow land in spring was unthinkable to a man who knew the planting seasons well. No other advertisement followed. His Midas touch still held.

Of course income from local rentals hardly supported the family's lavish lifestyle. For that Isaac needed slaves, and ships laden with all the sugar, molasses, and rum those slaves produced. He also had diversified, purchasing large tracts of land in western Massachusetts with a group of wealthy business partners. But as the political situation deteriorated and the economy began to sink he thought better of dabbling in distant real estate and moved to dump some of that property. On April 6, 1767, his name appeared in the *Boston Evening-Post* again, this time offering a "good House [in Medford] . . . convenient for a Trader in Lumber, Tar, Bricks & c." for rent, as well as a "valuable Tract of Land in South Hadley, containing about 900 or 1,000 acres," which he promised to sell "very reasonably." For the latter property there were no takers. These were years of contraction, not speculation, and few men wanted to invest in remote land deals at a time when the culture itself was sliding on a rink of uncertainty.

Even as Isaac scrambled to limit his own financial risk, he never gave up hope the crisis would blow over. To him, there *were* signals of good will (or at least capitulation), and these gave him faith cool heads would finally prevail. Not a year after the Stamp Act was imposed, Parliament repealed the measure. In Boston, noted the diarist John Boyle, the news was met with cannon blasts and fireworks on the commons. The "Liberty Tree" (so-named after those effigies were hung a year before) was now festooned with something far more cheerful: lanterns and streamers heralding success, he said. Underneath its leafy canopy, the Sons of Liberty cheered and danced in celebration.

Still, the matter of taxation was far from resolved, and London's change of heart proved fleeting. In the fall of 1767 Parliament acted again, this time slapping duties on tea, glass, paper, and painters' dye and establishing a board of commissioners to enforce the law. Once again, resistance came. And once again John Boyle was left to make a note of troubling new developments: "Arrived . . . ," he wrote within a month of this new order, "a most unwelcome cargo":

Off a ship from London strolled three commissioners charged with the collection of those duties. Once on shore the men were threatened and harassed. On moonless nights Patriots with blackened faces and white caps terrorized officials charged with enforcing this new act. Some among those British fled.

Around Isaac Royall's table at Ten Hills Farm, the growing political fever in town was cooled by four miles' distance. With Isaac on the council and prominent men constantly stopping by, there is no question the family knew every detail of the growing crisis. Yet life at "Royallville" continued much unchanged; and as always, there were pleasant diversions. On October 30, 1767, the couple's youngest daughter celebrated her twentieth birthday. She was shortly to be married.

Betsy Royall's fiancé was a Harvard graduate from a storied Maine family, the Pepperrells, who owned at least thirty miles of coastline running from the town of Kittery south, as well as thousands of acres inland used for farming and the timber business. William Pepperrell was heir to part of that estate and an enormous shipping enterprise as well, businesses that connected him seamlessly to a world in which the possession, control, and trade of slaves was a central fact of life. The groom's uncle, William Pepperrell II, on occasion transported slaves as well as other goods, and not always successfully. In a flowing hand the man had once informed a client all his slaves were dead. Most of them, he allowed, had sickened and died at sea for lack of proper cover during a cold voyage.

"Sir," he advised his client, "I received yours by Captain Morris, with bills of lading for five negroes and one hogshead of rum. One negro woman, marked Y on the left breast, died in about three weeks after her arrival, in spite of medical aid which I procured. All the rest died at sea. I am sorry for your loss. It may have resulted from deficient clothing so early in the spring."

Such were the vagaries of trade. Though a few thick woolens may have saved the men and women on that vessel, such minimal care was not the norm, and the loss of slaves in transport was most easily dismissed as just the cost of doing business. In Boston that grisly voyage was viewed as a practical matter, nothing more or less than a failed investment. It did not nick the family's reputation. On the contrary, the family Betsy would now marry into was held in high regard. The Pepperrells moved easily within the circles of New England power and, like the Royalls, seemed to rise with each succeeding generation. Betsy's new mate would shortly join the Benefactor on the Governor's Council and cleave yet closer to a world of wealth and influence. First, though, the couple's wedding brought a flurry of activity to Ten Hills Farm.

For Belinda and other slaves toiling beside the Mystic River, it was an intensely busy time. There was a grand celebration to prepare for, silver to polish, food to cook, a hundred small details to attend to as well as all the extra duties preceding winter. On top of that, of course, daily chores did not stop. Long days of work grew longer still. In the midst of that activity Belinda and other slaves must have whispered of a changing world. From Boston came a rain of news: *A man was tarred and feathered! There is much talk of freedom!* Many spoke of liberty. What might it mean for them? No topic would have mattered more.

Over at the big house, such stirring talk changed nothing. Orders spilled in a cascade and there was always more to do. Elizabeth's wedding was a major event. It brought Isaac Jr. powerful new contacts and promised the family one more step up the all-important social ladder. The groom (after aggressively petitioning the king for a lapsed title once held by his grandfather) would soon become a baronet, one rung below baron, one rung above a knight. The day when William Ryall had to burrow into the earth for shelter was forgotten. After five generations in America, the Royalls now stood at the threshold of the highest reaches of society. To help prepare for this ascent, slaves were sent scuttling to answer Betsy's every whim.

On a crisp November day the chariots came, and all the wealthy, well-connected people in them. Up the pebble drive they rumbled with their laughter and their dark-skinned coachmen, beneath the elms, past the garden with its boxwood walks and carefully tended flower beds, past the fine gazebo with its ice stored strategically beneath the floor, and the slave house towering and busy in the night. As guests swept through those doors, there to meet them (just as it had been a generation earlier) were slaves with skin as black as coal. With a nod (or hardly that), ladies trussed in yards of glistening cloth were pulled into a noisy crowd. Inside the towering three-story mansion mahogany tables groaned with food and the finest wine and spirits money could procure. Guests marveled at the luxury.

It is easy to imagine who might have been among them. The Benefactor's sister Penne and her husband Henry Vassall would have come with their daughter Elizabeth, and likely several slaves to tend. Their stepsister Ann almost surely made the trip north from Dorchester with her husband, the Antiguan planter Robert Oliver, and perhaps their son Thomas, an eligible bachelor of refined taste and a dignified air. Their coachman and any other slaves who came would likely have known the slaves at Ten Hills Farm. They may have even been related, just as it was for Penne's slaves and perhaps others who were brought from Brattle Street that day. The Benefactor's uncle and one-time tutor, Jacob Royall, surely came from Boston with his wife (a woman who also carried the surnames Adams and Winthrop). And there were others, bending over plates of oysters, great silver platters heavy with roasted meat, huge bowls of punch, interrelated, interconnected, interdependent, of a piece.

Slaves who came as coachmen and attendants with these guests were given a simple meal in the slave quarters. There and in the barns and stables on that day they would have spent their time sharing news and gossip from the town. Upstairs. Downstairs. Always ready for their masters' call.

For Isaac Royall and his family it was easy, for a blink, to ignore the political ferment of the day. After the wedding the mansion house at Ten Hills Farm was full and busy. Elizabeth and William Pepperrell moved into the estate. Betsy soon announced that she was pregnant. Celebration was muted by the fact that her husband would be absent for the birth. He was off to Europe then and would be gone almost two years. Betsy begged to join him for the trip, but he refused. London was in the middle of a smallpox scare, he chided. At Ten Hills Farm Betsy would have her sister and parents to watch over her, and a new baby for her company.

She would hardly lack for entertainment! The couple argued. But William Pepperrell did not relent.

Three months after that wedding there was another more modest affair in Cambridge when Penne's daughter Elizabeth married a doctor named Charles Russell. This match was not as lofty as the Royall-Pepperrell union, but Penne and Henry Vassall cheered the union anyway. And well they might. The groom had recently come into a sizable inheritance from his uncle, Superior Court Judge Chambers Russell, who had died suddenly during a trip to England. He left the young man a large estate in the town of Lincoln fifteen miles west of Cambridge. In his will the judge had a very particular order relating to his slaves: "My Negroes shal not be sold," he commanded. Neither did he set them free. Instead he ordered: "if any of them through Age or other Bodily infirmity should become in part or Wholly useless; they shal be *comfortably* supported on my said Farm in Lincoln during their natural lives."

The provision was much discussed, and up at Ten Hills Farm where Belinda then was growing old, perhaps it set her thinking: *In old age, or through bodily infirmity . . . Shall be comfortably supported. . . .*

For Henry Vassall, teetering on the edge of bankruptcy by then and only barely keeping up appearances, the marriage could not have come at a more propitious time. He rushed to take advantage. There was nothing more to sell or leverage. The house at No. 94 was just a shell disguising debt. He sold the acreage across the Charles River, spent the money gambling and keeping off his creditors. Penne, frightened of the family's decline, gave her Antigua property in trust to her nephew Thomas Oliver at Elmwood, who made sure any profits from the operation went to Henry's many creditors. That arrangement bought the family breathing room, but little more. In Boston and across New England, meanwhile, the economy lurched downward. The political situation appeared insoluble. Smart money started moving elsewhere. Then matters got worse.

On September 30, 1768, someone spotted a warship on the bay. Soon there were several more. At the docks two regiments of soldiers unloaded in a blur of red, gathered at Long Wharf, and stomped into the people's midst, their weapons raised and loaded. Behind them, those ships' cannons pointed toward the shore. Harsh measures were installed to put these people back to heel.

Paul Revere, witnessing the scene, felt certain there would soon be war. That evening he retreated to his shop to make a note of it. By lamplight he smoothed a sheet of copper on his workbench, arranged his tools, and etched the scene in fine detail. A dispatch from Boston printed that week by the *Connecticut Journal* described a city under siege. "We now behold the representatives' chamber, Court house, and Faneuil hall, those seats of freedom and justice, occupied with troops and guards placed at the doors; the common covered with tents, and alive with soldiers . . . , in short the town is now a perfect garrison."

Stunned by this invasion, Isaac Royall and his colleagues on the council drafted a letter to the troops' commander. In carefully diplomatic language they pleaded with General Thomas Gage to please remove his soldiers. The letter, reprinted in the *Connecticut Journal* on October 31, opened with a deferential tone. "In this time of public distress," the councilmen began, "when the General Court of the Province is in a state of dissolution; when the metropolis is possessed by Troops, and surrounded by Ships of War; and when more troops are daily expected, it affords general satisfaction that your Excellency has visited the province," that he might see "we are in a peaceful state."

Since that state continued, the legislators wheedled, could his Majesty's man "please to order them to Castle William, where commodious barracks are provided for their reception. . . ." Or better yet, might the general see fit to dispatch them to a "different part of North America"? *That* would solve it.

Nothing of the sort happened. Instead, the soldiers stayed, and month by month their aggressive display on Boston streets only raised the temperature. In an atmosphere of military siege, everyone could feel the heat. The local economy collapsed. Real estate prices fell to almost nothing. Still, creditors demanded what was due. In Penne's house the fact of chronic debt now became a pressing crisis. Desperate for help from any quarter, Henry tried another fix, another mortgage, and sought out his new son-in-law to plead for cash.

Charles Russell, soon to be a father, agreed and signed a £964 mortgage for the already heavily mortgaged property. The amount was just enough to tide the couple through another season. Yet what a season it would be. On the streets and in the smoking rooms of Boston, talk of liberty intensified.

In late winter Henry fell ill. His daughter, a new mother now, came to visit him from Lincoln. On the last day of her father's life she tiptoed into his sickroom carrying the infant in her arms. Later, she would bend to write a letter. Maybe now, she mused, her father's death might heal old wounds. Among Henry Vassall's pallbearers were some of the most prominent men in Boston. But Isaac Royall was not there. Those enmities ran deep.

WITHIN THE BOWELS
OF A FREE COUNTRY

◆

By the time of Henry Vassall's death in 1769, the Sons of Liberty had created an organized force intent on resisting British acts that worked against the colony's best interests. Month by month they harried British troops and shouted their profound distaste for England's bullying. Discontent across the colonies meant tinder scattered everywhere. All that tinder needed was a spark; and it was struck one night in March, a year after Henry's death, when a crowd of protesters in Boston threw snowballs, rocks, and oyster shells at British soldiers; and those beleaguered soldiers fired back.

A crack of muskets brought eleven protesters down. Six among the victims died. One was Crispus Attucks, a black man, a runaway slave who on that day had stirred the crowd with talk of liberty. Described two decades earlier in a notice of his escape from his Framingham master as "A Mulatto fellow, about 27 Years of Age . . . , 6 feet 2 . . . ," Attucks, by then in his late forties, had managed to live free for twenty years by disappearing into Boston's black community and cadging work as a sailor and rope maker as opportunity allowed. But on that night his luck ran out. Crispus Attucks' decision to risk his own freedom to join the broader call for liberty cost him his life. "The first to defy, the first to die," Irish journalist and poet John Boyle O'Reilly wrote approvingly a century later. Even at the time, Patriots called the man a hero and proudly buried him alongside his fellow victims in a cemetery otherwise reserved for whites. "A most horrid and inhuman massacre!" scribbled Boyle in his journal. Paul Revere bent to his work again, this time making an engraving of a Henry Pelham drawing showing the encounter in all its drama. The "Boston Massacre," as that event was provocatively named, would galvanize the population. From north to south white Americans began to band together with a powerful wish—freedom from the "masters" *they* had known.

In this growing mood of revolution, some slaves, stirred by all the rhetoric of liberty, began to think an end to bondage might be near for them as well. Freedom for the one should mean freedom for the other, they reasoned. Indeed, the idea of liberation was so sweet (and talk of it so universal), that Boston's black community began to stir. Some free men like Prince Hall, a skilled negotiator who sought education for black children and helped establish the first black freemasonry society in Boston, would push a radical agenda. In Massachusetts at long last, the slow clock of slavery was finally ticking down. But first, whites wanted freedom for themselves.

Ensconced in his quiet retreat in Medford, Isaac Royall Jr. knew of the debates but had no incentive to destroy the status quo and no moral attitude to do so either. For him these arguments were nothing but pestering distractions. What he wanted was appeasement. Freedom for the slaves? Ridiculous. Who would do the work? He loathed this air of change. He wanted peace. He wanted to be patriarch and grandfather. At Ten Hills Farm his daughter Betsy was busy with her newborn and dreaming of the new coach or chariot her husband promised to send back. Now he had a grandniece as well. And soon enough his other daughter would be married, too.

In Cambridge, Penne was in no mood to free her slaves either. Instead, she found she needed them for income as she faced the piles of debt her husband left. In this period she sold her slave Cuba and Cuba's children down the block to serve John Vassall Jr. Toby, the children's father, would remain behind at No. 94. Penne needed him.

In the halls of politics the talk of liberty grew yet more heated. Isaac Royall Jr. could feel the energy rising. Yet still he wavered. And for a moment, at least, it almost seemed the danger might still pass. In Boston, after some maneuvering, the king's soldiers were ordered to stand down. Ministers in London repealed most taxes except for one on tea "so small," wrote historian David Hackett Fischer, that London officials "believed even Boston might be willing to swallow it." They were wrong.

Instead, the tax on tea became a rallying point. Boycotts and rioting spread. Agents of the Crown were tarred and feathered and carted through city streets as people jeered. Distrust thickened into hatred. Issues before the Governor's Council grew more complex and more divisive. Increasingly, Isaac Royall Jr.'s seat stood empty.

In the summer of 1770, the Benefactor's wife Elizabeth fell ill. The *Massachusetts Spy* would soon announce her death: "At Medford, Mrs. Elizabeth Royall, the virtuous and amiable Consort of the Hon. Isaac Royall Esq." She left behind a husband, her sister Mary McIntosh Palmer, two daughters, half the Surinam plantation called Fairfield, and wealth enough to buoy generations. Two weeks later, William Pepperrell finally returned from his long sojourn. After "a very disagreeable passage of eight weeks," he reported in a letter he sent back to England, he arrived safe at Ten Hills Farm to find his little daughter "finely grown," standing well, and just starting to speak. Before the seasons turned his wife was pregnant with a second child.

Pepperrell's absence had covered an eternity in political time. When William sailed away the conflict between England and America seemed grave, but soluble. Now on his return it spun out of control. Like his father-in-law, Pepperrell found himself caught between allegiances and tried to thread that needle in a letter to a powerful figure of his acquaintance back in Britain. "Though I am a friend to America," he said cautiously, "I am no enemy to Britain." Two men on a tightrope. In that day it was impossible to play both sides. *We will not be slaves*, the rebels said, *come what may.*

This language had been used for years. By 1770 it sparked on every tongue. Like a noisy mantra punching myth into reality through cleverness and repetition, it was adopted with unthinking urgency. Those brave men who struggled under England's thumb, the *Boston Gazette and Country Journal* thundered one September morning in 1771, would certainly be praised by future generations. No man of dignity, that writer sneered, would ever submit to "the disgraceful state of *SLAVERY*."

Across the colonies, of course, the idea of enslavement was anything but abstract. Many Patriots who used the term owned slaves themselves. The famous Patriot Dr. Joseph Warren, for instance, five years *after* angrily denouncing Britain for enslaving citizens of the colonies with the provisions of the Stamp Act, set about to purchase "a negro boy" for his own use. The details of the transaction are preserved in a yellowed two-page bill of sale held at the Massachusetts Historical Society. The paper sets the boy's price at thirty pounds, paid upon delivery, with another ten pounds owed "in potters' ware" three years after the boy's delivery. Should the doctor not be satisfied with his new slave, he could skip the final payment and return the fellow for a refund.

Patriots like these knew what they were talking about. Yet glaring as that disconnection was (and tempting as it is to imagine America's famous freedom fighters shocked into wakefulness by the force of their own rhetoric), slavery's hooks were set too deep to easily dislodge. Though slaves did try. From 1773 forward, a score of blacks asked Massachusetts leaders to put an end to their enslavement. The first such plea, submitted on January 6, 1773, was signed by an anonymous slave named "Felix." Presented to the governor's council, the petition would have gone before Isaac Royall Jr. and his new son-in-law, the wealthy baronet William Pepperrell, among others. It must have packed a punch for men with just such property at stake: "Although the language was clearly diplomatic," observed historian Emily Blanck, "the petition called for the government to *abolish* slavery—a radical goal."

A second proposal followed not much later. This one asked the council to grant each slave one free day a week so they might earn enough to buy their freedom and return to Africa. "Subsequent petitions," noted Blanck, "became more demanding and confident." Some included talk of compensation for what one such document described as "all our toils and sufferings."

In these and other "freedom suits" put before the courts or taken up by the legislature in that period, British Loyalists most often represented slaves, while Patriots routinely represented masters. Patriots, explained Blanck in her study of this phenomenon, tended to consider the suits within the context of property

rights—without stopping to weigh the rightfulness of that property. Loyalists more often argued the cases in terms of "natural
rights," though they were emphatically "*not* abolitionists," said
Blanck. In fact, neither group sought slavery's end; and neither perceived that end as either attainable or necessarily good. Slaves and
free blacks knew this, of course, but used any wedge they could;
and their best wedge yet was to turn the fiery rhetoric of these men
of liberty against them in a blaze. And that they did.

In June 1773, a petition filed by a group of Massachusetts blacks
demanded freedom for all slaves. The rationale was vaguely religious. The approach was deferential. Framing their request as a
"humble petition," the supplicants declared they knew "in common with other men" they had the basic right to exist "free and
without molestation." And yet that right was brutally denied so
long as they were slaves "within the bowels of a free country."

The petition failed.

Three months later the matter was up again, this time framed not
as a "humble petition" but a set of "instructions" presented with sly
eloquence: "We expect great things from men who have made such a
noble stand against the designs of their fellow-men to enslave them,"
this group said. Letting political expediency rule, they stopped short
of calling for reparations even as they made it clear they knew quite
well what must be due. "It would be highly detrimental to our present masters," they acknowledged in a bit of bald-faced politicking,
"if we were allowed to demand all that of *right* belongs to us for
past services." Instead, they would settle for freedom so they might
leave the place of their confinement and start new lives in Africa.

That petition failed as well.

Despite rejections by the courts, petitioners like these slowly
gained ground—and new supporters. Tacked onto one petition,
notes historian Roy E. Finkelbine, was the eighteenth-century
equivalent of an amicus brief in the form of a pamphlet written by
the Patriot James Swan, who argued not only for emancipation,
but payment, too. In *A Disuasion to Great Britain,* Swan cited
the Bible to underscore his point. Deuteronomy 15:13–14 required
that slaves go free after a term of seven years, the colonial essay-
ist reminded readers. Nor should those former slaves be sent off

empty-handed. "Thou shall furnish him out of thy flock . . . and out of thy floor, and out of thy wine press; of that wherewith the *Lord* thy *God* hath blessed thee, thou shalt give him. This is in token that thou dost acknowledge the benefit thou hast received by his labours." That argument failed, too. Slavery kept its grip, for now, at least.

Isaac Royall Jr., then in his mid-fifties, watched this shift with mounting worry. Slavery was the world he knew, and it provided almost all the profits he enjoyed. "Sensitive and Pacific measures" were needed, he declared, not hotheaded talk of war. He had no taste for battle. He would rather run. And so he shuffled off the stage, resigned from public life, and made a plan to travel to his boyhood home in Antigua, where he might find sanctuary until the crisis passed.

He did not go soon enough. On the first day of September 1774, 260 of Britain's best soldiers swept across Ten Hills Farm on their way to seize stocks of ammunition stored at a powder house just beyond the farm's periphery. The troops left Boston before dawn. They traveled up the Mystic River by boat, unloaded at the foot of Ten Hills Farm, and made their way across the Benefactor's property. By noon they had taken what they came for and were marching home. The raid was a success. But it brought trouble in its wake.

As news of the seizure spread, bonfires sparked throughout the region. They signaled an emergency. Hundreds then thousands of men responded. By the next day these men gathered at Cambridge Common, where they made a rowdy crowd to sweep down Brattle Street. Outside the gates at Elmwood they called for Thomas Oliver, the Benefactor's nephew, recently named lieutenant governor. As he stepped out onto his front porch a cluster of men rudely served an ultimatum. If he did not quit his post they could not guarantee his safety. Seeing no way out, Oliver signed the paper they provided, but above his signature he scribbled this frequently cited remark: "My house at Cambridge being surrounded by about four thousand people, in compliance with their command, I sign my name."

Power may have fallen to him by accident (historians believe British officials mistook him for another Oliver with a more impressive political pedigree); now it was stripped from him by force.

Still the people's anger did not break. Instead of safeguarding England's rule, the powder house raid merely pulled another thread. Within the year the unraveling would be complete. Meanwhile, all across the colonies, the Sons of Liberty flexed their muscle with more confidence.

In England at that time, ship after ship brought news of fresh resistance. The scope of the crisis finally came clear. Small measures were pointless, war almost inevitable. On the floor of Parliament, the brilliant orator Edmund Burke warned England's leaders that only one action could avert full-scale revolt. America must have its freedom. "Slavery they can have anywhere," he thundered. "It is a weed that grows in every soil. . . . freedom they can have from none but you."

England would not give it.

At Ten Hills Farm Isaac Royall also understood that truth at last. Diplomacy and prevarication would no longer work. Money, power, property, and connections—the four stars he was born with, the four stars that guided his every action—could no longer keep him safe. He looked about his stately mansion and through the windows to those gorgeous fields that spread in waves down to the waterfront. How could he leave all this? How could he not? After some deliberation he made the same choice his great-grandfather, the Immigrant, had made when faced with grinding poverty; the same choice his grandfather made in Maine, when faced with war; the same choice his father, the Master, made in Antigua, faced with slaves plotting revenge. He would leave as well. The world that he knew best no longer held him safe. What could he take if he must flee? What should he leave behind?

Friends in Cambridge who ran from the mob that morning after the powder house raid had no warning for their exit. One moment they sat down to dine, the next they were fugitives, running for their lives. Even his old friend, the powerful and proud William Brattle, was now reduced to sending mawkish letters to the newspapers, saying he had quit his residence in that troubled moment and wanted to go safely back. He never would return.

The Benefactor swore his own fate would be different. *He* would leave in an orderly way, heading for a destination that he loved. Still he hesitated. His daughter Betsy was pregnant again. There was another wedding in the offing, too. His elder daughter, nicknamed Molly, was marrying George Erving, a Boston widower with a four-year-old son. For one last time, the house at Ten Hills Farm was busy with festive preparation. Once that bond was sealed, Isaac would tell his slaves to pack for him.

On April 18, 1775, Isaac Royall Jr. dined in Boston with a British captain and considered what might come. He did not have to wonder long. Boston was anything but quiet on that night. British troops had been ordered up and out. They were preparing for a major operation. Paul Revere knew of the plan. As Isaac sat to dinner, the famous silversmith (whose work adorned the Royalls' Medford table) was rowing silently across the Massachusetts Bay to Charlestown and then beyond to sound a powerful alert across New England.

On the far shore a man stood waiting with a horse. She was a fast horse, one of the fastest in the region, a young mare, and she would carry Paul Revere on his famous "midnight ride" thirteen miles to Lexington, where the first major battle of the American Revolution would soon start. Revere's intended path was to move from Charlestown due west to Concord. But as he set out on that night in the dark up the main road and past the withered remains of a slave named Mark (executed twenty years before for the murder of an abusive master and left to hang for all that time), the silversmith spotted British scouts barring the way ahead. Urgently, he wheeled his horse about, spurred her hard, and turned directly north. After thundering across a grassy marsh the horse touched solid ground again, and raced ahead on "full gallop for the Mistick road," Revere would later write. The route took him down the length of Ten Hills Farm, past Winter Hill, where Winthrop once had kept his house, along the main road, past the Royalls' mansion, then over Cradock Bridge and into the town center, where he alerted Isaac Hall, a captain with Medford's minutemen. British troops are moving, he told the man. With a kick, he sped down High Street at a gallop. Behind him the steady pop of gunfire and a sudden throb of bells alerted all to rise.

Isaac Royall did not hear the commotion. He was miles away in Boston, sound asleep after a large dinner. When he woke, a war had started. In Lexington and Concord years of tension finally crystallized. The muskets fired. The wounded fell. The dead were many.

After the battle, roads were closed. The flow of goods to Boston slowed to a trickle, then stopped entirely. British troops were ordered to throw a protective cordon around the city. No one was allowed in or out except a loyal few. For a time a stalement held. Then the Patriots determined it was in *their* interest to keep those exits closed—and firmly. A chokehold was applied as they moved to starve the British out. The siege of Boston would last almost a year.

Isaac Royall Jr., all his careful plans now fouled, found his way to Salem in those first few hectic days. There he struggled desperately to find a captain who would sail him to Antigua. No one would. Instead, he boarded a ship for Halifax, heading north and hoping to sail south from there. In a letter written that May, he recalled the chaos of the start of war in an unpunctuated gush:

> I packed up my Sea Stores and Cloathes for the passage and came to Boston after attending the public Worship on the Lord's Day Evening before the Battle of Lexington to take leave of my children and Friends in tending to have gone thence to Salem to embark for Antigua but unfortunately staid in Boston two or three Days and din'd with the Honble Capt. Erving the very Day the battle happen'd after which it was impossible to get out of Town for Gen. Gage had issued Orders to prevent any one coming in or going out.

Even as he bent to dip his pen, someone new had made his bed at Ten Hills Farm. This man, tall and angular, fierce and seasoned, was a colonel from New Hampshire, a veteran of Indian wars, a soldier who also wrote a letter on that day. Colonel John Stark did not look behind him to describe the chaos at the start of war, but thought ahead to how his men could possibly survive it. To American officials in New Hampshire he wrote an impassioned plea for blankets, for money and supplies.

Death Is Not the
Worst of Evils

In the weeks immediately after the battles at Concord and Lexington, the population at Ten Hills Farm swelled tenfold and more.

First came refugees. By nightfall on April 19, while Isaac Royall watched the unfolding events from his vantage point in Boston, more than one hundred men, women, and children gathered at Winter Hill seeking shelter where John Winthrop once had kept his home. Uncertain of their future, perhaps not even sure whom among them they could trust, they huddled in the dark. Then, by daylight, just as quick as they had come, they scattered. Some moved up the road to stay at Isaac Royall's house until they found their bearings and could sketch a plan. Others trudged away to stay with relatives or friends or went back home to dwellings they would shortly lose to fire, to cannon shot, and all the other wrenching dislocations of the war.

Next came soldiers. Within a week of the Revolution's start, men and boys came streaming from New Hampshire carrying knives and muskets grabbed in haste. John Stark was among them. He was working at his sawmill when he heard the news. A veteran of the French and Indian War, the forty-five-year-old New Hampshire farmer and mill owner dropped his tools and went straight home. There, he "changed his dress, mounted a horse, and proceeded toward the theatre of action," the general's grandson Caleb wrote admiringly in his *Memoir and Official Correspondence of Gen. John Stark*, published in 1860. As Stark rode south, men called out to him that they might volunteer as well. The lean-faced captain, fifteen years removed from combat then, urged them on and told them to meet up with him at Medford.

Hundreds followed. Farmers, printers, woodsmen, sailors, carpenters, and priests all pressed forward to the Mystic River, then moved across it to the Benefactor's property. Within a week, scores of these new soldiers poured into a Medford tavern. There, in a raucous meeting with a show of hands, they made John Stark commander of the force. Next they made him colonel, a rank the New Hampshire Provincial Congress formalized several weeks later when it officially granted him command of the colony's "first regiment of foot." John Stark now controlled thirteen companies with a total of eight hundred men. And so as Isaac Royall gathered his belongings and struggled to secure a passage out, his well-kept grounds were smothered by strangers who swept across the farm like a rare migration, eating up existing stocks of food, pushing into any warm place they could find.

The farm could not support this unexpected weight. Stark's men were cold. They were hungry. Many among them fell ill and could not join the morning muster. Even before the troops set eyes on their new enemy, they sank into a crisis.

Writing home to the Provincial Council on May 29, 1775, Colonel Stark pleaded for blankets, money, and basic supplies. The siege of Boston was already a month old by then, and more fighting appeared inevitable. The colonel worried his men would not be ready. Taking up a quill in Medford, he outlined his regiment's many difficulties. "As to fire Arms," he wrote, "the greatest part . . . [are] furnished." More guns were expected. But basic shortages remained. "A considerable part of the Regiment is destitute of Blanketts," Stark wrote urgently, "and [they] are very much exposed." Some soldiers were unfit for duty. Stark feared more might drop away before the guns were fired. Unless his troops' most basic needs were met, the colonel warned, "their courage will fail and they will return, and by that means, we shall work our own destruction."

Yet it was bullets, not blankets, the soldiers needed most. And that shortage would be all too clear before the month of June was out.

Still, more volunteers arrived.

Among the newcomers was the Patriot colonel's eldest son, who grew up in the care of slaves at his grandfather's house in New Hampshire. On June 16, 1775, one day before the Battle of Bunker Hill, Caleb Stark resolved to slip away. His grandfather (and guardian through adoption) did not want the boy to go. The grandfather, Caleb Page, a wealthy merchant, had already lost one son in the French and Indian War and could not bear to lose another. The two argued and then dropped it. But Caleb's grandson and namesake had a lot to prove, and he could not prove it sitting home. And so that morning in the dark the boy grabbed a small valise, pushed the stable gates ajar, then turned his stallion south and galloped hard toward Ten Hills Farm.

When young Caleb arrived in camp, his father asked why he had come. According to a descendant's account of these events penned so many decades later, the son responded with the father's pluck. *I'm here to fight,* he argued. "I can handle a musket."

"Tomorrow may be a busy day," the colonel answered. He summoned a captain and instructed him to take the boy into his company. "After that we will see what can be done with him."

Shortly after sunset young Caleb heard men moving. Soon he was among them. After weeks of anxious waiting, the regiment's orders finally were clear: They were to dig in at Bunker Hill on Charlestown Neck and lure the British into battle. Scores of fighters made the trek from Cambridge. Hundreds more moved quietly through Ten Hills Farm to stand nearby as reinforcements. Near midnight, the first among them pushed past Bunker Hill and halted on a second rise closer to the water's edge. There, on top of Breed's Hill, they set to work to make a crude redoubt. Directly in the enemy's line of sight and well within the reach of British guns, they worked until the dawn.

Early the next morning, a lookout with the British Navy sent up an alarm. He had spotted movement on the hill, he told his captain. Gunners aboard the *Lively* fired first. Her heavy cannons woke up officers in Boston, who learned to their dismay that more than a thousand rebel soldiers suddenly bristled within taunting distance. As troops in Boston rallied, more guns sounded as one by one the *Glasgow*, *Somerset*, and *Falcon* added fire from their snout-nosed cannons to the din. American fighters—curled in small depressions or crouched behind stone walls—found scant protection from that whistling crush; well before the heat of day was up, the smell atop Breed's Hill was not the "sweet ether" Puritans had cheered so many Junes before but the vile stench of human suffering. The worst of it still lay ahead.

Volley after volley came throughout the morning. But it would be for the infantry to tend to this eviction. In Boston as the sky gained color, British soldiers frustrated and stale from months of living in close quarters buttoned up their uniforms, checked their weapons, and clambered stone-faced into boats. The main assault would come on foot from men as organized and smartly trained as any soldiers in the world.

While those men prepared for battle, King George's officers ordered Charlestown put to the torch. Rebel soldiers on Breed's Hill could only watch those fires burn. For some among them, the homes and churches, shops and stables crackling in the distance were their own. Nothing to be done for it. Just brace for what came next: great lines of red along the shore; the thud of crude explosives; a moan from somewhere near.

Every soldier hunched beneath the rage of British guns now waited for his turn. Every gun was loaded. Every knife was sharp.

On city streets in Boston on that bright June day, Britain's faithful clambered onto rooftops for a better view. A film of ash at times obscured their vision. It settled in a dusty film on their clothes and in their hair. Four miles to the north, other men and women (enemies of England now) crowded into Isaac Royall's upper floors to press against the rippled glass, to see. Oh, there was never anything like that!

On Breed's Hill as the sun rose high, men who a month before had toiled in woodsy isolation or labored in the dusty industry of village shops held kerchiefs at their noses to try to block the shocking smells of this new work: the urine and the shit, the blood and vomit, the open gore of wounded men. Some soldiers retched and doubled over from terror and disgust. Others did not flinch or move but stood like stone to wait as hordes of red-clad soldiers scrambled off their longboats down below and arrayed themselves like ants in distant rivulets so full of purpose.

Twenty-five hundred British troops landed in Charlestown that morning. They would face those ragtag rebels with the best weaponry civilization had yet devised. It was a daunting display of power, of empire, of arrogance. But still the Patriots held tight. Every one among them knew the basics of that confrontation: Outnumbered and outgunned, they must wait until the last; then shoot to kill. And so they waited. And finally the troops approached and then the signal came, and they poured their lead like lava down the slope.

After several tries to take the hill, the tidy British lines collapsed. But still the soldiers came. American commanders, shouting to be heard, called desperately for reinforcements. Stark's troops raised their guns and made ready to join in. On the colonel's signal they would run, each one, straight into the mouth of it. Yet King George's officers had much to lose in a military humiliation on that day; and so as the Americans scrambled and reloaded and fired and fired again, British officers in full regalia pushed their soldiers up the hill into relentless storms of lead that caught those English soldiers in the face, at the throat, the chest, the legs, until they fell, or worried through it.

Stark's men, fresh and ready, were ordered up and into it. But as the New Hampshire regiment headed for the center of the fight, the colonel spotted a potentially grave vulnerability on the northern flank. A beach beside the Mystic River lay exposed. It offered a handy landing spot and the means to choke off any exit. If British soldiers landed there, Stark knew, they could squeeze the Patriots from east and west and cut them into ribbons at their leisure. Stark moved quickly, sending two hundred of his best men to the riverside and instructing them to put up a defensive barrier as fast as they could build it.

As the sun reached its zenith, those men built a rough, low wall by dragging stones into a line and ramming bales of hay against them. Anything to dull the thump of bullets. While the soldiers heaved and sweated, their commander walked forty feet onto the beach and pushed a stake into the sand. Back at the line he shouted out that no man should fire until the enemy had passed his mark.

It was a risky gamble to divert so many men at the very peak of battle. But it proved a brilliant bit of strategy. While Stark and his soldiers hid, eleven companies of light infantry landed on that beach. The only thing they saw to stop their progress was an ungainly line of stone and straw, perhaps a farmer's hat or two. British officers surveyed the scene, then ordered their men forward. With a flash of steel the redcoats dropped their bayonets and charged, advancing unopposed until a streak of crimson passed the colonel's mark.

It was not one man who fell then. It was not two. It was the whole first line that tumbled in a tangled mass, as soldiers lost their footing, their bearings, pummeled by shot, their faces distorted in shock. The second line fell almost as abruptly. John Stark used a trick he had learned in the French and Indian War to ensure the bullets did not stop. He organized his line three deep so that when each man fired and fell back another gunner was already shooting. The rotation made for an efficient slaughter. By the time the British troops withdrew, ninety-seven of their men lay dead or dying on the sand. It was one of the bloodiest encounters of the day.

Atop Breed's Hill the fighting was now equally intense. As British soldiers finally made their way to the hill's summit, they set upon the shooters with a fury, slashing with their bayonets and choking men with their bare hands. The resulting melee opened a space for yet more soldiers to pour through, and casualties on both sides mounted. In the confusion Colonel Stark was informed his son was dead. He pushed ahead without a pause. He knew the cost of war. Later he would learn his son survived the fight unharmed. It was other men who fell. Among the victims was a recently promoted general, Joseph Warren, the Boston doctor who spoke so eloquently against the enslavement of America even as he negotiated to buy a black boy for himself. By the time Dr. Warren fell, American troops were running low on ammunition. Their commanders, sensing the fight turning, shouted orders to retreat and pulled at those who would not go: *Come now!*

British troops chose not to follow.

Survivors on the American side gathered at the foot of Ten Hills Farm to recover and to count their missing, their wounded, and their dead. The guns were finally quiet. But both sides had suffered terribly. Among the British, the casualties were overwhelming. One man lay dead for every two who charged the hill. Americans lost one in three defending it. Now, where John Winthrop once had planted grapes and sent his wolfhounds running, men and boys lay moaning in the dark, or staring without speaking, rocking back and forth. The shock of war was fresh and total. Most of those injured on that day had only ever shot a turkey, a bear, a deer, a rabbit, or a wily fox before, not human beings whose language and whose culture they had shared. The force of that hit hard and put the cost of liberty in a difficult new light. What they wanted they would have to bleed for. That would be their compass now.

By traditional rules of engagement, the British won the Battle of Bunker Hill. They made those rough New Englanders give up their turf and flee. But instead of being perceived as a defeat, the misnamed Battle of Bunker Hill would stand forever as a signal of American determination. "Live free or die," John Stark would later say, capturing the spirit of that battle and so many others; "Death is not the worst of evils." That famous toast, written in 1809, provided New Hampshire with stirring words ("Live free or die") to press on every license plate.

Stark's legacy lives on in other ways as well. Here is his statue, cast in bronze, standing on the New Hampshire State House lawn. Another, showing him astride a horse, forever gallops near his grave in Manchester. A local high school bears his name, and in 2004 when the owners of the Flag Hill Winery in Lee, New Hampshire, created an apple vodka from local harvests, they put the soldier's flinty image on every bottle sold. A reviewer from the *Wine Enthusiast* two years later gave the beverage high marks in a review. He liked that General John Stark Vodka well, he wrote: "The mouth entry is viscous, nicely astringent on the tongue, and tastes of fruit peel. The aftertaste is dry and cleansing."

Whether the owners of the winery knew it or not, they had stumbled onto a fitting tribute to this savvy fighter. For Stark did like to take his drink. Legend has it the colonel so enthusiastically gulped his way through Isaac Royall's cellar he earned a personal reprimand from George Washington. Then again, Washington almost certainly sipped from the same bottles. For as the siege of

17.1 General John Stark Vodka.
Courtesy, Flag Hill
Winery & Distillery.

Boston dragged on and America's top generals pondered how to pry the British loose from Boston Harbor, General Washington called on his men from time to time to meet with him at Ten Hills Farm. There in Isaac Royall's house beside the Mystic River, the sharp-nosed New Hampshire colonel (later general) welcomed his superior officers with savories and wine from the Benefactor's cellar served up on Isaac Royall Jr.'s china and fine crystal, some of which was dug up centuries later by archeologists who, shard by fragile shard, puzzled together fancy glasses finished off with gentle swirls running circles down the stems.

The siege of Boston lasted for eleven months. In that time, war changed everything. In Boston, where British troops and those loyal to the Crown struggled through a hard winter with only minimal supplies, many succumbed to cold or illness. Among them was the Benefactor's daughter, Betsy, who chose to stay behind with her husband, the Baronet William Pepperrell, since she was four months pregnant as the fighting started. Two weeks after the

Battle of Bunker Hill, Betsy gave birth to a son. But her health failed soon after, and by November she was dead.

"It pleased God, the fifth of July, to grant deliverance of a dear boy," William Pepperrell wrote in a letter from that time. Yet the war would have its tithing. That summer, as the fields outside Boston lay thick with wheat and vegetables, the roads were closed and his frail and so-long-pampered wife was "able to get no other nourishment than that of salt provisions, which brought on a fever," the baronet complained. Month by month Betsy's condition weakened and her mood grew dark. In her last few weeks of life, her husband said, the miseries of the poor, the tragedy of war, and anguish over all she lost ruled Betsy's thoughts.

William took the loss hard. To his relative Thomas Palmer (who had retreated to the family's slave plantation in Surinam with Molly by then), William admitted he no longer had much taste for life. When last he wrote, he said, he was a happy man. By early fall it was no longer true. "Look now where you will, I believe one more miserable is not to be found. My dearest wife has bid me an everlasting farewell. . . . I still breathe—*live* I never can again." In February he packed his children up, said goodbye, and sailed for England on the *Trident*. It was a voyage he would make in profound, unshakeable sorrow.

In those first few months of war, the landscape around Boston was transformed. Betsy's childhood home, where she had posed all trussed in silk beside her sister Molly, functioned as a busy military camp now. Fields were trampled; trees were downed for firewood; sheets were ripped for bandages. Inside the mansion, where elegant rooms so recently were filled with music and amusing gossip, talk now floated in a fog of death and violence. Fine houses along Brattle Street in Cambridge fared no better. Seized by revolutionary forces and pressed into their service, those dwellings were remade.

George Washington claimed No. 105 for his military headquarters. That splendid establishment now rattled loudly with the thump of military boots. Penne's house across the street at No. 94 was turned into a hospital. So was Elmwood, Thomas Oliver's mansion up the river, where rooms accustomed to gentle entertainment were converted into crowded wards for suffering soldiers. With few medical supplies available and the invention of antibiotics still 150 years away, those men healed slowly, when they healed, and many a bed came free only after gravediggers showed up with their carts.

Along the streets of Cambridge, the exterior landscape was so altered that returning visitors at times became disoriented on ground they once knew well. Magnificent homes remained. But everything around them was laid waste. Formal gardens lay as grizzled remnants of more glorious days. Trampled, neglected, and abused, they were dotted now with tents and fires. Muddy paths sprang up on shortcuts that had never seen the stamp of feet; and shivering soldiers wrenched old fences from the ground and chopped them into pieces for the flickering hope of warmth. Even ancient trees long cherished for their graceful shape and ample shade were hacked and used for fuel. Town streets appeared denuded. Nothing but survival was sacred in that season.

But what of the slaves who lived in those old houses and remained behind when masters fled? Did they stay to fight? Did they run? Did they hide? Did they serve new masters at old quarters? Or side with the British, lured by a promise of freedom? Were they sold? Or traded? All of it. Certainly. Uncertainly. We know but do not know. For many slaves this was the first moment they could exercise a choice. Yet what choices they made, we can only wonder.

Here the god of memory has closed his eyes again.

It may be that someone's attic holds a trove of letters cradling answers to these questions; or that a mislabeled cabinet in a quiet municipal building, or a junk shop somewhere, or some obscure descendant's closet in America, in England, Antigua, or Surinam contains as-yet-to-be-recovered details fit to tell the tale of slaves at Ten Hills Farm and down on Brattle Street during the war. More familiar sources do not divulge much. An entire library could be filled from floor to ceiling with printed matter stemming from the Revolution; but almost none of it addresses the fates of families whose lives were made of unpaid labor and a lack of basic rights. If there *is* a wrinkled pile somewhere holding answers to these questions, generations have not found it, and a thorough scouring today leaves almost every detail hanging. Since few slaves could either read or write, they left minimal records of their own and therefore little likelihood these holes will *ever* fill. And so these are America's *desaparecidos,* parents and their children lost, as though they never were.

Records do show blacks fighting with distinction in the battles of Concord and Lexington, at Breed's Hill, and elsewhere. Some black soldiers among them, men like Crispus Attucks, won admiration for their service. But most slaves and many free blacks found only derision and contempt as they volunteered to risk their lives to help America pursue the cause of freedom. In Massachusetts, the Committee of Safety barred slaves from fighting well before that famous southern gentleman George Washington arrived, his favorite slaves beside him still. To allow a slave to fight, the Massachusetts committee members jeered, would go against the "principles to be supported, and reflect dishonor on this Colony."

George Washington agreed. In October 1775, he and other generals from up and down the Atlantic coast voted unanimously to "reject all Slaves & by a great Majority to reject Negroes altogether" from fighting in the war. Washington followed up with a formal order lumping black men in the prime of life with young boys and frail old men: "Neither Negroes, Boys unable to bare Arms, nor old men unfit to endure the fatigues of the campaign are to be enlisted," the general's order stated.

Within two months, that order was reversed. The raw need for men proved more compelling than shared prejudice. With British officers busy assembling an "Ethiopian Regiment" in Virginia and offering slaves their freedom if they took up arms, American officials suddenly found themselves at a marked disadvantage. Grudgingly, General Washington addressed it: On December 30, 1775, he took up his pen again at No. 105, this time allowing free blacks to enlist, so long as recruiting officers approved.

These were general policies. They give no clue to the fates of individuals. Nor do they illuminate any of the particular challenges enslaved men, women, and children faced at Ten Hills Farm during the war. There the void is almost total. Though slaves constituted the majority population on that ground, and had for many years, only the barest trace of their existence can be tweezed from scanty records that remain. In one letter the Benefactor instructed his

Medford lawyer to sell off several men at a deep discount. Selling slaves had always brought the family an exceptional return before. It was a natural path in times of trouble. Writing from his stopping point in Halifax, Isaac Royall Jr. tried that route again, to gin up cash for his time of exile. But prices plunged. Men he bought for £60 he was now willing to sell for a fifth the price, he grudgingly instructed Simon Tufts, a Medford neighbor and his lawyer in such matters. War did that. With so many people struggling and the future full of terrible unknowns, the market had soured.

John Stark during his time at Ten Hills Farm was altogether silent on the subject. In letters written from his post (and carefully preserved today by the New Hampshire Historical Society), he makes no reference to these people; who they were, how they fared, where they went. Instead the colonel speaks of blankets, of money and men's will.

Perhaps the very banality of slavery ensured there would be so little mark of it on history's skin. The Patriot hero John Stark certainly understood the slave system as a natural part of life; a prerogative of wealth and class. His wife Molly was raised by slaves in New Hampshire, a state that did not formally abolish the practice for another seventy-five years or so. Caleb, the couple's eldest son, grew up in that same home, where he was likewise tended to by men and women who were never free. Why would someone like John Stark mention a fact so common, so unremarkable? A soldier like him was more likely to write about his horse.

And so we know of guns and blankets, wounded soldiers, even the minutiae of shifting battle strategies amidst the chaos of a war. We know the death tolls and who won and who was falsely rumored killed and who survived to drink a toast instead, bear children, make a life.

But of these men and women—almost nothing.

So much is gone.

Only a few anecdotal accounts survive to give a clue. The archeologist Alexandra Chan writes this way of a slave at Ten Hills Farm who killed himself on the eve of being sold: "Unbeknownst to Isaac [Royall], Jr.," she explains in her 1996 study of the Royalls and their property, "George, who may have served the family for

as many as 38 years and may have been by this time well into his
eighties, had perhaps anticipated his master's course of action and
slit his own throat the day before."

May have served. . . .

May have been. . . .

Perhaps.

There is so much we do not know.

We know George was the Benefactor's slave. We know he killed
himself. We know his buckles and his buttons all were sold and
that, together, they fetched one pound, seven shillings, and some
pence; enough to pay for his funeral. After that we face the yawning void of our own ignorance.

Yet the slenderest of threads can help to bring this population
and its struggles into focus. Here and there lie scattered clues. One
is the story of a black boy named Darby, Cuba's son, who grew
up at No. 105 after the Benefactor's sister sold her housemaid and
her several children down the block. Darby was traded away from
No. 105 when he was barely old enough to walk—his second sale
before the age of ten. His new owner died in that first summer of
the war. Darby wandered home again after the man's death, to
Brattle Street, where the slight, black eight-year-old found a towering white general now in charge. When the general asked the boy
if he would like to stay and work for him, Cuba's son inquired
what wages the mighty freedom fighter was prepared to pay a boy
like him. The answer, Samuel Batchelder recounted in his speech
before the Cambridge Historical Society in 1915, was such a sting-
ing rebuke that Darby ("the pickaninny," as Batchelder called him)
would remember it until the day he died. *Famous* George Washington might be, Darby complained. But that imposing leader was
no gentleman to him.

Reparations

❖

In time, of course, the British left. The war moved on and all the soldiers with it. That strange intrusion lurched away. For seven years and more, violence swept south and west, extracting its ungodly toll, burying tens of thousands. Then at last the war was done and Ten Hills Farm reclaimed its marshy silence.

Despite the language of freedom embedded in the U.S. Constitution—*We the people . . . in order to form a more perfect union, establish justice . . . promote the general welfare, and secure the blessings of liberty to ourselves and our posterity . . .* —slavery did not end. In the South a deeply entrenched labor system firmly kept its hold, defying the lofty wording of the nation's founders for many generations more. In General John Stark's home state of New Hampshire, too, slavery remained legal, if almost nonexistent. No final order issued from the bench or from New Hampshire's new state capital would command an end of human bondage there until the verge of Civil War.

Beside the Massachusetts Bay, where Belinda still belonged to the absent Isaac Royall, the shift toward freedom for the slaves was gradual and initially quite vague. In Belinda's case, it came not from a new government, but from her master, who with a stroke of his pen allowed her to choose freedom for the first time in her adult life. Other of his many slaves would not be so fortunate. In his will, the Benefactor passed those men and women on to other owners.

By the time the guns stopped firing, Isaac Royall Jr. was dead. He had never managed to get home. Instead, he stayed in England and visited often with his daughter Mary Erving and her husband George, who had settled in the town of Froyle near the island's southern coast. In 1781, while war still raged, the town was visited by smallpox, a disease that had terrified Isaac Royall Jr. all his life. Now it took him. On October 17 that year, just as General Charles Cornwallis prepared to surrender with his seven thousand troops at Yorktown, the Benefactor was buried beside a fourteenth-century church an ocean's distance from the fighting. There, a weathered chest tomb set above his grave identifies this man—born on a slave plantation in Antigua, long-time master at Ten Hills Farm, a member of the Massachusetts Governor's Council for twenty-two years, dandy, dilettante, father of two, owner of slaves, collector of art, and the founder of Harvard Law School— only as a native of Medford in New England, dead at the age of sixty-two. But terse as his memorial is, that mossy stone, carefully refurbished and set plumb in 2005 (and clearly identified on the church's website), completes a circle of sorts. It rests just thirty miles from where John Winthrop sailed 150 years before.

It was not the Benefactor's wish to die in England. Instead, he dreamed of going home but hedged his bets by seeking money and support from Britain while he lived upon her shores. In 1777 he wrote a letter to Lord North in London requesting aid from the king's coffers. What money he could gather was already spent, he informed the baby-faced prime minister, since he had fallen ill and used it for his doctors' bills. But once he was a rich man. In America he'd had a farm worth £30,000 sterling, and men and women to serve his every need. Now he lived in exile, was nearly destitute and in ill health. He needed help. Oh that God might bless "his Majesty's measures with success," he prayed, that these misguided colonists would see their "true interest" and renew their sense of "duty to the Mother Country and to the best of Kings."

But could Lord North please use his considerable powers to grant him just a little cash meanwhile?

To friends and acquaintances in New England, the Benefactor sang an altogether different tune. Alarmed by a rumor that traitors who returned without permission would "suffer Death without benefit of Clergy" ("I am informed," he wrote with shock, "my Name is mentioned in the Act"), and disturbed by news the government had confiscated his beloved Medford estate, he scribbled hopeful pleas to influential men in Boston. Some among those letters survive and are held in Harvard University's Houghton Library among a trove of rare and crumbling documents. In them, in great flutters of delicate script, Isaac Royall Jr. professed his loyalty to America (not the king), and recounted his many services to Massachusetts. He *never* intended to go to England, he protested, but was swept up in a tide of circumstance. Now all he wanted was to live among his countrymen and find a wife so he could end his days "among you and be buried with my Father and the rest of my dear Friends."

To sweeten these entreaties he sent tokens. With one letter to Edmund Quincy the Benefactor mailed "the best Temple Spectacles with Silver Bows in a Case with the Initials of your Name." In other missives he explained how he had included significant gifts to Harvard College and the town of Medford in his will. Pages carefully preserved at the Houghton Library show him spelling out those gifts in minute detail. To Oliver Wendell, an executor of his estate, in 1778 he wrote: "I think it proper to inform you what I had left to the College. . . ." What followed in a second letter written one year later was a meticulous accounting of the acres granted and how he had come to buy them from the province twenty years before. Great tracts of land would go "toward the endowing of a Professor of Laws . . . or of a Professor of Physic and Anatomy, whichever the said Overseers or Corporation shall choose." Harvard College chose the law.

When the Benefactor was not busy with his correspondence, he steadily reworked the provisions of his will, eventually producing a document that dragged on for many pages. All he had amassed in life would scatter at his death, tracing a great spider's web of bloodlines laced with and attenuated by love, ambition, and the imperatives of trade. By the late 1770s, his extended family stretched from England to Maine, Massachusetts, South Carolina, the Caribbean, and beyond. He traced those lines with gifts and

18.1 Isaac Royall Jr., 1769. John Singleton Copley.
Photograph © 2010 Museum of Fine Arts, Boston.

carefully outlined his plan for the distribution of fabulous riches born of two generations of slave trading and slave labor.

Land and men in Antigua should be sold, the Benefactor ordered. Proceeds from the sale would be used to pay his debts, with any excess distributed among various descendants. Slaves who served at Ten Hills Farm would mostly stay within the family. Yet to his elderly slave Belinda he offered manumission. His daughter Mary would inherit the woman, his will declared, "in case she does not choose her freedom." But if that slave chose liberty, so be it, he allowed, "*provided she get security* that she shall not be a charge to the town of Medford." Other Africans were given out as tokens of his love. Some among them were already in the possession of family and friends. The Benefactor now diligently confirmed these gifts: of his "Negro boy Joseph" and "Negro girl Priscilla" to his son-in-law the baronet (now in England); of "my Negro girl Barsheba and her sister Nanny" to Mary (down the road in Froyle) along with land, furniture, a chariot and chase, a Bible, formal china, and so many other treasures collected through the years.

On and on he went, doling out his farms, his vacant lots, his paintings, his baubles, his plates and tea sets, his milk pots, his kettles and snuff boxes, his men and women, his carriages, his crystal, silk and velvet, his furnishings and more, all the things that smoothed the daily pattern of a pampered life. Recipients ranged from his daughter and sons-in-law nearby to relations in New England and South Carolina where the Benefactor's first cousin, William Royall (the family's only Harvard graduate and a direct descendant of John Winthrop through another Royall branch), lived on an elegant plantation with his wife and many slaves.

How he must have paced those distant floors in Halifax, Kensington, and Froyle in those last few years, thinking of his death while longing for his home. *Sell them!* he ruled of slaves who had served his interests for so many decades. Give them away. Free them. Just be done with it. It was not the slaves he cared for now. It was the land he pined for in this exile. It was the *ground* he wanted back. It was America and Ten Hills Farm, the friends, the parties, and the history, his vaunted sense of self and this place that he called home. Royallville! He had even named it for himself and included a provision in his will requiring anyone inheriting the property to keep the name and take his surname, too, since he had sired only girls. Meanwhile he hoped to die upon that ground and be laid to rest beside the Massachusetts Bay. Ill and homesick, he wanted once again to sit beside the Mystic River's icy race come spring, to see the green-backed hills of summer, the flights of geese, the great pure drifts of snow as seasons turned. Home. Instead, as he lay dying his property was held by other men. Descendants would eventually reclaim the ground. But that was of no use to Isaac as he fretted over letter after letter pleading to return.

Of course Isaac Royall Jr. was not the only exile with his wants. In England, William Pepperrell made a new career by helping men seek compensation for possessions lost in war. As president of the Loyalist Association and head of its bewigged governing board, it was Pepperrell's job to push the claims of men just like himself. The work consumed him. Many of his ilk had abandoned everything at the start of war. But now they wanted their possessions back. And if they could not get their land, their cattle, their furniture and slaves, they wanted reparations. No less a document than the Treaty of Paris, signed in 1783, acknowledged these demands: America's new Congress, stipulated article 5, should push each state to "provide for the restitution of all estates, rights, and properties, which have been confiscated."

Loyalists, in other words, should be made whole. And if state legislatures failed in this respect (as of course they often did), exiles had another arrow in their quiver. Men like the Benefactor's sons-in-law, William Pepperrell and George Erving, could also clamor for remuneration from the British government, which tended to look kindly on the plight of distressed members of the upper class. In time, many among them won their claims. Before the books were closed, more than three million pounds would pass from royal accounts into the hands of families who chose to flee when the war came.

Across the Atlantic in a nation just then forming, there were other demands, too, altogether different ones fueled not by assumptions of privilege but by powerful rhetoric that on its face favored all men equally. In Massachusetts, where Belinda chose freedom upon hearing of her master's death, the new state constitution began with this bold claim: "All men are born free and equal, and have certain natural, essential, and unalienable rights. . . ."

In 1780, when that document was written, the language did not necessarily reflect an intention to liberate all slaves. Rather— just as it was in the arguments leading up to war—those words in the constitution's preamble signified "essential, and unalienable rights"—for *whites*. Nor was there any expectation this new government would deliver reparations to the region's enslaved blacks if those slaves were finally released. Nonetheless, the words were sharp enough to send a chilling message to men like William Royall (another of the Benefactor's relatives—this one a distant cousin on his father's side), a Massachusetts farmer who, like his more affluent namesake in South Carolina, did not leave when the war started.

Isaac Royall Jr. had managed to sidestep the crisis over slavery by getting out of town. But his cousin the farmer faced it squarely and responded to the document's novel language with an ancient strategy. When he realized the new state constitution's wording might presage the end of bondage at his Stoughton farm, the Benefactor's cousin hired a gang to capture all his slaves, bind them up, and ship them to Barbados or Antigua to be sold. Surely he did not consider these men members of his family. On the contrary, lore has it he was so frightened of them at times he could not leave his house.

That sudden exile and sale came just in time; for men like the Benefactor's cousin were just about to lose their hold on humans held as property. After the Revolution, some in Massachusetts moved to take the language of the new state constitution at face value. Vermont's constitution, passed in 1777, had explicitly addressed the question of enslavement in its preamble. Now some in Massachusetts wanted the same clarity. Two important lawsuits in those early days of statehood pushed the matter to the fore.

One case involving a female slave named Mumbet ("Mother Elizabeth") transfixed citizens in a small town in the western part of Massachusetts best known today as the one-time home of that iconic early twentieth-century American painter Norman Rockwell, whose work, for the most part, depicted a lighthearted, sweet-tempered, and almost exclusively white America. In the town of Stockbridge in 1781, the slave Mumbet, Elizabeth Freeman, sought the help of the lawyer Theodore Sedgwick in filing a claim against her owner. She asserted that the language of the constitution meant that she was free. The defense claimed she was not. The trigger for the case, however, was not war and the passage of a powerful new constitution, but an ugly incident of domestic violence. Not long before Mumbet filed her suit, the elderly slave, in trying to protect her daughter from harm, was struck by her mistress with a hot iron shovel, a blow that left her arm disfigured. The confrontation snapped whatever patience she had left.

Mumbet's case was tried in nearby Great Barrington, the birthplace of W.E.B. DuBois. Her lawyer set the wording of the Constitution front and center. "All men are born free," he thundered, echoing the state and national constitutions. The law demanded it. A judge ruled in Mumbet's favor, and the outcome was held as hope by other slaves who sought relief from their own toil and bondage. So the ripples spread.

Yet still the claws of slavery did not release their grip. Instead, the institution lumbered on, challenged here and there, but hardly eradicated by a single decision in a lower court. In 1783 the question went before the Supreme Judicial Court of Massachusetts, a derivation of the Court of Assistants on which the Puritan had sat so many years before, when that body took up a case involving a slave named Quok Walker, a slave severely beaten by his master during a confrontation over whether he was free. Like Mumbet, Quok Walker won his case and took his freedom. Now a powerful message came down from the highest level of the judiciary. As a result, less and less could any owner claim he had a legal right to own another human. Even so, there was no immediate emancipation. Rather, some owners ignored the dictates of the court. Others used a rhetorical dodge. They renamed their slaves indentured servants, yet changed almost nothing of their status and responsibilities.

In the end the practice fell out of favor and quietly petered out. It was a process not so much mandated by the courts as it was a shift made farm by farm, family by family, slave by slave. Unpopular, diminished, gone. In Massachusetts, five thousand souls were freed. Not even a newspaper story marked the end. The termination of the practice was so piecemeal, so gradual, so incredibly unremarkable, hardly any whites made note of it.

Nor, for the slaves themselves, would freedom prove a simple matter. Slow as this transition was, profound as it was, *welcome* as it certainly was, emancipation heralded no easy future for people like Belinda who could only look ahead to a life with no guarantee of home, no money, no provision for retirement, and no prospects for their final years. Belinda was free. But she was destitute, and even what was due her did not materialize. No bills or silver came her way. No comfortable "security" (promised in the Benefactor's will) was granted by executors of the man's estate. There was no William Pepperrell to press her case, no language in the Treaty of Paris encouraging legislators to make amends and pay for what was lost.

Still, this slave wanted something of what should have rightfully been hers. And so she sought an advocate in her own community and put her mark on a petition asking for a pension from her owner's sizable estate. Belinda's petition was filed on Valentine's Day, 1783, just as, across the sea, politicians and generals hammered out the terms to end the war, sitting in Paris to sign a treaty including provisions for compensation due. No mention was made there of slavery.

Five days after Belinda's petition was filed with the Massachusetts General Court, a payment to her was approved by Samuel Adams and John Hancock, who ruled she should have a pension of fifteen pounds, twelve pence, to be paid annually by "the treasury of the Commonwealth out of the rents and profits arising from the estate of the late Isaac Royall." Some scholars have seen Belinda's petition as the first legal case in America involving reparations for slavery. In fact, it was something humbler. Belinda only wanted what her former master had already promised. Even with a court ruling in her favor, however, she would not get it. Though the pension was granted, the money was not paid after that first year. In time, Belinda was back before the court again, beseeching those powerful white gentlemen to press compliance in the matter.

There is no further record of her case, or of her life.

PART V

THE
LEGACY

CITY UPON A HILL

On a warm winter's morning in January 2007, a handsome, square-faced Harvard graduate climbed the steps of Boston's State House to deliver his inaugural address as Massachusetts' seventy-first governor. A native of Chicago, Deval L. Patrick was the first person of African descent to win the title since the commonwealth's founding; and he won by a wide margin. So he was confident that day, and full of plans as he talked about John Winthrop's centuries-old notion of a "city upon a hill" and what it meant to him, a black man, rising to the role of governor.

"My journey here has been an improbable one," the new governor declared. Raised on Chicago's South Side near a massive housing project that was home to some of the poorest citizens in the nation, he had moved "from a place where hope withers," as he put it on that day, "through great schools and challenging opportunities, to this solemn occasion."

A thunder of hands responded. This audience knew his story well.

"America herself is an improbable journey," Governor Patrick continued. There was the material wealth, of course, and the military might, and the blending of so many cultures into one. But there was always more than that, he said, for the land was marked forever by notions of "equality, opportunity and fair play—ideals about universal human dignity." He laid those cherished goals directly at John Winthrop's feet. "Massachusetts invented America," Governor Patrick told the crowd. "American ideals were first spoken here, first dreamed about here. . . . Our legislature is the longest continuously operating democratic body on the face of the earth. . . . Our struggle, our sacrifice, our optimism shaped the institutions and advanced the ideals of this nation."

Like others before him, Governor Patrick talked about the *May-flower* and the *Arbella* and the building of a nation from raw wilderness. His listeners knew this story, too. A binding myth, it made them one. In the crowd a few heads bobbed. Someone said "Amen." Then the governor spoke about another ship, the *Amistad*. He told his audience that when he took his oath of office he laid his hand across a Bible given by slaves from that ship to John Quincy Adams, who took their case for freedom to the nation's highest court, and won. "I descended from a people once forbidden their most basic and fundamental freedoms," the governor continued, "a people desperate for a reason to hope and willing to fight for it. . . . So, as an American, I am an optimist. But not a foolish one."

Ten months later, Governor Patrick donned a red tie and elegant dark suit as he prepared for an equally important passing of the wands of power. This time it would be Drew Gilpin Faust, a disarmingly unpretentious scholar of the Civil War and slavery in the American South, ascending to the presidency of Harvard University. Like the new governor before her, she crafted her installation carefully to reflect a change of season. Like him, too, she quoted the Puritan and called his "Model of Christian Charity" a source of inspiration. Even before she reached the stage, signs of a new era were already in evidence. After a thirty-five-minute bagpipe performance during which the university's elegantly robed faculty filed through a pouring rain, the tall historian, dressed in the heavy, double-breasted robe reserved exclusively for Harvard's president, was preceded down the aisle by two lines of students wrapped in kente cloth dancing to the thump of African drums.

Religion professor Diana L. Eck (a newsmaker herself when she became the first member of a same-sex couple named master of a Harvard residential house) was charged with narrating the scene

19.1 Drew Faust moves toward the stage for her inauguration as President of Harvard University. 2007. Photograph courtesy Jim Harrison.

along with a colleague from the chemistry department, James G. Anderson. Together they provided an archival record of the day, noting the long train of scholars, artists, and other luminaries winding toward the stage. Among them were some of the brightest lights in the world of African American arts and letters: Toni Morrison, John Hope Franklin, Natasha Tretheway, Henry Louis Gates Jr. As seats filled, the narrators chatted amiably about the rain and the various university icons displayed for the occasion. Here was the college charter penned in 1650; there, the president's chair, a spiky relic used to signal the moment of ascension; and there the college seal with its three open books arrayed beneath the Latin word for truth: *veritas*.

As the university's top leadership pressed forward at the end of this long train, Professor Eck, the master of Lowell House, gave an account of their slow progress. But it was the sight of the African dance troupe that prompted her most ardent response: "This is fabulous!" she said. "Look at this! *They* don't care that it is raining at all! They're delighted and exuberant. . . . A cheer is going up!"

Three gray-haired former presidents, Larry Somers, Neil Ruden-
stine, and Derek Bok, came into view between the dancers, moving
slowly, each identified in turn. But it was the performers who held
the crowd's attention, not the bemused older white men moving
through those swaying, jumping figures toward the stage.

Briefly, the camera showed five Harvard males who had smeared
the letters F-A-U-S-T in red across their naked chests. Then it
moved back to the main scene to catch Governor Patrick slipping
a rain poncho over his head, hailing a friend. At last Drew Faust
came into view, her mouse brown hair cropped short, her pale
complexion clear, eyes bright behind rain-splattered lenses. Even
in her presidential robes with all their weighty symbolism, she
moved with a light step that day and reached repeatedly to touch
the dancers to confer a fond anointment of her own.

When it was time for the governor to speak, Deval Patrick
waved a hand across the field of glistening umbrellas before him.
"This institution," he boomed, "has played a special role in so
many lives—including my own improbable journey from a two-
room tenement on the south side of Chicago to the high honor of
serving this commonwealth today." He was first in his family to
attend college, he informed that erudite assembly, "and I still remember receiving the acceptance letter and calling home and getting my grandmother on the phone and I said, 'Gram! I'm going to
college next year! I am going to Harvard!' And she was so excited.
And she carried on, and she made all kinds of noise. And then she
paused and she said: 'Now, where *is* that anyway?'"

The thunder again. And this time, laughter too.

"At first I was hurt that she didn't appreciate the news," the
governor admitted. "In time I came to realize she understood that
milestone better in many respects than I did. Because what she was
excited about was not the prestige, it was the opportunity. That's
what mattered. *That's* what lasts. And I ask you, President Faust—
as your governor, your graduate, and your friend, to remember my
grandmother's wisdom and all those waiting for a chance. Use the
strong foundation your predecessors have built for you—and lean
forward. . . ."

The rain had almost stopped by the time Drew Faust stood at the podium. After a short preamble she did exactly as Governor Patrick had done ten months before. She talked about the Puritan and his famous vision of America. "As John Winthrop sat on board the ship *Arbella* in 1630 sailing across the Atlantic to found the Massachusetts Bay Colony," Harvard's newly annointed president explained, "he wrote a charge to his band of settlers, a charter for their new beginnings." In that speech (an excerpt of which her son had read in the Harvard chapel that same morning) John Winthrop had offered "a compass to steer by," she told the crowd gathered there for her anointment, adding: "I aim to offer such a 'compass' today, one for us at Harvard . . . for we are inevitably, as Winthrop urged his settlers to be, 'knit together in this work as one.'"

Heads nodded in assent.

It had always been appealing to use the Puritan's sweet vision as a guide. His words rang through the years with the uncomplicated clap of moral rightness. Yet the thoughts and principles of freedom he articulated so beautifully aboard the *Arbella* on that famous voyage were disconnected from his own experience as a master over other men just as much as they were at odds with the wording contained in the Massachusetts "Body of Liberties," which disallowed bondage in John Winthrop's colony "unless. . . ."

What a mad paradox for Winthrop's slaves at Ten Hills Farm and those of darker skin who sailed aboard the *Desire* and so many ships that followed her: all this talk of liberty and none of it for them. Yet Massachusetts had long since shed the taint of slavery. By the time Deval Patrick and Drew Faust mounted their respective stairs, hardly anyone recalled that slaves were sometimes purchased by the inch: £26 10s. for a black slave four feet, four inches and up; £21 for "Boys & Girls" who ranged from four feet tall to four feet, four inches; just £17 for any child under three feet, nine inches, wrote Medford merchant Timothy Fitch in a letter to his ship's captain in 1764.

These details did not linger in the public consciousness. Instead, they died when the slaves died, leaving only the faintest trace—and even that visible only to those who went out looking:

"The Governor has leave to keep. . . ." "I have fixed mine eye on this little one with the red about his neck. . . ." "Willed she, nilled she. . . ." "Come up in the night with them. . . ." "I give unto my daughter my Negro Woman. . . ." Mostly, though, for several hundred years, these thinnest of remnants were dwarfed by legends of the Puritans, the stylish merchants, the Revolutionary heroes, the abolitionists, the grand industrialists and towering literary figures for which Massachusetts was always so well known.

Historians have worked diligently in recent decades to unearth these other stories and dispel the myths of Northern slavery, or its lack. Yet still the powerful mythology retains its hold.

And so it is John Winthrop's words we hear today and not the thoughts of slaves. And those words still ring with elegance and force, whether voiced on the steps of city hall or in a Harvard chapel on a morning to make history. Nothing could change that. It was natural, given this history of amnesia, that the Puritan was still embraced by people of sophistication across the spectrum of American politics as a hero of national conception, "an early freedom man," as Reagan put it, the great designer of that city upon a hill, the city which, in time, became America.

"There are four essential American stories," wrote Robert Reich, the secretary of labor under President Clinton and today a frequent commentator on American politics and culture. "The first two are about hope; the second two are about fear." Reich, in a blog posted February 8, 2008, credited the Puritan with creating basic story No. 2: America's story of "The Benevolent Community."

> This is the story of neighbors and friends who roll up their sleeves and pitch in for the common good. Its earliest formulation was John Winthrop's "A Model of Christian Charity," delivered on board a ship in Salem Harbor just before the Puritans landed in 1630—a version of Matthew's Sermon on the Mount, in which the new settlers would be "as a City upon a Hill," "delight in each other," and be "of the same body." Similar communitarian and religious images were found among the abolitionists, suffragettes, and civil rights activists of the 1950s and 1960s. "I have a dream that every valley shall be exalted, every hill and mountain shall be made

low," said Martin Luther King Jr., extolling the ideal of the national community. The story is captured in the iconic New England town meeting, in frontier settlers erecting one another's barns, in neighbors volunteering as firefighters and librarians, and in small towns sending their high school achievers to college and their boys off to fight foreign wars. It suffuses Norman Rockwell's paintings and Frank Capra's movies. Consider the last scene in It's a Wonderful Life, when George learns he can count on his neighbors' generosity and goodness, just as they had always counted on him.

And so, four centuries after John Winthrop's famous journey, his legacy—somewhat edited—remains and holds its power still. "And how stands the city on this winter night?" inquired Ronald Reagan on January 11, 1989. "She's still a beacon, still a magnet for all who must have freedom, for all the pilgrims from all the lost places who are hurtling through the darkness, toward home." How well he spoke. How many hearts he moved. Yet where was Belinda in his story? Or her family? Or descendants? Certainly she and her kin did not come to America "hurtling through the darkness toward home." They went away from home, toward darkness.

"We've done our part," President Reagan cheered in that last White House speech. "And as I walk off into the city streets, a final word to the men and women of the Reagan revolution, the men and women across America who for eight years did the work that brought America back. My friends: We did it. We weren't just marking time. We made a difference. We made the city stronger. We made the city freer, and we left her in good hands." And then he shuffled off the stage himself, and left his own deep mark behind.

"Whites stand on history's mountain," President Lyndon Johnson observed in December, 1972, in the last speech he delivered before dying, "and blacks stand in history's hollow. Until we overcome unequal history, we cannot overcome unequal opportunity." It was a Texas-sized prescription for a nation with its blinders fixed. But in various ways this remedy seemed to finally gain traction at the start of this new century. Signs of the shift were subtle, but occasionally transformative.

Just a month before Drew Faust donned her presidential robes, a rather quieter installation took place beneath the gaze of Isaac Royall Jr. and his family in the Casperson Room at the Harvard Law School Library. On the afternoon of September 18, 2007, a cluster of people gathered underneath the portrait of the Benefactor to watch the "ascension," as Law School Dean Elena Kagan put it, of a new Royall Professor of Law. Like Faust, the appointee was a woman who used the moment to send a message of changing times. For one thing, she dressed for the occasion in a black leather jacket, loose pants, and scoop-neck top, not the bow-tied-buttoned-down-pressed-and-tended uniform favored by her predecessors. More importantly, she spoke not so much about the law as about the history that got her there, the money made and slaves sold and all that deep entanglement of trade.

The new holder of the chair was Janet Halley, the first Royall Professor of Law in two centuries who did not also serve as dean. This was not a slight. Rather it was a deft maneuver on the part of Elena Kagan, who had declined the chair four years before when she was named to head the law school just as it was buzzing over issues of reparations for slavery in America's corporate past. When Dean Kagan got the nod in 2003 (and the offer of the university's Royall Professorship with it), attorneys advised by Harvard professors Charles Ogletree and Cornel West (who later moved to Princeton) were busy supervising a massive lawsuit against the insurance provider Aetna Inc., the railroad giant CSX Corp., and FleetBoston Financial Corp. seeking reparations for profits dating back to the days of slavery. The wording of the suit raised the threat of waves of reparations litigation yet to come, and suddenly what no president would dare, what Congress would not do, what many in the general public only ridiculed, loomed as a potentially serious threat to organizations of all kinds—including Harvard.

There were other rumblings then as well. In the same month that Elena Kagan took the reigns in Cambridge, Ruth Simmons, the newly appointed African-American president of Brown University in Providence, Rhode Island (the first black to lead a college in the Ivy League), sent a letter to a small group of professors inviting them to consider the issue of reparations as it might specifically relate to Brown, which had its own deep history in that regard. "I hope," she wrote in the opening lines of a letter dated April 30, 2003, that you "will help the campus and the nation come to a better understanding of the complicated, controversial questions surrounding the issue of reparations for slavery." The president's mere mention of the word so unnerved some alumni they threatened to choke off further contributions. Soon enough the talk of reparations was snuffed out, and a careful retooling of the school's public relations message emerged in its stead. And so what began as a bold, indeed even a radical initiative, gradually morphed into a more familiar form—a parade of conferences and panel discussions that ended with the issuance of a lengthy report. Though some members of the committee remained determined to push for action of some sort, the political climate proved too cold for that.

At Harvard, too, the mere mention of the word "reparations" sent a chill down the spine of many an administrator, and in that atmosphere it was not only morally acute but politically expedient for the new dean of the law school to decline the Royall Chair. Kagan did so, awarding herself the Charles Hamilton Houston professorship instead, thus signaling an alignment not with a family that owned and traded African slaves throughout the 1700s, but with a black Harvard graduate who fought against Jim Crow laws and went on to lead Howard University Law School in Washington, DC.

And so the matter of the Royall Chair was left to hang . . . and hang. Suddenly, what had always been a distinction bearing high prestige was a sticky mat no one knew quite how to touch. Of course, whether the dean took the title or not, the history could no longer be so deftly sweetened. Nor would it go away. Echoes of that past lay everywhere for anyone who knew to look. There it was in the Law School seal (topped with its stern imperative, *veritas*) and featuring the Master's seal—three sheaves of wheat to signal plenty. There it was there in the Feke painting in the Casperson Room where the Benefactor, born in Antigua, stood above his wife (heir to a slave estate in Surinam) and her sister (co-heir) and his own sister Penelope (who not only shared the inheritance of the Master's operations in Antigua but married a man, Henry Vassall, whose money poured out of slaves and sugar in Jamaica, and whose relatives were strung like pearls down Brattle Street).

Janet Halley, a scholar whose work explored diversity, feminism, gay rights, and issues of discrimination, was hardly one to duck a fight. And so in accepting the Royall professorship on that September afternoon, she did not dodge. Instead, she opened her remarks by naming every holder of the Royall Chair (an impressive list of accomplished white males) and ended with the name of every Royall slave whose name was known (an impressive recapitulation of obscurity). In between she talked about the Benefactor, the plantation in Antigua, the buying and selling of workers and their children, and how it all related to the law school's founding. For months, research assistants had combed archives and college records. She came to her ascension well prepared.

Questioned about this history afterwards, the new Royall Professor of Law answered without pause: "I want to grasp this thistle. . . . This is a hard legacy. But I promise you. I am going to have fun with it."

Ill-chosen as those last few words were, times were changing, and the change was not confined to Harvard Square, where the distant noise of reparations still sometimes troubled administrators' sleep.

Up in Medford, at what remained of Ten Hills Farm, a similar time of reappraisal had begun. There, the force of President Johnson's words was keenly felt. *Until we overcome unequal history. . . .* On that ground, 368 years after John Winthrop "was given leave to keep . . . ," the lives of slaves were finally being brought into the light to whatever extent possible by scholars, archaeologists, and guides at what had become a National Historic Site operated by the Royall House Association. At last on that old ground, the story of the farm was changing in important ways. It was changing to become more true, more complicated, and more difficult.

Of course all that was left of the farm by then was a scant bit of land bordered on all sides by urban sprawl and humming traffic.

The six hundred acres of the original property were long since sub-sumed in the urban landscapes of Medford and Somerville. What remains today is just the Royall House, the slave quarters, and a fragment of an acre of open space. Yet on that small plot bordered by George and Royall streets, the Master's mansion still stood proud. The elm-lined drive was gone. The fabulous gardens? Gone. The carriage houses and barns and rolling fences to the riverside? All gone. The fetching octagonal gazebo was no more. Of its eight sides only one remained, freshly painted, set up beside a brick wall, hinting at those glory days. The sculpture of Mercury, the god of commerce, that once stood optimistically on the structure's roof, one hip thrust out, a quiver at the ready, was armless now, pitted with weather marks, stuck unceremoniously in a dusty attic space where slaves once slept, a place away from the insistent stare of those few tourists who came by.

The main house, painted a cool gray-blue, its slender walk-ways freshly swept, remained largely unchanged. Electricity never made it there. The window glass was rippled, still; the floorboards wide and dark. Though the slave quarters now had electricity and hosted a simple caretaker's apartment on its closed-off sec-ond story, the wide fireplace where Belinda and other slaves once cooked still wore the carbon mark of many fires. But now it was the slave building that was the center of attention, not the fabulous mansion to its side. "Georgian mansions are a dime a dozen in Massachusetts," explained Peter Gittleman, a preservationist with Historic New England. Indeed, the farm's last paradox was that it was George and Belinda who would likely save it.

By 2007 the slave quarters had become the property's prime at-traction, touted by the Royal House Association as "the only such structure in the Northern United States." The boast—and it was one—was almost certainly overstated. Scholars with more reason for caution limit the claim to the Northeast, and should be quick to add the qualifier "still standing." Even with that asterisk, the boast may not be true. Few places rush to make the claim or hold that history up for public view. Yet even at the Royall House, trying as it was to replay history in some broadly elaborated way, there were odd limits on public memory. Despite the energy generated by various investigations of the property's slave past, the slave quarters still doubled as a gift shop and lecture hall, and across the way in the main house the clocks were moved back only to the time of Loyalists who fled, no further, a stopping point that wittingly or not left many a contemporary visitor with an almost subconscious feeling of relief: *Well, we got rid of that!*

Which was true, but never the whole story.

And so, while Drew Faust moved into Elmwood and Janet Halley vowed "to grasp this thistle," in Medford the Master and his son remained the focus of attention. The Master's slaves; the Master's history in Antigua; the Master's importation of the twenty-seven; his construction of the slave quarters; his son's ascension to the highest echelons of prewar society, and the family's departure on the eve of war, were all described in some detail in plaques and in the occasional lecture, while still a deep and seemingly impenetrable silence attended John Winthrop's history in this regard. And of John Usher and his illegal importation, there was not a word.

Despite these rather extraordinary omissions, the history of slavery yet lingered in plain sight. Anyone mailing a package at the Medford Post Office on Forest Street all these centuries after Henry Winthrop first sailed for Barbados (and Samuel, the youngest, settled in Antigua as lieutenant governor) waits for the privilege underneath the *Golden Triangle of Trade*, a wall-length triptych painted during the Great Depression by the New Deal artist Henry Billings.

In that mural, panels to the left and right exhibit the region's rise to wealth. On one side lies a shipyard and the image of a still; on the other, a more primitive scene depicts a cane press, thatched hut, palm tree, and the mast of a great schooner. At the center stands a map. It shows a triangle made of gold that stretches from the coast of Africa to the Caribbean, turns abruptly north to the Massachusetts Bay, then angles back to Africa in endless repetition. On a beach in the foreground, a tall black man bends forever underneath a load of cane, his muscled form clad only in a pair of tattered knee-length pants, shackles lying open next to his bare

19.2 Medford Post Office, showing WPA mural, 2008. Author's photo.

feet. At his left, a trimly uniformed white sailor, one hand in his pocket, his frame slumped casually against a hitching post, forever watches that man work.

But what are those shackles in the sand?

Unlocked?

A sign of freedom?

A wish?

A lie. Freedom never turned that engine. But memory can be tricked.

By the time of the Great Depression, when Henry Billings raised his brush, Medford was becoming a busy city of the working class. In the midst of that transformation, many older white residents longed for a fantasy past, a happier era marked by status, refinement, elegance, and wealth. To be sure, the change had happened

19.3 Detail of Medford Post Office mural, 2008. Author's photo.

fast. Between 1890 and 1920, Medford's population doubled, then tripled and quadrupled under a press of impoverished immigrants from Italy and Ireland who came to stoke the fires of a new industrial era. They sought a place to put down roots. For thousands, Medford was that place. The change at Ten Hills Farm was swift and almost total. The land was sold. Bulldozers scraped at ancient fields and turned a rural bower into a grid of streets and tangles of new housing.

In the midst of this upheaval, the Royall House stood as an isolated reminder, albeit a decrepit one, of the town's more genteel beginnings. The mansion, though its frame was old and its grounds were much diminished, retained a certain elegance as though it simply would not bow to depradations. After the Revolution, the house had functioned briefly as a boarding school. Then, in 1804, after protracted legal negotiations, one of Isaac Royall's grand-daughters reclaimed the property, put it up for sale, and went off with her profit. In 1810, a wealthy Boston merchant named Jacob Tidd bought the farm to be his summertime retreat. There he spent his free time in the gentle passion of cultivating fruit. For him the magic of the place still held, as did the pedigree, as did the triangle. Rum was how he made his fortune; and rum in 1810 was still the oil that slicked the trade.

When Jacob Tidd died, his wife moved to Medford and settled at the farm. She lived at Ten Hills Farm another forty years, an aging widow allowing her old manse to fade as she did. On the eve of the Civil War, she died and the farm was sold; it would be resold and eventually whittled down by a sequence of new owners. Then the developers came. By the 1890s the land was barely recognizable, the last remnant just a rattle-filled old house set back from Main Street. That house was not called "Royallville" as the Benefactor had commanded in his will, or even the "Royall House" as it is known today, or Ten Hills Farm, but "Hobgoblin Hall," a casual tag that made a playful stab at the ancient structure's creaking eaves, dusty passages, and restless ghosts.

In 1898, as immigration spiked, local members of the Daughters of the American Revolution decided to preserve this threatened relic. For almost a decade, they laid their plans and gathered funds. Then, in 1907, the Royall House Association was formed. The group bought the mansion and slave quarters and the three-fourths of an acre the dwellings sat on. Next came projects to allow for the site's refurbishment. Meetings and teas were held. The group hit on a bold idea. They would host a three-day theatrical extravaganza to gin up interest in American history and raise funds for the mansion's preservation and repair. Planning sessions were held in the slave quarters, just as meetings are today.

"The Pageant of the Royall House" took place in June, 1915. It was a grand event, and it endeavored to trace the property's history from the era of its first inhabitants until the dawning of the Revolutionary War and the appearance of George Washington at that front door.

John Winthrop was there, of course. He wore a hat and smoked a "peace pipe" with Indians who gave him—*vacuum domicilium*—what he had already given to himself with the king's express approval: "Six hundred acres of land, to be set forth by metes and bounds, near his house in Mistick, to enjoy him and his heirs forever."

At the pageant young women played the spirits of the seasons, of the river and the woods. They danced in white with flowing scarves and flowers in their hair. Isaac and Penelope were there, of course. They strutted across the lawn in full costume, prim in silks and wool and powdered wigs, then danced a minuet among their friends. As time rushed forward over those three days, the Benefactor would agonize about the coming of a war and foolishly elect to leave. John Stark came next. Then George Washington showed up on his horse. Like Isaac Royall and his kin, those famous Patriots were gently tended by Belinda and by George, the slave who killed himself on learning that his master planned to sell him off the farm.

The drama closed on a Saturday with what the program described as a "full chorus of Pageanters" singing of the "abiding woodland" (gone), the stream (buried) and mead (replaced by roads and businesses), and the Royall House itself "Like an old mother," her ancient boards and glistening windows a "mellowing shrine of Medford's memories."

"Mellowing," indeed. Two or three hundred people were expected to participate in the pageant, according to a note written by finance committee chairman Charles S. Taylor seeking funds. He was confident the occasion would prove "the most notable affair in the annals of Medford." Sure enough, even in the Royalls' time no more ambitious a gathering was ever hosted at the site. And this event, a newspaper account approved, was different in one important aspect. The "Pageant of the Royall House," the paper said, would represent "the entire city; the cast, dancers, choruses, as well as the committee in charge being drawn from *every part of the community*."

Well, not quite.

19.4 Boys in blackface; from the 1915 celebration at the Royall House.
Courtesy Historic New England Library and Archives.

Though the 1910 census reported more than four hundred blacks making their homes in Medford in that era, a blizzard of postcards, photographs, and other surviving records of the three-day extravaganza shows not a single black man, woman, or child involved. This is not to say there were no black *faces* in that crowd of reenactors. Belinda and George were represented by whites—in blackface. They showed up to bid Isaac Royall goodbye and help General George Washington dismount from his horse. Belinda's 1783 petition was read aloud, perhaps to show the dawning of a more benevolent era. But did those Medford actors add that she was never paid in full?

Unlikely.

The broader slave community was shown as well. Yet none of those performers hailed from Medford's African-American community. Instead, it was white boys from the high school glee club who played slaves "singing for their dinner" back by the "out-kitchen" door. Images of the event preserved in the archives of Historic New England show the boys in blackface on a bench outside the slave quarters, grasping the thistle in their way. Several of them are squirming. Others grin for the camera, thinking who knows what? And a few are making faces. One boy, seated to the right, his hat mashed back to show a nappy wig, thrusts his lips out thick and makes his eyes go wide. He is the thistle, too.

Afterword

Letter from Antigua,
Easter Monday, 2008

◆

There is an old man who works at the Sunsail Club Colonna down by Royall's Bay who is known to pour a bit of beer on the floor every time he passes the place where long ago a sturdy, gnarled tamarind tree was used for hanging slaves. The beer is a mindful offering to ancestors who perished there, an emollient to some lost relative or distant god, or the ghosts of times long gone. *Jumbie, jumbie*. Ghost. Ghost. The word trips off the tongue of many an Antiguan, signifying restless spirits troubled by the past.

On this Easter Monday (the same day, I think idly, John Winthrop sat to write the first pages of his journal), I go to see a place called Devil's Bridge on Antigua's southeast tip. It is a rough, natural place, a span of rock across an open drop to boulders, waves, and water. The bridge is sharp and bumpy underfoot, and it is narrow. The fall would be quick and possibly deadly, especially for anyone who could not swim. White spray flies overhead. Salt catches on the tongue. It is hot and dry and windy.

On an island that claims 365 beaches made of the finest powdered sand (a different beach for each day of the year, tourists are cheerfully informed), this place is an aberration, full of the race of water and the possibility of injury. Today the waves are high and the wind is strong. On the desiccated point of land just past Devil's Bridge, families have gathered to celebrate the holiday by flying kites. The crowd is loosely formed and interracial. But here, as it is everywhere in Antigua, black faces dominate. Music blares from

A.1 Kite day at Devil's Bridge, Antigua, 2008. Author's photo.

an amplifier hooked to a truck battery. Under a small canopy, a man is selling kites. People stop to chat with him and sometimes buy a plastic triangle that lifts into the air with a sudden exhilarating jerk. Some groups carefully tend kites that stretch in three dimensions: here a puppy, there a fish, the fluttering figure of a scuba

A.2 Kite day, father and child, Antigua, 2008. Author's photo.

diver, a pair of disembodied legs (wind billowing through an open waistband at the hip), a dragon, a tire, a fluttering black ghost.

I had asked Gwendolyn Payne, an elderly black woman who had folded towels at the Mill Reef Club for forty years, to tell me the story behind Devil's Bridge. The question ended our conversation. "There *is* a story," she answered. "Nobody knows if it is true." But here, the man hawking kites repeats what I already know. "Slaves came here to commit suicide when they couldn't stand it anymore," he says, yanking at a bit of string and bending forward to help a customer.

Isaac Royall's plantation, like Ten Hills Farm in Massachusetts, is built up now. On his hundred acres by the sea—all the land it took to build such wealth—there is a relatively new development called Royall's Garden, full of stucco houses, chain-link boundaries, and large dogs that roam the fence lines. Cows munch on grass beside the road. An occasional goat cries out of sight. All the sugar is gone. Instead, scrub, dry grass, and bushes litter the landscape where it is not tended. The road is made of shells and bits of rock and it is bumpy enough to slow down every car that passes.

The place where Isaac Royall lived is set considerably back from the water. The towering stone mill is there to mark the spot. It stands intact, though the machinery has long since been sold or stolen and the sails and their wood frames are missing, too. The main house is less than a memory. Most likely it was carted off by people who wanted dwellings for themselves and tore the thing apart over the years, cannibalizing its contents and chipping away at its foundations. Where the big house stood, now there is a small veterinary clinic run by the daughter of the man who got it in his head in 1988 to rebuild an old estate house for his home. Though the Royall House was already gone, the manager's house was standing. He chose that, and took a seventy-five-year lease from the government and set about his lengthy renovation. It has been his family's home for several decades now.

When I arrive to visit, seven dogs rush toward the gate. Lotte Edwards, white-haired, smiling, wearing a loose cotton dress, green-striped apron, and red sandals, shoos the dogs off with a sharp command and extends an exceedingly warm welcome. Every hopeless case her daughter takes, she shrugs, ends up as a family pet. Still, there are so many dogs on the island it is not clear at first there is anything at all unusual about the density on this particular fenced-in plot.

Lotte flurries me inside for a piece of apple tart and a tour of the refurbished house. But before we enter through the back, I spot something familiar and bend to pick it up. It is a shard from some previous era at the estate, blue and white and covered with fine cobalt painting. "Oh, those are everywhere," Lotte tells me dismissively. "I'll give you some." Later she hands me a plastic zip bag full of fragments.

At the kitchen table, her husband Malcolm Edwards is enjoying a glass of midday wine. He rises, offers me a chair, and pulls out several old photo albums. And so the story begins, or begins again, or begins somewhere in the middle now. Malcolm is a man meticulous in his personal habits and careful in his speech. An electrical engineer by training, he met Lotte, who is Danish, in London, where they both were studying fifty years ago. They fell in love, and when Lotte told her friends that she was leaving, "everyone had to ask me where Antigua was!" she laughs.

As Malcolm flips through old photographs of the renovation project, he describes something of his own past, unprompted. "I had a grandfather who was Irish. I've gotten that far," he explains. "One of my grandmothers was Portuguese. The other two halves of my family were black." He carries all this history in his light amber complexion, his graying tight-curled hair, and a certain calm bearing that implies he would feel at home in almost any environment or circumstance.

In the 1980s, when Malcolm started looking for an old estate house to refinish, most were already gone: appropriated by government officials and members of the elite, spirited off stone by stone and board by board by homeless people in the night, too far gone for renovation. These, Malcolm explains, were not some icon of the past to be preserved, but a tug of troubling history (like the sugar mills, 109 of which still stand, roughly one for every square mile on that dry and gorgeous island). "I looked at fourteen," Malcolm explains of his 1980s house hunting experience. "They were all subsequently destroyed," He blames Antigua's first prime minister, V. C. Bird, for that. At the Royalls' place at Hodges Bay, the manager's house was in relatively good condition. At least it was still standing. The main dwelling, on the other hand, was just a puzzle in the ground, recognizable only when Malcolm found the remnant of the cistern here, an outline of the old foundation there. "I was lucky to find this one." He pushed the album forward across the table. Color photographs from thirty years ago capture tangles of tropical growth, an abandoned stone façade, trees growing through its open windows.

"After working on this building for a year," Malcolm explains, nodding toward the kitchen, "she was crying."

"No!" Lotte calls back energetically. "I was screaming!"

They both laugh. The renovation took almost two years. Lotte slides several plates of apple tart onto the table and holds a bottle of wine aloft. It was, she says with a meaningful look, "just bees, mongooses, and mud."

The conversation drifts. They had a jumbie, too. That ghost was a tall, thin black man who told the Edwards' helper he used to eat from metal plates. Lotte contributes another detail. "Every night when I hung out my washing, it would be on the ground by the next day. I always wondered if it wasn't the jumbie. That he just didn't want us here. . . ."

"Oh, Lotte," interrupts her husband. Crazy talk of ghosts.

Up on the second story, the couple's bedroom window looks out on Isaac Royall's sugar mill on one side and to the coastline on another. It is possible, standing in that room, to imagine the land as the Master and the Benefactor and Ann and Penne may have known it. In their day the island was planted coast to coast in cane. Great vistas of waving green were interrupted only by the white cut of narrow roads. That sight, for them, meant safety. For in the tangle of the hills where maroons carved out a rudimentary living, it was possible to hide and launch attacks.

From Malcolm and Lotte's bedroom window only the thinnest glint of blue is visible. Houses, trees, and scrub now block the water's view. But I find myself considering how the Master directed Jacob to drain the marsh down by the Mystic River back in Medford and plant a lawn of grass down to its banks, building a familiar vista. I recall, too, how he arranged for the renovation and expansion of John Usher's house and finished it with a wood façade cut to look like stone, another echo of that life he knew.

At the National Archives here, a modern building set just outside the low and bustling city of St. John's, the Codrington Papers offer thousands of documents detailing the ways and patterns of slavery on this island. Among the papers (the originals of which

A.3 Entrance to the Mill Reef Club, Antigua, 2008. Author's photo.

reside in England, with only microfilm for viewers here) are several letters between the Master and his son and that much wealthier and more influential family. The letters show these families' business ties. They are dry fare, full of tight script that talks in a gentlemanly way about the price of rum, the price of sugar. Nothing in that material shakes my understanding of the family and its time on this dry soil. Yet when I ask the archives' director, Dr. Marion Blair, to check baptismal records for St. John's, she produces what I seek, but also something more, something I had not expected. There is the notation for the master's son John, who did not survive into adulthood. And there is the entry, 23 September, 1719, showing "Isaac, Son of Isaac Royall and his Wife" being christened on that day. But Dr. Blair has scribbled something else beneath that

A.4 Malcolm and Lotte Edwards and family, Antigua, 2008.
Courtesy Ricardo Sealy.

note. I bend to read her script. She has transcribed the record of another Royall baptism on that September day in 1719. This one is for "Mary a negro living at Isaac Royall."

Why, I am left to wonder, among the scores of men, women, and children the Royalls bought and sold and worked and gave away and willed to relatives and buried, is there just this single record of a "negro" baptized?

On the car radio at noon a talk show host is fielding questions from as far off as New Jersey. The subject of the moment is why the Antiguan pay scale is so low. Much of the discussion is taken up with an argument about the Mill Reef Club. The talk spins down a familiar curve. Some callers are defensive. They believe the government set wages low years ago so the island could compete with other tourist destinations of the Caribbean. People at Mill Reef wanted to pay more, they argue earnestly, but they were stopped. Other callers are angry, and blame a system that always has exploited black workers on the island. The conversation, though impassioned, is restrained and unflaggingly polite.

But it circles in a loop, caller to caller, with no sense that anything will change.

As the program ends the station switches to quiet music and its noontime fare. A woman's voice reads aloud a list of names of people who have died. It is a small island and the intimacy compelled by size comes home in this gentle ritual. Though relatives are scattered, they are acknowledged on the airwaves here: *beloved sister of . . . ; beloved mother of . . . ; beloved uncle, aunt, grandfather, son, daughter, niece, nephew. . . .* Friends and relatives are named. They live here on the island still or in Miami, the Dominican Republic, Trenton, Barbados, Chicago, Detroit, Tampa, Paris. Bermuda. Beyond.

Out on a rough soccer field on the Royalls' old estate a group of boys in yellow shirts kicks up a cloud of dust as the sun drops down in the turquoise sea not far away. It is dry again this year. The price of gasoline is up. Along the roadways people walk for miles wearing holes into their shoes.

Note to Readers

Many of the quotations in this text have been altered to reflect contemporary spellings. I have made these edits to allow the reader to move easily through the narrative without having to constantly struggle to decipher perfectly familiar words. In places, however, I retain spellings faithful to the original in order to deepen the sense of life as it was experienced in another era. These inconsistencies are intentional. Readers will also note rather radical changes to Boston's shoreline in the maps presented here. Boston's landscape expanded over the centuries as marshland was filled and the ragged contours of the harbor were smoothed and extended toward the sea. Readers interested in that aspect of Massachusetts history will want to find *Gaining Ground: The History of Landmaking in Boston* for a detailed explanation of how the city grew.

Most Americans remain unaware of the North's extensive links to slavery and the slave trade. For myself, though I was born in Boston and privileged with a fine education, this history was new. And so I embarked on this project to fill a troubling void in my own consciousness. I began, too, with the simple aim of telling the story of a farm. For me, this work has been a revelation. I will never see America in the same light again. For that awakening I am grateful, and profoundly humbled.

In the years during which my life was given over to this project I came to appreciate how many historians have explored this material before me. In addition to books cited in the following notes, I commend the following authors for their groundbreaking work. Elizabeth Donnan's remarkable four-volume set, *Documents Illustrative of the History of the Slave Trade to America (1930–1935)*, and Lorenzo Johnston Greene's *The Negro in Colonial New*

England, 1620–1776 (1942) paved the way for many scholars. Jay Coughtry's *The Notorious Triangle: Rhode Island and the African Slave Trade* (1981), and *Black Yankees: The Development of an African-American Subculture in Eighteenth Century New England* (1988) by William Dillon Piersen awakened another generation. In the 1990s, *Root and Branch, African Americans in NY and East Jersey, 1613–1863* (1999) by Graham Russell Hodges and *Disowning Slavery: Gradual Emancipation and "Race" in New England 1780–1860* (1998) by Joanne Pope Melish added immeasurably to our understanding of slavery in the North. More recently, the journalists Anne Farrow, Joel Lang, and Jenifer Frank at the *Hartford Courant* exposed Connecticut's earliest ties to slavery and the slave trade. Their important series from 2002 is now the book *Complicity: How the North Promoted, Prolonged and Profited from Slavery* (2006), with an introduction by Evelyn Higginbotham. Readers seeking the latest scholarship in this field as well as material on highly specific topics in this vein are encouraged to search the database of the *William and Mary Quarterly*, which contains an extensive repository of articles on early American history and culture. Also of use is the relatively new web resource, *Early American Books Online*, which provides readers with exactly what its title promises.

In 2005–2006 the New York Historical Society's extraordinary exhibit "Slavery in New York" drew national attention and enlightened millions of Americans to the difficult realities of slavery in that important city. Though the exhibit has closed, the website and book accompanying the exhibit remain. *In the Shadow of Slavery: African Americans in New York City, 1626–1863* (2003) by Leslie Harris and Jill Lepore's *New York Burning: Liberty, Slavery, and Conspiracy in Eighteenth-century Manhattan* (2005) provide a deep and nuanced sense of New York City's history in this regard. Readers will also want to see Shane White's *Somewhat More Independent: The End of Slavery in New York City* (1995) and Ira Berlin's exceptional work, *Many Thousands Gone* (2000). For those seeking a broader grounding in the roots of colonial life (including the roles and experiences of the Spanish, Dutch, and French), there could hardly be a better book than *American Colonies: The Settling of North America* (2001) by Alan Taylor. This work, part of the Penguin History of the United States edited by Eric Foner, does a truly masterful job of laying out the settlement of this region using the best new scholarship available. It is an awakening.

Why then, does this void persist, and so many Americans not know this aspect of our past? There are probably as many answers to that question as there are people to ponder it. More important to me is the notion—indeed the hope—that we may finally close this gap. Textbooks and general histories have too often dismissed references to slavery in the North with a parenthetical acknowledgment, or dismissed the fact in just a few short sentences. That should change. Some of the best historical overviews in print today continue in that pattern. It is not enough. We need this knowledge, to be whole.

NOTES ON SOURCES

This book was written with the generous support of the National Endowment for the Humanities, the American Antiquarian Society, Harvard University's W.E.B. DuBois Institute for African and African American Research, and the Newhouse Center for the Humanities at Wellesley College. I thank each institution for providing funding, time, space to work, and access to their exceptional collections. Harvard University, where I was a research fellow in these years, provided unlimited access to its extensive library system both in person and via the Internet. My gratitude and humility in the face of those resources is profound. Google Books must also be mentioned here as it provided, with the touch of a computer key, access to materials that otherwise would have taken weeks to procure, if they were available at all. The search engine in that tool, while not flawless, is impressive and saved me countless hours better used for other work. Every month now more materials come online. Bravo to the individuals who make it happen.

To create a weave of the kind I have attempted here I needed to cull materials and information from an unusually wide range of sources. These have included rare documents dating back to the 1500s made available to me during the year I spent as a fellow at the American Antiquarian Society in Worcester, Massachusetts; original materials including letters, diaries, shipping accounts, wills, inventories, newspaper articles, legal records, and advertisements dating from two, three, and four centuries ago and available through various archives and online engines; and eighteenth-, nineteenth-, and twentieth-century histories and multiple other secondary materials contained in libraries and other repositories throughout the northeast United States. To round out this work I interviewed a range of individuals including museum curators, preservationists, scholars, archeologists, and some of the people who now inhabit the homes and acres that take up room within these pages.

No character or bit of dialogue here is fictional, nor were any events imagined or invented to help in the telling of this tale. Where I occasionally felt compelled to employ imaginative devices to smooth the narrative or provide the reader with a more visceral sense of this ground's history I have indicated as much, as when I describe the specific details of the farm by urging the reader to "Imagine a man passing there in summer. . . ." In that instance, my understanding of the farm's aspect in that time was gleaned from detailed descriptions of the property appearing in old letters as well as property deeds held at the Middlesex County courthouse in Cambridge, Massachusetts.

At several points I allowed myself to imagine what might have passed through a character's mind at an important juncture in life, as when I pictured Isaac Royall first considering the ground that would soon become his plantation in Antigua: "He must have stood on salty ground there, out by Beggars Point, with his back to the warm sea. . . ." The attentive reader will see that I have made such flights of fancy clear in the language I employed. On the very rare occasion when I found it necessary to imagine a character's language or specific thoughts (John Stark's son saying, *I'm here to fight . . .*) I employed italicized text to signal a departure from the standard conventions of nonfiction. Lastly, in one or two cases I adopted dialogue imagined by another writer, as when I quoted John Stark and his son Caleb in conversation before the start of the Battle of Bunker Hill. The dialogue comes from a memoir about the general's life penned by his grandson one hundred years after the battle, a fact that I noted in context.

Throughout, I have taken pains to provide readers with guideposts to sources. These often include folding references to sourcing into the body of the narrative. However, to cite the source of every quotation and fact within the narrative would render the work leaden and, I believe, unreadable. Too, to cite every source in a work that attempts to traverse so much history in so few pages would take a volume almost as large as this one. In my effort to find a balance between credibility and narrative flow I therefore have incorporated some source citations into the text and held others aside. Quotations that appear in the text with no indication of source are credited below with the exception of material so broadly reproduced that a citation is virtually meaningless. I do cite some widely available material, however, to give readers a springboard if they wish to do further study. Citations appear below, arranged sequentially, chapter by chapter. It is my wish in the following notes and citations, as it has been throughout the writing of this book, to make my process transparent.

LETTER FROM ANTIGUA

In the spring of 2008 I traveled to Antigua to complete the final phase of my research. There I drew on my years as a journalist and foreign correspondent to take the island in through every sense. The letters that resulted were written in Antigua and are grounded almost solely in scenes witnessed, conversations held, or materials studied while there. In these pages I drew from formal interviews and casual conversations, official island records, and research conducted at the Antigua and Barbuda National Archives and the Antigua Public Library in St. John's. In addition, I trolled through the bookshelves of my host, the Antiguan attorney John Fuller, an avid historian with a remarkable library and a highly nuanced perception of the island's past and present. It was John who first took me to the Royall estate and introduced me to Malcolm and Lotte Edwards. The warmth and welcome they extended and John's generosity were welcome gifts in a visit filled with unexpected treasures. The island and its people moved me deeply. Chance encounters, snatches of talk radio programs, and other ephemera proved useful as well. Where I found it necessary to confirm facts and assertions, I did so. For example, after witnessing the protest march winding up the road outside the National Archives building, I scoured local newspapers and then went online to do further research. At the National Archives I owe particular gratitude to Dr. Marion Blair for her patient assistance and willingness to let me copy some of the rare materials that institution keeps.

PART I: The Puritan

The American Antiquarian Society in Worcester, Massachusetts, contains more than three million items of historical interest, including books, letters, pamphlets, broadsides, newspapers, maps, and other print materials covering American history from colonial times through the Civil War and Reconstruction. I arrived at this extraordinary institution as a fellow in the fall of 2005 having only the vaguest sense of where this book would lead. I could have wished for no better embarkation. When I was curious about something dating to America's earliest days of settlement oftentimes I had only to ask a librarian and she or he would dart back into the stacks and emerge with an original copy of some obscure but helpful text. This proved an exquisite window into a far-gone time. During my year with the society I pored through antique maps, early histories, collections of letters, and original copies of newspapers, finding a trove of material that helped me build a picture of the struggles, realities, and mores of that time. Key general sources there included the group's many shelves of books from the New England Historic Genealogical Society (NEHGS). The NEHGS online research engine, available at NewEnglandAncestors.org, eventually made my research easier and faster; but those first days of flipping through actual pages provided many a serendipitous moment and proved crucial to my awakening understanding of the importance and complexity of the ties and relationships that linked so many of the first families who settled in America. The American Antiquarian Society's map collection also provided invaluable help in that it allowed me to see geographical and historical relationships I might otherwise have missed. Several early maps of Antigua, for example, show where every major estate was situated on the island and allowed me to understand viscerally who was a neighbor to whom. Slowly, I came to appreciate more and more why that mattered.

Several works were of particular importance to me in my year at the AAS and they remained for months on the trolley that held my most treasured sources. John Winthrop's journal contains remarkable details of his journey across the Atlantic as well as myriad insights into the struggles and triumphs of the first years of colonization. Many editions of this work exist and I consulted most of them, but the 1996 edition of this material released by Harvard University Press and edited by Richard S. Dunn, James Savage, and Laetitia Yeandle was far and away my most trusted and visited source. Most of John Winthrop's quotations and nearly all of my general sense of the momentous voyage he led came from these journal pages. Also key were the *Life and Letters of John Winthrop* (1864, 1867) edited by his descendant, Robert C. Winthrop; the six-volume *Winthrop Papers*, published by the Massachusetts Historical Society in 1947; and *The Winthrop Family in America*, edited by Lawrence Shaw Mayo, released in 1948, reissued in 1989. The *Massachusetts Historical Collections* and other multivolume sets regarding Massachusetts history rounded out my understanding. I leafed through these volumes time and time again. Biographies and histories were, of course, useful as well. Francis J. Bremer's *John Winthrop: America's Forgotten Founding Father* (2003) stood out among the many histories I read about Winthrop's life and work. Other important sources included Edmund S. Morgan's *The Puritan Dilemma: The Story of John Winthrop* (1958); the 1930 classic, *The Planters of the Commonwealth* by Charles Edward Banks, which includes lists of passengers on early ships; and the *History of Cambridge, Massachusetts 1630–1877*, by Lucius R. Paige, published in 1877. Material regarding the scandal involving John Winthrop's devious manager James Luxford came from, among other sources, the *Proceedings of the Massachusetts Historical Society*, second series, volume 7.

General information regarding early laws and noteworthy events is available in *Records of the Governor and Company of the Massachusetts Bay in New England Printed by Order of the Legislature* (1853), edited by Nathaniel B. Shurtleff. *Gaining Ground: A History of Landmaking in Boston*, by Nancy Seasholes (2003), an eminently readable examination of Boston's changing shoreline, provided a gritty understanding of the city's physical growth. It is a fascinating book.

Margaret Ellen Newell's wonderful study of early America's evolving economic life, *From Dependency to Independence: Economic Revolution in Colonial New England* (1998), provided countless insights into financial realities of the colonial period and how those realities affected the lives of early settlers. Bernard Bailyn's 1955 classic, *The New England Merchants in the Seventeenth Century*, proved exceptionally useful as well.

For details of daily life including food, dress, housing styles, and other banal but crucial elements of the settlers' lives I relied heavily upon *Every Day Life in the Massachusetts Bay Colony* (1935) by George Francis Dow. It was Dow, for example, who described the early dwellings of settlers just off the boat, and Dow who provided images of ships and lists of store inventories that helped me imagine life almost four hundred years ago. Information about Medford in that day came in part from the *History of the Town of Medford, Middlesex County, Massachusetts, from Its First Settlement in 1630 to the Present Time, 1855*, by Charles Brooks. A later edition of that work released in 1886 and edited and updated by John M. Usher also proved useful at times. Various other materials held at the Antiquarian Society in Worcester and the Massachusetts Historical Society in Boston helped me complete my view of Massachusetts during John Winthrop's time.

The Younger John Winthrop by Robert C. Black III, published by Columbia University Press in 1966, Richard S. Dunn's *Puritans and Yankees* (1962), and letters and other original materials from the six-volume *Winthrop Papers* published by the Massachusetts Historical Society provided material on John Winthrop Jr. from his youth through his rise to the position of governor of Connecticut.

Finally, Alfred A. Cave's *The Pequot War*, published in 1996, provided important important information on that early conflict. The magnificently gripping story of the first settlers told in *Mayflower: A Story of Courage, Community, and War* by Nathaniel Philbrick not only provided me with an elegantly written account of the colonies' earliest roots and those first settlers' relationships with the indigenous population but with a model of nonfiction written with assurance and grace. All these books and institutions buoyed me, informed me, and set my compass right.

Chapter 1: The Land

chief proprietor and commander-in-chief. . . . Robert C. Winthrop. *Life and Letters of John Winthrop.* Vol. 2 (1869): *From his Embar-*

kation for New England in 1630, With the Charter and Company of the Massachusetts Bay, to his Death in 1649. Page 34.

pleasantest island in all the West Indies. . . . This quotation appears in multiple sources. Here I quote from a letter from Henry Winthrop to Thomas Fones. *Collections of the Massachusetts Historical Society.* Vol 8. Fifth series. Page 179.

We are very glad to hear so good news. . . . Letter from Margaret Winthrop to her husband. Robert C. Winthrop. *Life and Letters of John Winthrop.* Vol. 1 (1864): *Governor of the Massachusetts-Bay Company at Their Emigration to New England, 1630.* Page 247.

I have found two sturdy youths. . . . Letter from John Winthrop to his son. Winthrop. *Life and Letters.* Vol. 1. Page 250.

So ill-conditioned, foul, and full of stalks. . . . Letter from John Winthrop to his son Henry. Winthrop. *Life and Letters.* Vol. 1. Page 285.

I have no money. . . . Letter from John Winthrop to his son Henry. Winthrop. *Life and Letters.* Vol. 1. Page 285.

. . . adventurers or traffickers. . . . Life and Letters. Vol. 1. Page 346.

We see how frail and vain. . . . Letter from John Winthrop to his wife. Winthrop. *Life and Letters.* Vol. 1. Page 290.

not one quarter of an hour's time. . . . Letter from John Winthrop to his wife. Winthrop. *Life and Letters.* Vol. 1. Page 334.

We are now agreed. . . . Letter from John Winthrop to his wife. Winthrop. *Life and Letters.* Vol. 1. Page 334.

. . . it hath pleased the Lorde. . . . Letter from John Winthrop to his wife. Winthrop. *Life and Letters.* Vol. 1. Page 340.

I have conferred with him. . . . Letter from John Winthrop to John Winthrop Jr. *Life and Letters.* Vol. 1. Page 335.

Some would discourage us. . . . Letter from John Winthrop to his wife. Winthrop. *Life and Letters.* Vol. 1. Page 356.

We shall be as a city upon a hill. . . . Historians disagree whether this famous sermon, "A Model of Christian Charity," was delivered on the decks of the *Arbella* or on shore just before the ship set sail. Whichever the case, the text has been preserved and can be found in multiple sources, though perhaps most easily online at the website of the Winthrop Society.

The first keeper of the New England conscience. . . . Richard S. Dunn, *Puritans and Yankees.* 1962. Page 4.

. . . three shots out of the steerage. . . . This quote and almost all other particulars of John Winthrop's voyage aboard the *Arbella* are taken directly from John Winthrop's account of the sailing recorded in his journal and reprinted in various editions. I relied most heavily on the 1996 Harvard University Press edition edited by Dunn, Savage, and Yeandle.

We have many young gentlemen. . . . Robert C. Winthrop. *Life and Letters.* Vol. 2. Quoting from Winthrop's journal. Page 17.

The Lord's hand hath been heavy. . . . Letter of John Winthrop to his wife. Robert C. Winthrop. *Life and Letters.* Vol. 2. Page 36.

Chapter 2: Ten Hills Farm

Here is as good land. . . . Letter of John Winthrop to his son John. Winthrop. *Life and Letters.* Vol. 2. Page 43.

like a king, offering hospitality to all who came. . . . Edmund S. Morgan. *The Puritan Dilemma.* 1958. Page 59.

among the most tantalizing. . . . John Winthrop. *The Journal of John Winthrop, 1630–1649.* Richard S. Dunn, James Savage, and Laetitia Yeandle, eds. 1996. Notes, page 36.

flocks of wild pigeons. . . . Charles Brooks. *History of the Town of Medford, Middlesex County, Massachusetts, from Its First Settlement, in 1630, until the Present Time, 1855.* 1855. Page 24.

We began to consult . . . Everett Emerson, ed. *Letters from New England. The Massachusetts Bay Colony, 1629–1638.* 1976. Page 71.

... we are here in paradise! Letter from John Winthrop to his wife. Winthrop. *Life and Letters.* Vol. 2. Page 54.

are swept awaye by the small poxe.... David Shumway Jones. *Rationalizing Epidemics: Meanings and Uses of American Indian Mortality since 1600.* 2004. Page 37.

we may ... fix upon June 17, 1630... Emphasis added. Brooks. History *of the Town of Medford.* Page 43. (Usher edition.)

... much debt will lie upon us. Letter from John Winthrop to his son. Winthrop. *Life and Letters.* Vol. 2. Page 44.

recommended Gov. Cradock's men to plant.... Brooks. *History of the Town of Medford.* Page 39.

This arrangement.... Brooks. *History of the Town of Medford.* Page 33.

There is more than enough for them and us.... Alexander Young, ed. *Chronicles of the First Planters of the Massachusetts Bay, 1623–1636.* 1846. Page 227.

... the slightest trace of injustice, violence, or crime.... Brooks. *History of the Town of Medford.* Page 34.

refused to recognize the legitimacy of Indian claims.... Alfred A. Cave. *The Pequot War.* 1996. Page 35.

like well of our coming and planting.... Francis Higginson. *New England's Plantation. Or a Short and True Description of the Commodities and Discommodities of that Countrey.* 1630. Reprinted by the Essex Book and Print Club, 1908. Page 106.

divers thousands of acres of ground ... Higginson. *New England's Plantation.* [1630] 1908. Page 23.

a secular, legalistic argument.... Cave. *The Pequot War.* Page 35.

Acknowledge their many kindnesses.... Brooks. *History of the Town of Medford.* The full text of this deed is reprinted on page 73. A copy of the original deed is kept in the Middlesex County Courthouse.

all the land within the line.... Emphasis added. Brooks. *History of the Town of Medford.* Page 74. A copy of the original deed is kept in the Middlesex County Courthouse.

Chapter 3: Possession

raised such forts, built so many towns.... Sir Simonds D'Ewes. *Collections of the Massachusetts Historical Society.* Volume 1. Fourth series. 1852. Page 248.

drawing, ordering and making.... Lion Gardiner. *A History of the Pequot War, or a Relation of the War between the Powerful Nation of Pequot Indians, once inhabiting the Coast of New England, Westerly from near Narraganset Bay, and the English Inhabitants, in the year 1638.* 1860. Page 9.

Worshipfull sir.... Letter from Lion Gardiner to John Winthrop Jr. C. C. Gardiner, ed. *Papers and Biography of Lion Gardiner, 1559–1663.* 1883. Page 35.

... leave [at] the stake to be roasted.... Gardiner. *A History of the Pequot War.* 1860. Page 10.

War is like a three-footed stool.... Gardiner. *A History of the Pequot War.* Page 10.

The Lord God blessed their design.... Gardiner. *A History of the Pequot War.* Page 21.

The destruction of the Pequots.... Alden T. Vaughan. *New England Frontier: Puritans and Indians 1620–1675.* 1965. Page 153.

Our men cut off a place of swamp.... Letter from John Winthrop to William Bradford. Winthrop. *Life and Letters.* Vol. 2. Page 199.

we send the male children to Bermuda.... Letter from John Winthrop to William Bradford. Winthrop. *Life and Letters.* Vol. 2. Page 199.

The rest are dispersed.... Nathaniel and Thomas Philbrick. *The Mayflower Papers, Selected Writings of Colonial New England.* 2007. Page 87.

Among the prisoners.... Letter from John Winthrop to William Bradford. Winthrop. *Life and Letters.* Vol. 2. Page 200. This vignette is often repeated and often reprinted, and carries various interpretations. In some accounts, Winthrop saves the woman's life and keeps her family with his own. In others, the woman is mistaken for her husband, the sachem. These sorts of misinterpretations abound when there is so little factual material to build upon. Here, I have stayed as close to the original text as possible.

...Adam's degenerate seed.... Letter from Roger Williams to John Winthrop. *Winthrop Papers.* Vol. 3. 1929. Massachusetts Historical Society. Page 436.

We have heard of a dividence of women and children.... Letter from Hugh Peter to John Winthrop. *Winthrop Papers.* Vol. 3. Massachusetts Historical Society. Page 450.

By this Pinnace.... Letter from Israel Stoughton to John Winthrop. *Winthrop Papers.* Vol. 3. Massachusetts Historical Society. Page 435.

A breed of Negroes.... John Josselyn. *An Account of Two Voyages to New England.* 1674. Page 28.

The Governor had leave to keep.... John Noble, ed. *Records of the Court of Assistants of the Colony of the Massachusetts Bay 1630–1692.* Vol. 2. 1904. Page 91.

...lawful captives taken in just wars.... Charles W. Eliot, ed. *American Historical Documents 1000–1904.* Vol. 43. Page 88.

...as reasonable as you can.... *Winthrop Papers.* Vol. 1. 1929. Massachusetts Historical Society. Page 362.

A war with the Narraganset is very considerable.... *Winthrop Papers.* Vol. 5. 1947. Massachusetts Historical Society. Page 38.

PART II: THE IMMIGRANT

Materials on the lives of the Royall family are spread far and thin. There are tantalizing clues referencing diaries and shipping records carefully kept. I could not find them. Instead, my work on William Ryall and his descendants was pieced together from an eclectic smattering of letters and references tucked in national, state, and local archives and libraries in Antigua, Massachusetts, New Hampshire, Rhode Island, and Maine.

The Massachusetts Archives, located in a modern facility on a point of land jutting into the sea in Dorchester, holds an exceptional collection of vital records, wills, court documents, passenger lists, family genealogies, and other materials from which I was able to piece together important details about the lives of the Royalls and many other men and women who figure in this tale. Inventories in particular provided information on the estates of various members of the Winthrop, Usher, and Royall families. These documents show these families' wealth, kinship bonds, business ties, and ownership of slaves. They also generated leads to information I could then trace through other means.

At the Massachusetts Historical Society I found the *John Usher Papers* and the thirty-four-volume *Jeffries Family Papers* of particular importance. I could hardly have written about John Usher's life without these materials. They sent me on a journey of the sort every author longs to have.

One resource to which I returned time and time again was the family genealogy prepared by the Royall House Association. I have kept this unpublished study close at hand and am indebted to everyone involved in its compilation. Interestingly, as I returned to those pages over time, knowing more with each visit, they disclosed secret after secret lying in plain view, but waiting for me to have the wit and learning to connect important pieces of this tale.

Local histories and regional archives were key to my understanding of the early settlement of Casco Bay and the development of the New Hampshire woodlands. Though undervalued and often ignored (and, alas, sometimes littered with errors of fact), local histories provided a fascinating view to local pasts while at the same time affording glimpses of the prejudices and biases of the time in which they were written. I found them fascinating. In some cases I may be repeating factual errors contained in such volumes. I have done my best to avoid this pitfall, and come away from this project with humility and enormous empathy for any historian—local or world renowned—who faces the monumental task of trying to make sense of the particular details of any life lived centuries ago.

From the hushed and formal reading rooms of the Boston Athenaeum and the Massachusetts Historical Society in Boston, to the more cramped quarters of the Freeport Historical Society in Maine, and the august chamber that houses the New Hampshire Historical Society in Concord, I encountered librarians and archivists with boundless patience and key information. In these and other archives I was able to find enough facts, clues, and specifics to move the narrative constantly forward. While there was no single "Aha!" moment in these places, I did find that over time each thread found hidden here and there came together in a solid fabric.

Charles Brooks's *History of the Town of Medford* proved especially useful as I gained my initial sense of Medford. That book also helped me bridge the gap from one generation to the next, a task aided as well by Lawrence Shaw Mayo's *The Winthrop Family in America* (1948), which tells the stories of John Winthrop's many children. Samuel E. Morrison's *Builders of the Bay Colony* provided other useful sketches and details.

Details of the slave trade are now widely available. I have relied most heavily on the work of David Brion Davis and David Eltis. Each has produced numerous volumes examining the trade. I also used Elizabeth Donnan's four-volume *Documents Illustrative of the History of the Slave Trade in America*, published in 1930, and Lorenzo Johnston Greene's *The Negro in Colonial New England* (1966), for both a basic grounding in the subject and specific details regarding the trade in the North.

John Josselyn's remarkable travelogue, *An Account of Two Visits to New England: Wherein You Have the Setting Out of a Ship, with the Charges, the Prices of All Necessaries for Furnishing a Planter & His Family at His First Coming, a Description of the Country, Natives and Creatures, the Government of the Countrey as it is Now...*, provides a stunning sense of New England as it was in the days of the first settlers. Josselyn's chilling account of Samuel Maverick's order that a male slave in his possession should rape another slave on Noddles Island is told with subtlety and power in a 2007 article from the Journal of American History, "'The Cause of Her Grief': The Rape of a Slave in New England" by Wendy Anne Warren.

My understanding of the social, economic, and political pressures of early colonial times was derived from a variety of sources. The stunningly sudden drop in commodity prices during the 1640s, for instance, is described in various scholarly articles examining the economic challenges experienced by the first planters. Edmund S. Morgan's *The Puritan Dilemma* (1958), in which he specifically describes the effect of the economic downturn of the late 1630s on Governor Winthrop's relationship to Ten Hills Farm, and Margaret Ellen Newell's *From Dependency to Independence* (1998), which provides a fuller account of these vicissitudes as well as a well-considered explanation for them, were particularly helpful. Bernard Bailyn's *New England Merchants in the Seventeenth Century*, first published in 1955 and now considered a classic, proved useful, too, as were several histories of the Caribbean, which helped me view the period from an obverse perspective. To a lesser extent, I used William Babcock Weeden's *Economic and Social History of New England, 1620–1789* (1891). My reason for using similar books from different eras was to gain a sense of how historians from various generations have viewed the same material through different lenses.

Two wonderful books will help any reader understand the appalling devastation of King Philip's War. Nathaniel Philbrick's *Mayflower* (2007) shows the conflict's earliest antecedents. Jill Lepore's masterfully written and researched book, *The Name of War: King Philip's War and the Origins of American Identity* (1998), tracks the causes and the path of destruction as well as anyone perhaps ever could.

Chapter 4: The King's Forester

A neat and nimble ship. . . . Higginson. *New England's Plantation.* [1630] 1908. Page 60.

. . . *advantages of trade therewith.* . . . Vincent T. Harlow. *A History of Barbados, 1625–1685.* 1926. Page 268.

. . . burrow[ed] . . . in the Earth. . . . Dow quotes Edward Johnson, a clerk from Woburn, describing this pattern in 1652. George Francis Dow. *Daily Life in the Massachusetts Bay Colony.* 1935. Reprinted 2007. Page 17.

Coopers and cleavers of timber. . . . Brooks. *History of the Town of Medford.* Page 87.

. . . plenty of strawberries. . . . Higginson. *New England's Plantation.* Page 94.

. . . liberty from his father. . . . Edwin M. Stone. *History of Beverly, Civil and Ecclesiastical, from Its First Settlement in 1630 to 1842.* 1843. Page 315.

Chapter 5: Favors to the Few

One Mr. Ryall. . . . Winthrop. *The Journal of John Winthrop, 1630–1649.* Page 297.

It came over by divers letters and reports. . . . Winthrop. *The Journal of John Winthrop, 1630–1649.* Page 324.

the first gift of real estate. . . . The Harvard Guide/Finances. An online resource detailing Harvard's "History, Lore, and More." http://www.hno.harvard.edu/guide/finance/index.html.

forgery, lying & other foule offences. . . . Nathaniel B. Shurtleff. *Records of the Governor and Company of the Massachusetts Bay in New England.* Vol. 1. 1628–1641. 1853. Page 295.

the court (having no money to bestow . . .). Winthrop. *The Journal of John Winthrop, 1630–1649.* Page 326.

Among second-generation New Englanders . . . Dunn. *Puritans and Yankees.* Page 59.

There came in her the governor's wife, his eldest son and his wife. . . . Winthrop. *The Journal of John Winthrop, 1630–1649.* 1996. Page 59.

"neger". . . . Robert C. Black III. *The Younger John Winthrop.* 1966. Page 194.

. . . to be possessed and enjoyed by him. . . . Samuel Eliot Morrison. *Builders of the Bay Colony.* 1930. Page 282.

live comfortably in his profession. Darrett Bruce Rutman. *American Puritanism: Faith and Practice.* 1970. Page 58.

. . . keep sail with his equal. . . . Rutman. *American Puritanism.* Page 69.

only a single allotment appears to have been made. . . . Robert C. Black III. *The Younger John Winthrop.* 1966. Page 64.

For the untried, the speculative, the romantically grandiose. . . . Black. *The Younger John Winthrop.* Page 59.

Chapter 6: Happy Instruments to Enlarge Our Dominions

and the more they buie, the better able they are to buye. . . . *Collections of the Massachusetts Historical Society.* Vol. 6. Fourth series. 1863. Page 537.

Winthrop had it on good authority that men in Barbados. . . . Bernard Bailyn. *New England Merchants.* 1955. Page 85.

Winthrop and his colleagues looked to the West Indies. . . . Vincent T. Harlow. *A History of Barbados.* 1926. Page 270.

Barbados was suddenly leaping into phenomenal prosperity. . . . Harlow. *A History of Barbados.* Page 272.

Age now comes upon me. . . . *Proceedings of the Massachusetts Historical Society.* 1862. Page 384.

as if she had been muche abused. . . . Winthrop. *The Journal of John Winthrop, 1630–1649.* Page 712.

weaker than ever I knew him. . . . Robert C. Winthrop. *Life and Letters.* Vol. 2. 1869. Page 391.

All plantations were mean at the first. . . . Worthington C. Ford, ed. *Winthrop Papers.* Vol. 1. 1929. Massachusetts Historical Society. Page 105.

When I've been at that window upstairs. . . . Ronald Reagan. *Farewell Address to the Nation.* Delivered from the Oval Office on January 11, 1989. Full text available through the Reagan Library at http://www.reaganlibrary.com/reagan/speeches/farewell.asp.

Details regarding Hezekiah Usher's loan to John Winthrop Jr. can be found in Richard S. Dunn's *Puritans and Yankees,* page 201.

Elaborate speculations in sugar. . . . Black. *The Younger John Winthrop.* Page 194.

handsomely contrived. . . . John Josselyn. *An Account of Two Voyages to New England.* 1674. Page 162.

The Town is rich and very populous. . . . John Josselyn. *An Account of Two Voyages to New England.* 1674. Page 162.

as great a God with us English as God Gold was with the Spaniards. . . . John F. Martin. *Profits in the Wilderness: Entrepreneurship and the Founding of New England.* 1991. Page 118.

This, I fear, will be the ruin of New England. . . . John Demos. *A little Commonwealth: Family Life in Plymouth Colony.* 1999. Page 10.

Intermittent killings and burnings by the Indians. . . . Florence G. Thurston and Harmon S. Cross. *Three Centuries of Freeport Maine.* 1940. Page 19.

. . . there is some difference about the land. . . . Dorchester Antiquarian and Historical Society. *History of the Town of Dorchester, Massachusetts.* 1859. Reprint of a 1670 letter from Captain [Hopestill] Foster to King Philip of Mount Hope. Page 220.

Rage and fury of the enimy. . . . Colonial Society of Massachusetts. *Publications of the Colonial Society of Massachusetts.* Vol. 17. Transactions 1913–1914. Page 251. Jill Lepore describes this in *The Name of War.* See chapter 3: *Habitations of Cruelty,* pp. 71–96.

When the Indians were hurried away. . . . Samuel Adams Drake. *History of Middlesex County, Massachusetts, Containing Carefully*

Prepared Histories of Every City and Town in the County. Vol. 2. Page 188.

. . . bleak and cold, their wigwams poor and mean. . . . Jill Lepore. *The Name of War.* 1998. Page 139. This quote is widely reprinted. I cite Lepore, since she provides the best context.

great, naked, dirty beast. . . . Benjamin Church, Thomas Church, and Samuel Adams Drake. *The History of Philip's War, Commonly Called the Great Indian War of 1675 and 1676.* 2nd ed. 1840. Page 125.

. . . happy Instruments to enlarge. . . . Collections of the Massachusetts Historical Society. Volume 5. Fourth series. 1861. Page 32.

Chapter 7: Slavers of the North

There was some unpleasantness. . . . Dunn. *Puritans and Yankees.* Page 209.

The self-sufficiency of the imperial unit was to be maintained. . . . Bailyn. *New England Merchants.* Page 113.

Chapter 8: Come Up in the Night with Them

graceless, grasping son. . . . Bailyn. *New England Merchants.* Page 137.

million-acre purchase. Jeremy Belknap. *History of New Hampshire.* Volume 1. 1831. Page 116. Details about the "million-acre purchase" are scattered in various early histories of New England. None are particularly clear. What the deal does illustrate, however, is how a network of business and family connections in that time could generate extraordinary wealth for men with good connections. Some future student of history would do well to examine this particular transaction in detail for it speaks volumes about the system of the day and how it worked.

negroe woman. . . . Last will and Testament of Hezekiah Usher. 1676. Massachusetts Archives, Dorchester. Microfilm record.

having layn 4 months in the bay. . . . Letter from Cadiz. April 27, 1679.

Massachusetts Historical Society. *Jeffries Family Papers*. Vol. 2 Pages 142–50.

single interrelated family. Bailyn. *New England Merchants*. Page 135.

300,000 Englishmen swarmed across the Atlantic.... Nuala Zahedieh. "Economy." In *The British Atlantic World 1500–1800*. David Armitage and Michael J. Braddick, eds. 2002. Page 51.

In terms of immigration alone.... David Eltis. "*Free and Coerced Transatlantic Migrations: Some Comparisons*." American Historical Review. Vol. 88. No. 2. Page 255.

Come up in the night with them.... Letter from John Saffin, John Usher, et al. to Captain William Welstead. June 12, 1681. Massachusetts Historical Society. *Jeffries Family Papers*. Vol. 2. Page 149.

When you went hence.... Letter from John Saffin, John Usher, et al. to Captain William Warren. June 12, 1681. Massachusetts Historical Society. *Jeffries Family Papers*. Vol. 2. Page 149.

for passage of 6 negroes.... Invoice of John Usher. Massachusetts Historical Society. *Jeffries Family Papers*. Vol. 15. Page 86.

a burning for a burning.... Lorenzo Johnston Greene. *The Negro in Colonial New England*. 1966. Page 154.

Chapter 9: You May Own Negroes and Negresses

He used to make a show of hangeing himselfe.... Collections of the Massachusetts Historical Society. Vol. 7. Fifth series. 1882. Page 427.

I am forced to abide here.... Letter from Elizabeth Usher to her husband. Massachusetts Historical Society. *Jeffries Family Papers*. Vol. 3. Page 48.

You may ... own Negroes and Negresses.... The Report of a French Protestant Refugee, in Boston, 1687. E. T. Fisher, translator. 1868. Collection of the American Antiquarian Society.

An imaginary "hemispheric traveler".... David Brion Davis. *Inhuman Bondage: The Rise and Fall of Slavery in the New World*. 2006. Page 1.

. . . come in a coach from Roxbury. . . . Collections of the Massachusetts Historical Society. Vol. 5. Fifth series. 1878. Page 151.

. . . wearing Apparill, and all my Rings, Bodkins, Jewills and Orniments. . . . Massachusetts Archives. Probate of the will of Elizabeth Saffin. 1687.

dissatisfied with the Trade. . . . Collections of the Massachusetts Historical Society. Vol. 6. Fifth series. 1879. Page 16.

Originally, and Naturally, there is no such thing. . . . Samuel Sewall. *The Selling of Joseph: A Memorial.* Pamphlet. 1700. Digital reproduction available online through the website of the Massachusetts Historical Society. http://www.masshist.org/objects/2004september.cfm.

prone to revenge. . . . Mason I. Lowance. *A House Divided: The Antebellum Slavery Debates in America, 1776–1885.* 2003. Page 15.

Purchase them (for Toyes and Baubles) perhaps you may. . . . Samuel Sewall. *The Athenian Oracle.* 2nd ed. 1704. Page 2.

PART III: THE MASTER

In one of the many residual paradoxes of colonial rule, the most important collections of material regarding Antigua's history lie outside the nation's borders. Even the Codrington Papers, an extraordinary collection of more than eight thousand letters, invoices, maps, and other documents pertaining to that family's trade in slaves and sugar in Antigua and Barbuda from the seventeenth to the twentieth century, reside in Antigua only in the form of a grainy microfilm copy. The originals were put up to auction by Sotheby's in December 1980, and sold at an undisclosed price to an undisclosed bidder. Many materials that did remain in the country suffered terribly prior to the construction of the new climate-controlled archive in St. John's. Some materials simply disintegrated over time in the harsh conditions of the tropics. A powerful hurricane devastated the island in 1972, destroying the national library, a loss the writer Jamaica Kincaid chronicles bitterly in her book *A Small Place.* So chaotic was the scene, it was left to volunteers and those with a bent for history to wander into the sodden wreckage and salvage what materials they could.

As to histories of Antigua, there are sadly few. The enormous, leather-bound, limited-edition, three-volume *History of the Island of Antigua, one of the Leeward Caribees in the West Indies, from the First Settlement in 1635 to the Present Time,* penned by Vere Langford Oliver, though written more than a century ago, proved an extraordinary resource. Its pages are full of detailed general history, family genealogies (called "pedigrees" in these volumes), and numerous island records. Reissued in 2003, the set is now available to the general public for the prohibitive price of $1,600. I was lucky enough to find copies in the American Antiquarian Society, in the rare books collection of the Widener Library at Harvard, and on John Fuller's bookshelf in Antigua. The library in St. John's has another copy. Also useful to me (in part because of its extremely dated voice and view) was *Antigua and the Antiguans*, written by a woman whose name is alternatively cited as Mrs. Lanaghan or Mrs. Flannigan, an Irish visitor who traveled to the island in the early 1800s. Of more depth, sweep, and authority is the admirable book *Bondmen and Rebels: A Study of Master-Slave Relations in Antigua, with Implications for Colonial British America*, by David Barry Gaspar. That book, published in 1985, is filled with data, statistics, and acute insights into the dynamics of slavery during Isaac Royall's time. I learned much about the islanders' life from Gaspar's fine scholarship.

Richard S. Dunn's *Sugar and Slaves: The Rise of the Planter Class in the English West Indies, 1624–1713,* first published in 1972 and reissued with an introduction by Gary Nash in 2000, is another key work in this vein. In another era, *History of the West Indies: Comprising British Guiana, Barbadoes, St. Vincent's, St. Lucia, Dominica, Montserrat, Antigua, St. Christopher's &c. &c.* by R. Montgomery Martin, 1836, provided brief but useful sketches of each of the islands in this Caribbean region. Finally, no one traveling to Antigua or seriously interested in the island should be without Jamaica Kincaid's *A Small Place* (1989). This bitter memoir of her childhood home is as chilling and illuminating as it is, itself, small. Here is a work that proves books need not be long to be profound.

Readers interested in archeology will do well to look up Alexandra A. Chan's 2007 book, *Slavery in the Age of Reason: Archeology at a New England Farm,* which tells the story, inasmuch as it can be unearthed, of the lives of slaves at Ten Hills Farm. The book sprang from Chan's doctoral dissertation and work on the grounds of the Royall House Association where the slave quarters still stand.

For the Royall House in particular, the *History of the Oliver, Vassall and Royall Houses in Dorchester, Cambridge and Medford* (1907), by Robert Tracy Jackson, proved helpful, as were various articles published in the *Medford Historical Register* in the early 1900s. The 1894 book *Our Colonial Homes,* by Samuel Adams Drake, which identifies the residence as "Hobgoblin Hall," also proved useful, if somewhat prone to error. The same author's *Historic Mansions and Highways around Boston* (1900) was likewise helpful. Two books exclusively about the Royalls capture the family's history in an amber view. These are *The New-England Royalls* (1885), by Edward Doubleday Harris, and Gladys N. Hoover's rather gushy *The Elegant Royalls of Colonial New England* (1974). Hoover's book is quite good in its florid way, since the author went to great lengths to discover letters and other original documents pertaining to the family. Materials kept by Historic New England at the archives in the Otis House in Boston rounded out my research with a trove of photographs, pamphlets, and other wonderful original items spanning various eras. Jim Shea, the site manager and museum curator at the Longfellow House in Cambridge, shared his enthusiasm and his notes on slaves at that residence. He is one of the many quiet souls who work every day to fill the gaps in our understanding of slavery in the colonial era.

Newspaper articles and advertisements, once only available to the white-gloved researcher slowly turning yellow pages, are now largely available online through *America's Historical Newspapers, 1690–1820,* a resource I accessed through both the American

Antiquarian Society's website and my Harvard library account. Though I did spend some time at the Antiquarian Society leafing through actual newspapers, I found this online resource so exceptional that I eventually shifted all my research there. In a matter of moments I could execute targeted searches for individuals, subjects, and events; or I could peruse papers from an era of interest to get a flavor of the time. Nearly all newspaper articles and advertisements I cite were accessed in this way.

Chapter 10: Antigua

30 or 40 I shou'd think full enough for a first purchase. David Barry Gaspar. *Bondmen and Rebels: A Study of Master-Slave Relations in Antigua.* 1985. Page 89.

one of the most pretentious and elegant residences. . . . Henry Wilder Foote et al. *Annals of Kings Chapel from the Puritan Age of New England to the Present Day.* 1896. Volume 2. Page 161.

how it had been raised and treated, the kind of soil. . . . Gaspar. *Bondmen and Rebels.* Page 108.

improved to the utmost. . . . Gaspar. *Bondmen and Rebels.* Page 95.

The prettiest little harbour I ever saw. . . . Samuel Taylor Coleridge. *Six Months in the West Indies, in 1825.* 1832. Page 225.

. . . plenty of black boys, to grin and chatter. . . . Mrs. Lanaghan. *Antigua and the Antiguans.* 1844. Vol. 1. Page 156.

founder, patron, and benefactor. Edwin Mark Norris. *The Story of Princeton.* 1917. Page 28.

Negroes, Males and Females. . . . Many individual advertisements placed by Jacob Royall regarding the sale of slaves and other merchandise can be found through a search of old newspapers contained in the online repository, *America's Historical Newspapers.* All references to slave sales from the text come from that source. Readers seeking an overview of the role of newspapers in the sale of slaves in Massachusetts should also look for Robert E.

Desrochers Jr.'s article in the *William and Mary Quarterly,* vol. 59, no. 3 (2002), "Slave-for-Sale Advertisements and Slavery in Massachusetts, 1704–1781." In this article Desrochers explores what he calls the "close and synergetic relationship that made slave-for-sale advertisements a regular feature of the local press for most of the eighteenth century."

Dear Kinsman. . . . Letter of Isaac Royall to John Usher. *Jeffries Family Papers.* Vol. 3. Massachusetts Historical Society. Page 132.

Chapter 11: Crime, Punishment, and Compensation

As he was riding along the high road. . . . Mrs. Lanaghan. *Antigua and the Antiguans.* 1844. Vol. 1. Page 73.

Negroe Servant to Mr. Jacob Royall, Esq. . . . New England Historical and Genealogical Register. Vol. 102. Christ Church, Boston, Records. Page 35.

Antigua is in a most deplorable Condition. . . . . Gaspar. *Bondmen and Rebels.* Page 141.

Sold at fifteen shillings a Hogshead. . . . Gaspar. *Bondmen and Rebels.* Page 141.

NB: All statistics regarding slave ownership and census data in Antigua are taken from Gaspar's *Bondmen and Rebels.*

Chapter 12: Homecoming

send me in your schooner. . . . Letter from Thomas Worsley to John Jeffries. April 9, 1731. *Jeffries Family Papers.* Massachusetts Historical Society.

the negroe boy, which you will be pleased to send me. . . . Letter from Jonathan Belcher to Isaac Royall. *Collections of the Massachusetts Historical Society.* 1893. Sixth series. Vol. 6. Page 255.

This Island is in a very great Confusion at present. . . . Early American Newspapers Series I. *The Boston Weekly News-Letter.* November 25, 1736.

We are in a great deal of trouble in this Island.... Gaspar. *Bond-men and Rebels.* Page 28.

Boston's most active slave trader.... Robert E. Desrochers Jr. "Slave for Sale Advertisements and Slavery in Massachusetts 1704–1781." *William and Mary Quarterly.* Third Series. Vol. 59. No. 3. 2002. Page 629.

Chapter 13: The Benefactor

one of our Law School's most prized possessions.... Erika Chadbourn. "Robert Feke—In San Francisco?" Undated. Art Curator's Files. Harvard Law School Library. Isaac Royall and His Family research file. Reprinted by permission.

arguably the most influential colonial portraitist. Signage accompanying the Feke painting, Isaac Royall and His Family. Casperson Room. Harvard University Law School Library.

made a great fortune in the mercantile trade.... Ralph Peter Mooz. "The Art of Robert Feke." 1970. Ph.D. dissertation, University of Pennsylvania. Dissertations and Theses: Full Text database. Page 5.

2 negros, my chariot & horses.... Isaac Royall. Last Will and Testament. Probate records. Massachusetts Archives. Microfilm.

...To inherit a plentifull Fortune.... New England Historical and Genealogical Register. Volume 5. 1851. Dorchester Inscriptions. Page 256.

Chapter 14: Luxury on the Grandest Scale

WANTED, Two Pair of handsome, well made Coach Horses.... *Boston Evening-Post.* 1760. Early American Newspapers.

...rank ingratitude and treachery. Samuel Batchelder. *The Cambridge Historical Society Publications IX.* 1915. Including Batchelder's reading on the portraits of Penelope and Henry Vassall. Page 64. This lecture was published posthumously in the book *Bits of Cambridge History* (1930).

Six hundred and three Spanish Milld Dollars.... Batchelder. *The Cambridge Historical Society Publications IX.* Including Batchelder's reading on the portraits of Penelope and Henry Vassall. Inventory appears on page 65.

... less a presentation of character.... Carol Troyen. "John Singleton Copley and the Heroes of the American Revolution." *Antiques.* July 1995.

There was a tax.... Interview with Alexandra Chan. 2006.

... severe and tart master to his people.... Batchelder. *The Cambridge Historical Society Publications IX.* Including Batchelder's reading on the portraits of Penelope and Henry Vassall. Recollections of the slave Darby quoted in Batchelder's address to the Cambridge Historical Society. Page 35.

Biased and overdrawn as we may hope.... Samuel Batchelder. *Bits of Cambridge History.* 1930. Page 159. This work is an expanded version of the talk Batchelder gave to the Cambridge Historical Society in 1915. It was edited and revised for publication.

well-stocked matrimonial market. Batchelder. *Bits of Cambridge History.* Page 159.

PART IV: THE PETITIONER

So much material traces the role of Massachusetts in the first days of the Revolutionary War it is hardly worth listing general sources here. Instead, I leave it to the intrepid researcher to discover this material on her own. As to the particular characters within this book, however, among the most useful materials were these: *Massachusetts Historical Society Collections*, sixth series, vols. 1–10; *Medford in the Revolution: Military History of Medford, Massachusetts, 1765–1783*, by Helen Tilden Wild (1903); *The Day of Concord and Lexington, The Nineteenth of April, 1775*, by Allen French (1925); *Massachusetts Soldiers and Sailors of the Revolutionary War, A Compilation from the Archives*, published by the commonwealth in 1905; *Patriots of Color: African Americans and Native Americans at Battle Road and Bunker Hill,* a report prepared for that National Park Service by George Quintal Jr. in 2002; John Boyle's *A Journal of Occurrences in Boston,* available to me through the Houghton Library at Harvard; *An Imperfect God: George Washington, His Slaves and the Creation of America,* by Henry Wiencek (2004); and *Paul Revere's Ride* by David Hackett Fischer (1995). Each of these books was enjoyable as well as edifying. In this part of the book as elsewhere, I made extensive use of the Massachusetts Historical Society's collections, both sifting through materials at the society's Boston research library and reading materials published in the *Collections.* The digital sea of Early American Newspapers available online was also a central source, as were the collections made available at the Massachusetts Archives and the New England Historic and Genealogical Society.

A variety of scholarly articles and Emily Blanck's as yet unpublished dissertation on *Revolutionizing Slavery: The Legal Culture of Slavery in Revolutionary Massachusetts and South Carolina,* completed in 2003, proved of particular interest and help as I explored the end of slavery in New England following the American Revolution.

The slave Belinda, who appears here as "the Petitioner," has attracted significant scholarly interest in recent years. Though I may have missed an article or two, for my own purposes the article "Belinda's Petition: Reparations for Slavery in Revolutionary Massachusetts" by Roy E. Finkenbine, published in the *William and Mary Quarterly* of March 2007, did the best job of telling this story and analyzing its importance. By contrast, the almost bizarre piece, "An 'Animadversion' upon a 'Complaint' against 'the Petition' of Belinda, an African Slave" by Vincent Carretta, published in *Early American Literature* in 1997, left me literally speechless in the face of its errors of fact (he posits that Isaac Royall was "an American invention" cooked up as a "slur against the avariciousness, Jewishness, and royalist sympathies of the 'master'"). I can only say here, what *was* he thinking?

Stories of the military adventures of John Stark abound, but they are often skewed by the language of stirring heroics. Still, I was grateful to find the *Memoir and Official Correspondence of Gen.*

John Stark with Notices of Several Other Officers of the Revolution, written by his grandson Caleb Stark in 1860, and now available in its entirety through Google books. Though a thundering tone of righteousness rings throughout the book, it does provide a decent grounding in the man's life and military exploits.

At the Houghton Library at Harvard University I pored over John Boyle's *A Journal of Occurrences in Boston, 1759–1778*, which provides an incomparable sense of the tensions and excitement preceding the Revolution. The Houghton Library also shared letters written by Isaac Royall Jr. to Oliver Wendell in 1778.

Some assistance came unexpectedly from far afield. In June 2007 I sent an email to Professor Colin Nicolson, a lecturer in United States history and editor of the Bernard Papers at the University of Stirling in Scotland, and within minutes he emailed me back, offering whatever help he could. It was no empty offer. In the weeks that followed Professor Nicolson emptied out his files and sent me a huge package filled with letters and other documents he had photocopied during visits to the Boston Public Library and the Massachusetts Historical Society in addition to a book, self-published by one of the Pepperrell family's descendants, telling the story of that family through the lens of letters and papers, some of which had been left to the author by her "godmother-aunt" in 1960. While I could not make as much use of this material as I wished, Professor Nicolson's generosity was noteworthy, and the materials he shared saved me time and helped me obtain a deeper sense of the people and sensibilities that surrounded Isaac Royall Jr. as well as his sister Penelope and half-sister Ann in the last days before the Revolution.

Chapter 15: We Shall Not Be Slaves

valiant Brigadier Royall. . . . Edmund S. Morgan. *Prologue to Revolution: Sources and Documents on the Stamp Act Crisis, 1764–1766.* 1959. Page 126.

. . . destroyed almost every article therein. John Boyle. *A Journal of Occurrences in Boston.* Courtesy of Collection of Houghton Library, Harvard University.

a most unwelcome cargo. Boyle. *A Journal of Occurrences in Boston.* Courtesy of Collection of Houghton Library, Harvard University.

Although the language was clearly diplomatic . . . Emily Blanck. *Revolutionizing Slavery: The Legal Culture of Slavery in Revolutionary Massachusetts and South Carolina.* Ph.D. dissertation, Emory University. 2003. Page 95.

. . . I am sorry for your loss. . . . Usher Parsons. *The Life of Sir William Pepperrell, Bart., the only native of New England who was created a Baronet during our connection with the mother country.* 1855. Page 28. This letter is reproduced in full in *Pepperrell Posterity* on page 21. The original is kept at the Massachusetts Historical Society.

My Negroes shal not be sold. . . . Margaret Mutchler Martin. *The Chambers-Russell-Codman House and Family.* 1996. Page 97.

Chapter 16: Within the Bowels of a Free Country

. . . Mulatto fellow, about 27 years of Age. . . . Frederic Kidder. *History of the Boston Massacre, March 5, 1770: Consisting of the Narrative of the Town, the Trial of the Soldiers: And a Historical Introduction, Containing Unpublished Documents of John Adams, and Explanatory Notes.* 1870. Page 29.

The first to defy,the first to die. James Jeffrey Roche, with poems edited by Mrs. John Boyle O'Reilly. *The Life of John Boyle O'Reilly.* 1891. Page 410.

A most horrid and inhuman massacre! Boyle. *A Journal of Occurrences in Boston.*

. . . even Boston might be willing to swallow it. David Hackett Fischer. *Paul Revere's Ride.* 1994. Page 25.

a very disagreeable passage of eight weeks. . . . Virginia Browne-Wilkinson. *Pepperrell Posterity: Written 1964–1981 for Mary Theresa Caroline Browne-Wilkinson (1890–1978).* Self-published in 1982. Page 103.

a negro boy. . . . Massachusetts Historical Society. *Agreement of Joseph Warren with Joshua Green regarding payment for a slave, 28 June 1770.* The text of this document, as well as a digitized image of the original, are available online at the website for the Massachusetts Historical Society.

within the bowels of a free country. . . . *Collections of the Massachusetts Historical Society.* Vol. 3. Fifth series. 1877. Page 432.

. . . *great things from men who have made such a noble stand.* . . . Robin D. G. Kelley and Earl Lewis, eds. *To Make Our World Anew.* Vol. 2: *A History of African Americans Since 1880.* 2005. Page 99.

My house at Cambridge being surrounded. . . . Fischer. *Paul Revere's Ride.* Page 47. This quote is repeated in countless stories of the Revolution. I cite Fischer because the context he builds was particularly helpful in my understanding of those several weeks leading to the Revolution.

Slavery they can have anywhere. . . . Edmund Burke. *Burke, Selected Works.* Edward John Payne, ed. [1881] 2005. Vol. 2. Page 232.

I packed up my Sea Stores and Cloathes for the passage. . . . Letter from Isaac Royall Jr. to Edmund Quincy. May 29, 1779. Massachusetts Historical Society.

Chapter 17: Death Is Not the Worst of Evils

. . . *changed his dress, mounted a horse, and proceeded.* . . . Caleb Stark. *Memoir and Official Correspondence of Gen. John Stark.* 1860. Page 28.

As to fire Arms. . . . Stark. *Memoir and Official Correspondence of Gen. John Stark.* Page 110.

I can handle a musket. Stark. *Memoir and Official Correspondence of Gen. John Stark.* Page 346.

Live free or die. . . . The New Hampshire state motto, taken from a toast given by John Stark in July of 1809, was adopted by the legislature in 1945.

... no other nourishment than that of salt provisions. . . . Virginia Browne-Wilkinson. Self-published in 1982. *Pepperrell Posterity: Written 1964–1981 for Mary Theresa Caroline Browne-Wilkinson (1890–1978).* Page 114.

... reflect dishonor on this Colony. Henry Wiencek. *An Imperfect God: George Washington, His Slaves and the Creation of America.* 2003. Page 197.

reject all Slaves & by a great Majority. . . . Wiencek. *An Imperfect God.* Page 201.

Ethiopian Regiment. Wiencek. *An Imperfect God.* Page 203.

George, who may have served the family for as many as 38 years. . . . Alexandra Chan. "The Slaves of Colonial New England: Discourses of Colonialism and Identity at the Isaac Royall House, Medford, Massachusetts, 1732–1775." Ph.D. dissertation. Boston University. 2003. Vol. 2. Page 308.

Chapter 18: Reparations

... duty to the Mother Country and to the best of Kings. Letter from Isaac Royall Jr. to Lord North. May 31, 1777. Isaac Royall Papers, 1726–1789. Collection of the Boston Athenaeum.

I am informed my Name is mentioned in the Act. Letter from Isaac Royall Jr. to Edmund Quincy, May 29, 1779. Quincy, Wendell, Holmes, and Upham Family Papers, microfilm reel 31. Massachusetts Historical Society.

The best Temple Spectacles with Silver Bows. . . . Letter from Isaac Royall Jr. to Edmund Quincy, May 29, 1779. Quincy, Wendell, Holmes, and Upham Family Papers, microfilm reel 31. Massachusetts Historical Society.

I think it proper to inform you what I had left to the College. . . . Letter from Isaac Royall Jr. to Oliver Wendell. May 31, 1778. Copied by Isaac Royall Jr. and included in a second letter dated, Kensington, March 18, 1779. Houghton Library Collection. Harvard

University. Courtesy of Houghton Library, Harvard College Library. bMS Am 1953 (113).

toward the endowing of a Professor of Laws. . . . Letter from Isaac Royall Jr. to Oliver Wendell. March 18, 1779. Houghton Library Collection. Harvard University. Courtesy of Houghton Library, Harvard College Library. bMS Am 1953 (113).

in case she does not choose her freedom. . . . Details from Isaac Royall Jr.'s last will and testament dated May 26, 1778. Emphasis added. Massachusetts Archives. Microfilm.

provide for the restitution of all estates. . . . Treaty of Paris, 1783; International Treaties and Related Records, 1778–1974; General Records of the United States Government, Record Group 11; National Archives. The full text of the Treaty of Paris is available through various online sites, including that of the National Archives.

All men are born free. . . . The Massachusetts State Constitution is available online through the state government's website.

PART V: THE LEGACY

This book was written at a time when the quantity of research materials available through the Internet increased at a dizzying speed. Items I reviewed in libraries in 2005, and books I examined at that time, often were online three years later, and more become available each day. At the same time, the use of streaming video proliferated, a fact that allowed me to attend important events over and over in some kind of weird academic rendition of the movie *Groundhog Day.* When I learned of the appointment of a new Royall Chair at the Harvard Law School, for instance, I was able to view online the professor's speech delivered in the Casperson Room, where the Feke painting of Isaac Royall and his family rests. In this way I not only got the flavor and the specifics of an event I would have otherwise missed, but was able to generate a reliable transcript of Professor Halley's remarks. The inaugurations of Drew Gilpin Faust and Deval Patrick were also available online, and while nothing replaces the dynamic of being there, the web allowed me to fact-check remarks and study details I might otherwise have missed in the real time of a crowded public event. Much of the material in this section stems from these various sources.

Chapter 19: City upon a Hill

My journey here has been an improbable one. . . . Deval Patrick. Inaugural speech. January 4, 2007. Details are taken from videos of the event featured at the time by Boston.com, http://www.boston.com/news/local/massachusetts/articles/2007/01/04/text_of_governor_deval_l_patricks_inaugural_address/.

This is fabulous. . . . All material regarding the inauguration of Drew Gilpin Faust as 28th president of Harvard University is taken from a two hour, twenty-eight minute video clip detailing the occasion made October 12, 2007. This video can be accessed through the Harvard University web page, http://www.president.harvard.edu/news/inauguration/.

£21 for 'Boys & Girls' who ranged from four feet tall to four feet, four inches. . . . Mid-voyage letter and Contract for Captain Peter Gwinn. March 5, 1764. Medford Historical Society. A copy and the full text of this letter are available online at http://www.medfordhistorical.org/letterp7.php.

And how stands the city. . . . Ronald Reagan. *Farewell Address to the Nation.* Delivered from the Oval Office on January 11, 1989. Full text available through the Reagan Library at http://www.reaganlibrary.com/reagan/speeches/farewell.asp.

Whites stand on history's mountain. . . . Robert Dallek. *Lyndon B. Johnson: Portrait of a President.* 2006. Page 371.

I want to grasp this thistle. . . . Janet Halley. *My Chair and Your Chair: Reflections on Our Isaac Royall Legacy.* Speech delivered on the occasion of Professor Halley's acceptance of the Royall Chair of Law at Harvard Law School. A video of the full speech and Elena Kagan's introduction can be accessed through Professor

Halley's website at: http://www.law.harvard.edu/faculty/jhalley/speeches/.

Georgian mansions are a dime a dozen.... Interview with Peter Gittleman, 2005.

mellowing shrine of Medford's memories.... Program for *The Pageant of the Royall House.* 1915. Collection of the Library and Archives of Historic New England. Page 7.

... most notable affair.... Letter soliciting funds from Charles S. Taylor. June 2, 1915. Collection of the Library and Archives of Historic New England.

representative of the entire city.... Emphasis added. Microfilm. Newspaper clipping. *Pageant at the Royall House. Medford History Will Be Reproduced in June.* May 24,1915. No publication noted. Collection of the Library and Archives of Historic New England.

ACKNOWLEDGMENTS

Every journey, however solitary, has its fellow travelers. I would like to thank mine here. First, my warmest thanks to my superb editor, Brigitta van Rheinberg, for awakening me to this project, putting my gaze back to the blank page after an absence, and staying with me every step. It has been a singularly inspiring professional relationship. My thanks, as well, to her wonderful team at Princeton who always went the extra mile.

Ideas must begin somewhere. Mine began in an informal conversation with Ruth O'Brien in her office at the City University of New York in 2004. Of course, as with many books, this idea morphed over time and with deeper thought. For the morphing, my thanks to Neta Crawford, who pointed me toward the Royall House and helped me see the story in its earliest outline. She has a courageous mind. Many others have provided guidance and support along the way. I owe a special thanks to the patient staff at the American Antiquarian Society, who in the early days of this project cheerfully filled my many requests, indulged my dead-end turns, and humored my desire to work not in my quiet fellow's cubby but out under that glorious dome that fills the Society's central chamber with light and a temper of solemn magnificence. The AAS was the perfect place to start this work; and the staff's support gave me all I needed to rethink everything I knew. There I remain especially grateful for the support and kindness of Caroline F. Sloat, Director of Publications, and Marie E. Lamoureux, the Collections Manager, who tirelessly combed the archives on my behalf and continued to assist me long after I moved on. Marie also gave my young friend Rose a memorable tour of that facility so full of treasures. At Harvard I owe a deep bow of thanks to Skip Gates, who offered me a happy berth at the W.E.B. Du Bois Institute for African and African American Research and proved an enthusiastic supporter and friend throughout. During these years of work he arranged my unfettered access to Harvard's exceptional archives and libraries, a gift for which I could never thank him heartily enough. There, too, I am grateful for the support and assistance of Lisa Gregory and Dell Hamilton. While at the Institute I befriended Susan Reverby and her partner, Bill Quivers, a pair whose humor, sophistication, and edge sharpened my own, even at the most difficult of times. At the Newhouse Center for the Humanities at Wellesley College I found time and space to complete the manuscript and the funds to travel to Antigua where I was able to do a last—and crucial—piece of research. At Wellesley my warmest thanks to Susan and Donald Newhouse for their vision in establishing an important sanctuary for deep thought; to the director, Tim Peltason, for opening those doors to me; and to Deb Carbanes, who made everything possible—and fun. In these years I also worked with Jonathan Wyss and his partner, Kelly Sanderfer, of Topaz Maps. This pair bent their heads over a four-hundred-year-old sketch of the farm, and using their own wizardry—and modern tools—managed to trace the outlines of the farm on modern ground. That worked helped me in innumerable ways and led me to the startling realization that America's forty-fourth president, Barack H. Obama, lived on the farm's southeastern edge (365 Broadway) while he studied law at Harvard. Various people at the Royall House Association gave freely of their time, their files, and their insights. Among them I would particularly like to thank Peter Gittleman, Tom Lincoln, and Leslie Spaeth. At many a stop along the way I received gracious help from men and women who toil in local and state archives. I thank you all, and applaud the work you do. Thanks, too, to Clara Platter for reappearing in my life and helping to shepherd the manuscript home, to Terri O'Prey, whose patient oversight kept me sane at the end, and Maryanne Alos for her careful indexing. Lastly, a special *huzzah* to Barbara Goldoftas, who helped me through the eye of one last needle. How nice to be blessed with friends and colleagues of such warmth, intelligence, and generosity.

On a more personal note, I owe a great debt to my sister and neighbor, Deb Manegold, and all the Quayle family (Win, Katie, Will, and Peter) for all the love, shelter, help, support, laughter, and good cooking they showered on me throughout these years. My sisters Nina and Eliza, though further distant geographically, were always there as well, as were my parents. Thank you all. For myriad reasons that I have not the room to list, I would also like to extend my genuine gratitude to the following: Daniel M. Abramson; Andrea Akrib; "little Beanie" (for love, laughter, and children's stories every Friday afternoon); Albér Gaston Berét; John and Nancy Braasch; Karen Breslau; Rachel Brier; Deb Cramer; Steve Crowley (still my "bro" after all these years); David Brion Davis; Robert, Eliana, Vanya, James, and Natalie DeNormandie; Malcolm and Lotte Edwards; Frances Smith Foster; Shawn Garber (shiraz, merlot, grenache . . .); Charlie Haddad; Raul Jarquin and the kids (Emelie and Santi); Melinda Henneberger; Suzanne Hill; Jan and Dan Hoffman; David Kaiser; Trude Kleinschmidt; Cindy and Michael Kuppens; J-bird and Cayla Lambert; Vickie and Bob Lea; Carolyn Lee; Alexandra Lehmann; Joseph Lelyveld; Melinda Lindquist; Caitlyn Marsh; Colin and Ian Martin (who kept me alert with ever-escalating Scrabble challenges, taught me to love lacrosse, and made a million jokes about my overuse of "the herb," garam masala); Arlene Morgan; Susan Meyer; James M. Naughton; Kathy Neely; Martha Paine; Phil Pechukas; Deadria Farmer-Paellman; Gene Roberts; Stephanie Sandberg; Diana and Colin Smith; Bob Thomas; Augusta Tilney; Luisita Torregrosa; Heidi VanGenderen; Tris Windle; and in ending, which is really a beginning, Hope Wittman.

To each of you above, for reasons that you surely know, or certainly can guess, my head is humbly bowed.

csm
Lincoln, Massachusetts

ILLUSTRATIONS

Index